SECOND BEST

www.**transworldbooks**.co.uk

Calum Best was born in 1981, the son of the late British football legend George Best and his first wife, Angie Best, an English model. After a childhood lived in the spotlight and a successful spell as a model, Calum appeared in a number of reality television shows. After his father's death, he turned to drugs and alcohol – a period of his life which lasted several years and which he now speaks openly about in order to raise awareness and provide support for others. He is an actor, model and entrepreneur, and is involved in several charities including NACOA (National Association for Children of Alcoholics), Action on Addiction and the Elton John Aids Foundation. He lives in London.

SECOND BEST

My dad and me

Calum Best
with
Humfrey Hunter

CORGI BOOKS

TRANSWORLD PUBLISHERS
61–63 Uxbridge Road, London W5 5SA
www.transworldbooks.co.uk

Transworld is part of the Penguin Random House group of companies
whose addresses can be found at global.penguinrandomhouse.com

First published in Great Britain in 2015 by Bantam Press
an imprint of Transworld Publishers
Corgi edition published 2016

A CIP catalogue record for this book
is available from the British Library.

ISBN
9780552171397

Typeset in 12/15pt Adobe Garamond by Falcon Oast Graphic Art Ltd.
Printed and bound by Clays Ltd, Bungay, Suffolk.

Penguin Random House is committed to a sustainable
future for our business, our readers and our planet. This book is made
from Forest Stewardship Council® certified paper.

1 3 5 7 9 10 8 6 4 2

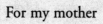
For my mother

'Every saint has a past, and every sinner has a future'

Oscar Wilde

Chapter 1

'I'm pretty terrified of what people will think of me after they read this. But those people should know that I loved him too.'

Calum Best

It's late summer 2008, nearly three years after my dad died. Losing him sent me into a bad place, the worst, lowest moments of my life. Months and then years slipped by in a dark blur, and I felt like I was dropping further and further into a deep hole. I was depressed, drinking and taking drugs, and living a wild life to try to cope with what I was going through. To try to mask the pain I felt. In the end, I began to believe I was worthless, that my life had no purpose. My dad rejected me, and compared to him I was nothing. I was ashamed of myself.

But in the past few months, I've started to change.

Almost three years after he passed away, I've begun to feel that there might be a way out of this. As an alcoholic might say, I've hit rock bottom, and now I'm on the way up. Slowly, but surely.

My mum started my recovery, simply by reminding me that she loves me and by being there for me. What I'm doing now is the next step: I'm making a documentary for the BBC as part of Children in Need about how parental drinking affects children's lives. It's called *Brought Up By Booze* and the goal is to raise awareness of the terrible impact alcoholic parents can have on their children's lives.

I know what my dad's alcoholism did to me, how awful he made me feel, and how the legacy of his drinking nearly destroyed me, but I've never spoken about it properly before. I've never really opened up to anyone. For the programme, I'll be speaking with children of alcoholics, alcoholic parents and the people who try to help them. I want them to tell me as much as possible, to talk in a way I haven't done. It's not going to be easy.

Before we start filming, I'm feeling positive, like I'm moving forward with my life, away from that dark place. I'm excited about the idea of confronting my own past while doing something that might help kids going through hard times because their parents are drinkers.

The programme starts with me and my mum watching some of my dad's football highlights. We're both smiling as he knocks in the goals, caught up in his genius and stardom like all his fans were and still are, decades after he stopped playing. My mum says she has goosebumps. This man we're watching is George Best the idol, and we're both proud of our links to him.

Then it cuts to a shot of him running out on to a football pitch at his testimonial in Northern Ireland in 1988, long after he'd left Manchester United and the glory days behind. The crowd is going wild for him, I mean absolutely crazy, and he waves back at them with a big smile on his face. 'The entrance of a superstar,' says the commentator.

Running along next to him is a little boy with blonde hair, who is looking at the ground, clearly terrified. That little boy is me, and I really was terrified. I'd never heard noise like that before, let alone been in the middle of it. I didn't know where to go or what to do, so I just stuck as close to my dad as I possibly could, thinking I'd be safe with him. It's my first memory of my dad and, while it wasn't much fun at the time, looking at it now fills me with pride, because this legend, this hero, was my dad.

Next, with the cameras rolling, my mum and I talk about something we've never discussed before: what it was like for her being the wife of an alcoholic. She's never told me this stuff because she wanted to protect me from the worst of what happened with my dad. She's always seen the best in people, even him, and wanted me to do the same, especially where he was concerned. Telling me how bad things were for her with him might have affected how I saw him, so she never did. As always, she put me first.

After some nervous laughs, we get down to it. Serious faces on. The first words my mum says explain why we moved to Los Angeles when I was five, which was to get away from my dad. She says, 'Your dad was drunk every single day for thirty years and I didn't want you to see the downward spiral that your poor dad was on. You were busy chasing your father, trying to develop a relationship. But developing a relationship with an alcoholic is impossible to do because they are inherently the world's most selfish people. You could never have done that.'

She believed my dad's drinking would hurt me less if I was in a different country to him. It's incredibly sad, but she was right.

Then she sums up my relationship with him. 'I always have this picture in my head when I think of you and your father, because any little things he'd give you, you'd just soak them up. Your father loved his fans, and they loved him. So there's the back of your dad, reaching up to the fans who are reaching down to George Best, and their hands are going towards each other. And there, in the bottom left-hand corner of the picture, tugging on George's trouser leg, is you. That's what it was like for you.'

This hits me hard. She's absolutely nailed it. Deep down, I always knew that was how it worked between me and my dad; I'd just never had it spelled out to me so clearly before. I tried and tried to get close to him, to build a relationship with him, but he always pushed me away. He was more interested in other things – his fans and alcohol.

I can feel the emotions boiling up, but I try to keep myself under control. I want to be professional for the programme.

I tell Mum it was hard for me, but I've learned to smile about things, laugh even. I put on my usual brave face. She replies with the point of the programme. 'You can do that,' she says, 'but there are so many children out there who suffer, so many kids going through that stuff, and their fathers aren't famous. They have nowhere to go and nowhere to turn.'

Her point is that I have always had her around to turn to, and that when I was a kid I had a life separate to my dad's because we lived in Los Angeles, thousands of miles away from him and his crazy world. But the flipside of living thousands of miles away meant I never got to know him properly. I never had the chance and so, compared to most sons, I don't have many memories of my dad. I hardly saw him when I was a kid; then, when I was a bit older, I would visit him every summer, but that was only for two weeks a year, and even then he spent most of the time drunk.

'Everyone is telling me about my dad,' I say, 'but I'm still trying to figure out who my dad was, and who he was to me.'

We talk about how my dad would always be so excited to see me whenever I went to stay with him in London, but once I was actually there he wouldn't know how to deal with it, so he would drink even more than usual. And whenever I tried to ask him about why he drank so much, he would shut me out. That's how it always went for me with him. Alcohol made him push me away, and so I have felt horribly rejected by him all my life.

My mum shows me some photos. First, one of four generations of Bests: me, my dad, his dad and his dad's dad. Next comes a shot of just me and my dad when I'm about eleven. I remember the time well – it was one of my annual trips to London to see him. My dad's face is bloated and his beard is thick. He's wearing that distinctive eighties-looking purple shell suit, the one he put on every single day before he went out drinking.

The picture was taken around the time I realized what his drinking meant, when it became clear to me that he didn't care about his appearance. If he had cared, there's no way he'd have gone out like that. No way. I remember how red his eyes were and how the skin on his hands used to peel. All thanks to alcohol.

'What a waste,' my mum says, as the photo of me and my dad is shown on screen.

Later, I go to London Zoo to meet some children who are affected by alcoholism. They're having a day out, getting their faces painted and looking at the animals.

I talk to some of the kids and tell a little girl that I was eleven when I began to realize what was going on with my dad's alcoholism. I ask about her moment of realization. She says it came when she was going round to her friends' houses and noticed that none of them had to make their own dinner like she did, and none of them

14

had to make sure their mum or dad were home from the pub and somewhere safe every evening, in bed or on the sofa, as she did. She said that was when it clicked that there was something wrong, but because she idolized her dad she didn't want to admit it. This sounds very familiar to me.

I listen to these children talk, and the deep, far-reaching consequences of alcohol abuse are hammered home to me. These are children talking, young people driven to the point where they're self-harming or comfort eating because of their parents' drinking and the terrible behaviour that comes from it.

A girl tells me how her mother would do a runner from the flats they were living in when she couldn't pay the rent, which meant this little girl missed so much school that she says she doesn't know anything. Those were her actual words: 'I don't know anything.' Her life is now messed up, and it's tragic.

Then there is a girl who hasn't set eyes on her dad for three years because she couldn't handle seeing him any more because of how he behaved. She wasn't even ten years old when this happened.

In spite of what they went through because of alcohol, some of the kids tried drinking themselves. They wanted to see what this amazing thing was, and what its effects were. One of them says she had some and threw up, and now thinks it's disgusting and can't understand why anyone would drink it at all, let alone every day.

All the children told me tragic stories and were

incredibly brave. I could see how talking openly was helping them. They could get advice and guidance from people who understood what they were going through.

I never spoke about my dad like this to anyone, because if I had, I would have felt like I was betraying him, the man idolized by millions of people, including me. As I talk to these kids, I begin to have doubts about whether or not I should be talking for the programme about his alcoholism and my own experiences of it. I feel guilty for sharing this stuff, as if it isn't something that should be talked about.

That, I find out, is common among the children of alcoholics. We want to hide things away. But then I am told it's a good thing to open yourself up. It helps you change your perceptions of your own experiences of alcoholism for the better, as well as affecting other people's views of what it means to live with alcoholism. That's before you get on to your perceptions of yourself. I can see from the way the girls are that talking is doing them good. Making this film is becoming an intense experience, and I've hardly started.

I speak to a mother and her son, along with a counsellor. The boy's father is an alcoholic and he's being taught to cope with the situation by taking control, by talking to people, finding his own voice and dealing with his anger rather than letting it take over.

I didn't have this kind of help. When I was fifteen, if I wanted to be with my dad I had to fit in with him, which meant going to the pub. I pushed my pain and anger way down, away out of sight, and got on with living my life. The consequences of that came later, and the worst of them are what I've been living through for the past three years since he died.

Next, I meet a seventeen-year-old boy called Dominic, who lives with his mother. Her drinking has made him feel completely helpless. He tells me how he once found twenty empty bottles of vodka in her room and how he stopped caring about himself – he missed school and sold his guitars, which he absolutely loved – because his mother didn't care about him. His mother was in hospital, seriously ill, on his fifteenth birthday. I feel so sorry for him.

Things were so bad that Dominic couldn't go out because he was scared of what would happen while he wasn't at home – he didn't know whether his mother would be OK or whether his stuff would be out on the streets because they'd been evicted. His mother eventually went for treatment and is doing all right now, but Dominic is still scared that she might start drinking again. I don't blame him. When alcohol has been so influential in his life for so long, it must be hard for him to imagine living without it, even though he's not the one drinking.

These stories are breaking my heart, and mystifying me too, because I wonder how a parent can start feeling that booze is more important than their children. How can alcohol make a person be like that? They are also making me realize how lucky I've been to have my mum. At least

I had one good parent. Most of these kids are from single-parent families and don't even have that.

I speak to a woman called Sally, who used to be an alcoholic and now works helping people with drink problems. She says things got so bad for her that at one point she was in hospital doubly incontinent. She tells me that at her lowest point, if someone had said she had to stop drinking or her children would be taken away or even that she would die, she would have carried on drinking. She was that far gone.

Sally tells me about a phrase from the Alcoholics Anonymous handbook (known as 'The Big Book') that describes the moment for an alcoholic when drink becomes life itself. The book says, 'He shall be at the jumping off point. He can neither live with nor without alcohol. He will wish for the end.' I wonder if this happened to my dad and, if it did, when? Was there a moment when he jumped off and decided he was going to drink until he died, no matter how soon that might be? And if there was, could I have helped him?

Sally tells me about the pain she felt when her son was taken away from her for five months while she tried to get off alcohol. While she was being treated, she was allowed hour-long visits with him every weekend. At the end of each one, the social workers had to physically pull her son away from her, while he shouted and screamed and grabbed on to doors as he tried to stay with her.

Eventually, Sally got sober, and when we talk she has

not drunk for six years. She has her son back and their lives have improved. She still feels incredibly guilty for what she put him through, but at least they are together now so she can try to make up for it, to repair some of the damage done.

Hearing how Sally made a huge change in her life makes me wonder why my dad didn't do the same. Did he try and fail, or did he not even want to make an effort? Was alcohol's hold over him that strong? Or did he just not care about me enough to want to change? I don't know the answer.

I'm relating everything I hear back to myself, and it's becoming harder and harder to keep myself together. I ask Sally if an alcoholic can stop themselves from drinking. She tells me it's the drinker's responsibility, no one else's, and maybe my dad just didn't want to give it up. There's a small chance that he might have done with a different kind of treatment, but Sally says what it boils down to is that he didn't want to. This is tough to hear, but I believe her. We end up hugging each other, which is not the kind of thing I expected when I started this.

Sally's example shows me that even people with awful drink problems can change, no matter how far gone things might seem. So I am now convinced that my dad could have changed, if he'd really wanted to. He could have chosen not to drink, but he didn't. He chose alcohol over getting better, and over me. He chose to drink, and it kept me away. My whole life was about trying to be closer to my dad, trying to get to know him properly, but alcohol stopped me from doing that. And he chose not to do anything about it.

Next, we go to film in Belfast. I love going there, because it's where he's from and where he's laid to rest. I feel closer to him when I'm in Belfast. But the day before, I get nervous because I don't know how I'll cope, and I do what my dad always did when he felt under pressure: I go on a bender. I have lunch at a friend's restaurant, have one drink and that one drink turns into thirty drinks.

At the moment my relationship with alcohol is different to my dad's and to his mum's – she too was an alcoholic. They both drank all day, every day, regardless of whether they were with other people or alone, until it killed them. But I'm different. My weakness is nights out. I never drink on my own, or first thing in the morning. I never even want to. But when I'm out, I go for it and get out of control. This is not how it started for my grandmother, who didn't drink at all until she was in her forties. My dad was different. He began much earlier, with parties and fun in his teens, and then the addiction gene he'd inherited kicked in and he destroyed himself. I worry about the same thing happening to me, because I have the same genes as my dad. But at the same time, I really don't think I'm the same kind of drinker as he was. I really hope I'm not, anyway.

I'm not feeling great when we get to Belfast, but there's nowhere to hide. We have to get on with making the film. We drive around the city and go to see a mural of my dad on the side of someone's house.

It's just the three of us – the two producers with a hand-held camera and me with a mic on – and we get to this mural, a huge painting of my dad. I walk up to it, stare a bit; they're following behind and ask me what it means to me. I say I'm super-proud of him, it's crazy how he brought everyone together like this, how big he was, and I miss him so much.

And then this guy walks past and shouts, 'Hey, Bestie!' I wave back and he comes over. 'I love your dad,' he says. 'Look at this.' He opens his shirt and he has a tattoo of my dad on his chest. Not a small one – this covers half the guy's chest. I can't believe what I'm seeing. This is how much my dad is loved – some random guy happens to walk past and he has a tattoo of him. And the guy isn't old either, so there's no way he was alive when my dad was playing football. It's amazing, truly amazing.

I've met five or six people over the years with tattoos of my dad, and every time I'm astonished by the effect he had on them.

While we're in Belfast, memories come back to me, of kicking balls around, of visiting his family and of his funeral. I go to the house where he grew up and see the plaque on the front. The house is up for sale now, which is very weird. The last time I was here was for his funeral. The family were inside, the front garden was full of flowers and there were thousands of people outside, but now it's quiet. The difference is astonishing. I can hardly believe it's the same place. On the day of the funeral, you couldn't move for people. It was crazy. But today it's empty. The silence brings my emotions to the surface. My memories of that day are still so raw.

The final part of the film takes place in Clouds House, a residential rehab centre in Wiltshire, which has been treating NHS and private clients for twenty-five years. Three hundred people come through the doors each year and over half of them have children at home who have been directly affected by their addiction. I talk to Clare, the head of treatment, and she tells me that for every addict there will be at least three or four people affected on the same kind of level as that addict – the people closest to them.

She shows me a board where people write things – a kind of thought-for-the-day place. The newest one says, 'One of the attributes of love, like art, is to bring harmony and order out of chaos.' Clare asks if I want to write something. I haven't planned this, but I say yes, I would like to. I write, 'Every saint has a past. Every sinner has a future.'

Clare shows me how addiction affects families by drawing a kind of family tree. She's interested when I say I'm an only child and tells me that for someone in my situation, where there is alcoholism in the family, a lot of emotion and distress lands on me. If I had brothers or sisters, we would take up different positions and share the problems among us, but I can't do that, so it's all on me. She says it's lonely, which is true.

She points to my grandmother and my father, but doesn't say I'll necessarily end up that way, which is a relief. The possibility that I'm fated to die like my dad did terrifies me.

I talk about my relationship with my dad, how tough it was, how difficult it was for me to be close to him, how I reached for him and reached for him all the time, and how I knew deep down he wanted the same thing I did – for us to be close – but the alcohol stopped him from being able to do it. There was a third party in our relationship – booze.

Clare says that means I didn't have a father figure in my life, which is true, although I searched and searched for it from him, and that has an impact on me too.

'As much as you did, and as hard as you tried, you couldn't get through,' she says.

She's right. She seems to know exactly what I've been through, and I can feel my emotions working their way up to the surface in a way they never have before. I've felt layers peeling back over the weeks I've been making this film, but right now, talking to Clare, it's the most intense moment. I am finding her very easy to open up to and, even though I'm now twenty-seven, it's the first time I've ever done this. Better late than never, I suppose.

We sit down to talk more. I say I have questions which I wish I'd asked my father, and I wish I knew the answers to them, but I know they will always be just questions. As we talk, what Clare says begins to affect me more and more. I say alcohol stopped my father expressing himself, especially towards me, but I stop myself saying any more, because my emotions are boiling up again. I don't want to break down.

'It's interesting you should say that,' Clare tells me. 'It's a story we hear many, many times. What he was probably doing was feeling very anxious and nervous about seeing you, and so used stress-reducing behaviour – getting drunk – but he chose one which actually invokes more stress.'

Clare saying my dad would have used alcohol as a stress relief because he was so anxious and nervous about seeing me gets me thinking. Why would he have felt like that? Maybe he had a low opinion of himself. Maybe he thought he was a terrible father, and alcohol numbed that pain. But if that was why he drank before I came to visit, what about all the other times? Was drinking always 'stress-reducing behaviour' for him?

Clare wants to know what I'm feeling, and I say anger and guilt, but I can't work out why. She says it's because I was let down by my dad and that it's normal to be angry if someone lets us down. But because I was let down by someone who was unwell, and it happened *because* he was unwell, I feel guilty for feeling angry at that person who was unwell and who I love. She's right. It's complicated, but it makes sense. I know my dad wanted to be a better father, but he couldn't do it. And he suffered too – it wasn't just me – so I don't like being angry at him. But I *am* angry, I can't deny that.

I try to get back to the questions I planned for this

interview. They're written on a bit of paper that I'm holding, and I read one out to her about the general effects of alcoholic parents on their children, but my voice is faltering. My eyes are going, the tears are coming. I rub my forehead in an effort to bring myself under control. Clare is calm and knows exactly what's going on. I'm not your typically impartial TV interviewer – we're talking about my life here.

I can't talk, so Clare does. She says my father's drinking will affect my own relationships. I don't know how much she knows about me, but she's right. I say I have real commitment issues, and she says that strikes a chord with her, because alcohol turns relationships on their head. Someone in my position feels like alcohol is being chosen over them, so that will affect how they go about having relationships with other people too.

That is how I've always felt, and for the first time in my life I say the words, 'My father chose alcohol over me.'

Clare's reply breaks me. 'Can you imagine how that would make you feel about yourself?'

Yes, I can.

I tell her I'm OK, but for the next thirty seconds I can't talk. The tears are flowing.

When I've composed myself a bit, I say, 'It's funny. Before I sat down with you I thought I can take it. It's been nearly three years since he passed away. But that's my stubbornness. I didn't think I'd actually . . . I find myself a lot saying laugh about it so you won't cry.'

Before we started work today, I'd texted my mum to say I really couldn't be bothered. I didn't feel motivated for filming. But Clare has tapped into my deepest feelings and they're all coming out now.

I say it's hatred that I feel towards my dad. There's a lot of hate.

'The thing is,' Clare says, 'it's not your fault.'

'I know it's not,' I say. 'It's just that it's too late.'

'It's not too late for you to deal with how you feel about these things.'

'My head turns into a wreck sometimes, and I just think get on with it. That's closure. My dad's passed. Deal with it. Move on. But these things affect you no matter how long down the line you are.'

Clare says, 'There's no one who has a rule book on closure, on how long it's going to take you.'

'I just wondered if it comes,' I say. That's what I've been searching for.

'It does come, for sure,' Clare says. 'But only if you can do this, and find a way to talk about things.'

Clare says she doesn't believe anyone starts drinking with the ambition of becoming an alcoholic. It happens as they get deeper and deeper into it – the idea of having a choice to drink or not disappears. She says my dad might have been so ill he'd lost sight of the fact that he had a choice. Maybe he was. I'm not sure.

I say I'll always see George Best, the footballer, and George Best, my alcoholic father, as one person. For me they're one big package. And that's where the show ends.

* * *

I knew as I was making the programme that the experience would be life-changing for me. It made me open up, understand myself better and want to do something good with my life. I learned that what I went through isn't unique and that it is possible for something positive to come out of all the bad things that happened. That means I'm a step closer to being happy and living the kind of life I want for myself.

The person I owe the most to for this is my mum. She was there for me when I needed her the most, and she encouraged me to make *Brought Up By Booze*. She went through all kinds of hell with my dad, when they were together and for a good few years after that. But she says that despite all that, she doesn't look on their time together as a mistake for one reason: she had me, which makes me a very lucky son.

She is a special woman and without her I don't know what would have happened to me. My dad was not a good father, but my mum gave me stability, security and unconditional love, and in the end that's what saved me.

In a lot of ways, this book is for her. But mostly, it's for me. A lot of things have been said and written about my dad and me. Some of them were terrible and true, and some were terrible and not true. The point of this book is simply to tell the truth about what happened to me. No more and no less. Some of it is ugly, but sometimes the truth is.

I'm not writing this to trash my dad's memory. I know

how much people loved him, and still do love him, and I don't want to change their opinions. In fact, I'm pretty terrified of what people will think of me after they read this. But those people should know that I loved him too, probably more than anyone else in the world did. He was and is my hero and my idol, and I am so, so proud to be his son. But he was also a shitty dad. There's no way round that.

I know my dad was a good man who wanted to do the best for the people he loved. But alcohol stopped him. It had a terrible effect on his life and the lives of people around him, including me. Maybe especially me. So this book isn't really about being the son of George Best, the legend. It's about being the son of a man who chose alcohol over his child. That man just happened to be one of the greatest footballers who ever lived.

Chapter 2

'Having Calum proved one thing – alcohol had become the most important thing in my life. More important than my wife and even more important than my new-born son.'

George Best

In late 1975, my dad is in Los Angeles playing football. Even though the peak of his career, his time at Manchester United, is behind him, he is still a star wherever he goes. But soccer isn't America's main sport so his fame there is on a smaller scale than back home. In the States, he can live a different kind of life. Instead of being constantly hassled by adoring fans, he can sit in a bar for a few hours on his own, relaxing quietly in a way that is impossible for him in the UK. By this time he owns a bar – Bestie's Beach Club – at Hermosa Beach, LA, and he loves spending time there. Even though his name is above the door, it's still peaceful for him.

He is a charming guy, and in LA he quickly makes friends with people who spend their spare time enjoying the same things he does, which are mostly related to alcohol and women. Among those friends is Ed Peters, who has one long party going on at his house. Booze and beautiful women, very often naked, are on tap. There are joints around too, but my dad doesn't touch those. His only poison is alcohol.

On a Sunday afternoon in October, my dad is kicking back at one of Ed Peters' house parties when two women he hasn't seen before walk in. One of them is tall, blonde and beautiful, and he immediately notices her. But both leave very quickly. The blonde – my mum – remembers the party as being made up of five men and fifty women, far too sleazy for her and her friend, and absolutely not her kind of scene, so they get out of there as quickly as possible.

This, in my dad's opinion, is the first time they've met. Actually, it isn't. That happened a few years ago, at a party in London. He had tried it on with my mum then, but she wasn't interested. She was still young and was slightly overwhelmed by his fame, but more importantly very turned off by how drunk he was. I assume my dad has forgotten about their first meeting because of all the booze he'd had, which is ironic in a sad way.

By the time this debauched Sunday party happens in LA, my mum is older and more mature. She moved to the US to be a model a couple of years ago and is making a life for herself out here on her own. She's much more confident and streetwise now. So when she gets a call from Ed Peters a few weeks later saying George wants her to come to a party at his bar, she accepts. Why not? She isn't the kind of woman to turn down a party invitation. But when she gets to the bar, there is no party. There's just George, waiting for her. This is his way of getting her on her own, and it works. They are attracted to each other immediately and my dad's 'party' becomes their first date.

But even on that first date there are complications, because after they've been sitting talking for a while an upset girl walks up to my dad and kicks him. My mum is smart enough to understand exactly what's going on – this girl has been involved with my dad previously and is unhappy about something he did – but she doesn't worry too much about what she sees, reasoning that his affair with this girl is in the past. She ignores the warning sign and lets their relationship develop.

By doing this, she puts herself in line for all kinds of heartache over the next few years. My dad is a drunk, a cheat, unreliable on an epic scale, and sometimes abusive. My mum will come to know all his flaws better than anyone, and he will hurt her in terrible ways, but through it all she will love him anyway. She thinks he is a really special person, one of a small number of truly original people, and that is why she has fallen for him in the first place.

Here's an example of how charming he is. Not long after my mum starts seeing my dad, she is working for

Cher as a personal trainer and assistant and they have become close friends. Cher, who my mum confides in, isn't impressed by her stories about George Best. Cher knows there are lots of rich, handsome, famous men in LA who are interested in my mum, and she thinks she would be much better off with one of them. Someone like Jack Nicholson, say, who meets my mum in LA and takes her out for dinner one night. They get on well and Jack sends her yellow roses the next day, wanting to see her again, but she isn't interested. She's just started dating my dad and doesn't have eyes for anyone else.

Cher is baffled. Why is beautiful Angie turning down famous movie stars to hang out with this little drunk Irishman? It is a mystery to her. But then Cher meets my dad, and he works his magic on her. After that meeting she tells my mum that she gets it. She understands the attraction. She can see what my dad has, how magnetic he is.

My mum thinks my dad is more than just an incredibly charismatic man, though. She carries on loving him through all the bad times because she is convinced he has a good heart and good intentions, and that it is alcohol that has turned him into a monster. That's why she sticks with him when he disappears for days on end on benders, or when he goes off with one of what turns into a procession of other women, or when he comes home drunk more times than she can count. And that's why she marries him in January 1978, even though by now she knows exactly what he is like. That is also why she has his son in 1981, and why she never, ever does or says anything that could make me think less of him. She makes sure I know that everything bad that happens is alcohol's fault, and that my dad is a good man who loves me, but who is trapped and cursed by his addiction.

My mum takes a long time to learn this. When they are together, she tries as hard as she can to make their relationship perfect, but she can't. At this point, she doesn't understand alcoholics. She doesn't know that you can't stop someone from drinking. They have to want to stop. And so for her their relationship is full of pain, anger and distrust.

This is it in her words: 'I knew very early on that George drank a lot, but I thought he was just one of the boys, and as all women would, I thought I could change him. I thought he needed to settle down, to be mothered, and I wanted to do that for him. I had Florence Nightingale syndrome, but I didn't know anything about alcoholics.'

My mum knows things hadn't always been easy for my dad, with his family problems and his career ending, and I suspect that makes her more forgiving. My dad is an idol to millions of people and has lived an amazing life, but he has suffered too. His mother died in October 1978 and he was devastated. He hadn't seen her for two years because, in his own words, 'I'd always run away from trouble and I wasn't inclined to run towards it.' Trouble in this case, of course, meant his mother's drinking. She hadn't had a drink for her entire life until her mid-forties and ten years later she was dead. It's incredibly sad, and must have been awful for my dad and the rest of his family. I guess he visited his family so rarely because he couldn't face seeing the state his mother was in. My grandmother's funeral was the first time my mother met my dad's relatives, and by that point they'd been married for almost a year.

By the time I am born, in San Jose, California, my parents have been married for three years. For my mum, it hasn't been a smooth ride. My dad's drinking is getting heavier. He even left her on their wedding night to go to the pub, and while she was pregnant with me he was out of control. He would get bored and go on huge benders, sometimes walking eight miles just to find a bar. Some nights he ended up sleeping on the beach while my mum was at home pregnant and alone. And there are still plenty of other women around. My mum tolerates this because she loves him so much and knows he always comes home to her. One time, though, she really loses it with my dad. She overhears him calling another woman to come over to their house when he thinks my mum is out, and she flies into such a rage that she ends up stabbing him in the backside with a kitchen knife. Given everything he put her through, I'm surprised it was only his backside and that it happened only once. Despite all this, they stay together.

On the day I am born, my dad is there with my mum all the way. He looks after her, supports her, and even cuts the cord. I arrive on 6 February 1981 at 7.02am Pacific Time, which is 3.02pm in the UK. This is pretty much exactly the same time and date of the Munich air disaster in 1958, when so many great Manchester United players died. This is a coincidence, obviously, but it pleases my dad anyway.

His drinking continues, to the extent that in March, when I'm a month old, he goes into rehab and is away from me and my mum for months. When he gets out, he is travelling backwards and forwards to the UK because his football career is up in the air. Teams still want him, but they're not at the highest level and that means my dad won't properly commit to them. He still has dreams of playing for Manchester United again, no matter how unrealistic that is. But he needs to earn a living and so he's caught between that harsh reality and the fact he isn't the player he was, which is hard for him to cope with. He is still drinking, but not quite so heavily.

A bit of luck sees him save my life when I'm eight months old. One day, I start wheezing. My mum takes me to the doctor and they say I'm fine and send me home again. By chance, that evening my dad is sober, and in the middle of the night he can't sleep, probably because he hasn't drunk anything. He decides to go and see me, and when he walks into my room he finds me standing up in my cot trying to cry but not making any noise because I can hardly breathe. He wakes up my mum and they take me straight to hospital, with them both scared I'm going to die. I'm put in an oxygen tent and it's a very close call.

It turns out I have croup, a swelling of the throat which makes breathing difficult. I'm in hospital for a week before they let me go home.

If my dad had been drinking that night, if he'd been out somewhere getting hammered or already home and passed out, the chances are I would have died. I was lucky.

At this point, my mum thinks her life with George is heading in the right direction. Before I was born, he made all kinds of promises about how things would be different when he was a father. I'm not sure if my mum truly believed him, but she wanted to, and the early signs are promising. He stops drinking for a few months and is there for her and me. He even tries feeding me on his own. Just once, though, because he forgets to follow my mum's detailed instructions about holding me in my chair while I eat – I was very energetic and active – and I end up falling out of the seat and landing on the floor on my head.

He means well but, as always, he crashes, this time on a trip to Las Vegas which he takes alone and which turns into a monumental bender. Not long after this, my mum has an epiphany and realizes she can't look after us both, after an incident she describes like this: 'I'm driving down the street in San Jose. It's raining, and is a really dreary, miserable day. In the middle of the street, on the two yellow lines which run along the centre, there's this creature walking towards me. It's a man, soaking wet, miserable, huddled over like a homeless person, wandering aimlessly down the street. At first I thought it was a tramp, and felt sorry for him. Then I realized it was my husband. I looked at you, and thought, "I can't do this any more. I can't look after two babies. The big one has to go."'

That's it – she's going. But before she has the chance to tell my dad she's leaving, he goes on a twelve-day bender, one of his biggest ever. My mum nurses him back to health and then tells him we're out of there.

A few days later he smashes the house up and begs her to stay. But she won't have any of it, and we stay gone. But something in her still thinks maybe this will be the almighty kick he needs to change his ways and that it's still possible that we'll be a family again. In January 1982, my dad is back in rehab for another month, but nothing really changes. A few months later, my mum finds out she's losing her home, because behind her back my dad has been spending money from the account meant for the mortgage. That moment, just before my mum's thirtieth birthday, is when she finally snaps and breaks away from him for good. She knows now that she will never go back to him.

Later that year, in November, my dad is declared bankrupt. He has been living on cash, spending it as fast as he earns it with no thought for things like tax or bills. It has been day to day.

For me, this situation and their break-up lay the foundations for what my father will always be in my life: a distant figure, someone mysterious and fascinating and dangerous who I don't see all that often. I can't know this, but my relationship with him is already defined – I will spend the rest of his life trying to get closer to him, and failing every time. I will love, worship, adore and idolize him, but I will also hate him.

In his autobiography, my dad wrote this about how he felt when I was born: 'Having Calum proved one thing – alcohol had become the most important thing in my life. More important than my wife and even more important than my new-born son. I felt guilty that I couldn't stop drinking even for him and probably drank even more because of my guilt, which is just about the worst vicious circle you could get.'

That's how it would be until the day he died.

A few months before my second birthday, my dad moves back to the UK when he is offered the chance to play for Bournemouth. He and my mum have separated on relatively friendly terms in the end, and he admitted he'd been a bad husband and father. As always, he wanted to be good, but something inside him meant he couldn't do it, and I expect he is relieved when he leaves Los Angeles and the pressure of being close to us is taken off him. By putting thousands of miles between himself and us, he avoids the constant reminder of what he's done, how absent he's been and how he broke up his family.

A little later, at the end of 1982, my mum and I go back to London, partly to see her family, whom she misses and wants around her, and partly so I can spend more time with my dad. I'm not sure if he asked for this, or if it was her idea. I expect it was her idea. Either way, things are quite smooth, except for the papers trying to stir up trouble between my mum and my dad's new girl-friend, Mary Stävin. The papers say Mary broke up my parents' marriage. The truth is they met months after it was over. But that's the papers for you. They don't care if something is true or not, as long as it makes a good story they can print.

In the months that follow, every now and then my dad appears at the London flat we're living in. It's usually late at night when he shows up, and he's always drunk. If he's being nice, my mum lets him in, but only to sleep on the sofa. If he's in a real state and she can't get rid of him, she tries to hide him from me, but it doesn't always work. On the odd occasion when I see him in the evening it's con-fusing, and on the days when I get up in the morning and find my dad there I'm so excited to see him I nearly burst. Every time my mum sees me going crazy over my dad with his stinking hangover her heart breaks a little bit.

This, 1983, is the year that my dad's football career officially ends. He plays his last ever game for an Australian team, Brisbane Lions, as they lose 0–4 to Adelaide City. Sixteen hundred people watch the match.

My mum and I spend Christmas with her parents in Southend, in Essex, and my dad turns up in the evening, dressed as Santa Claus, which I love. We open presents together, and he is as excited and happy as any father would be as he spends Christmas with his son. It's a special time because it's one of the very few Christmases the three of us spend together as a family.

Things are OK with my dad, but my mum can't help the fact she isn't happy in London. She misses her friends and life back in California. Things are so different here – the weather, the scenery – and, although she's working as a personal trainer, she has no job as good as the one she had with Cher, who has become a close friend and is also my godmother. My mum is becoming painfully aware that she left her whole life in the States. But she sticks things out in the UK. She has her family around her, I get to see my dad as often as possible and, eventually, as she starts meeting more people and doing interesting things, she gets happier.

By late 1984, my dad is possibly at his lowest ebb, and something happens which affects me deeply. My dad goes out one night and gets drunk, gets pulled over in his car, breathalysed, taken to the station and then released. Afterwards, he carries on as normal, sleeping in late the next day and then going drinking again. He completely forgets he was supposed to be in court that morning.

The morning after that, the police turn up at his place with a warrant for his arrest, because you can't just skip court appearances. First, my dad won't let them in, because he doesn't realize it's the police at the door. He thinks whoever it is should go away and leave him in peace. Then, when he understands who it is, he decides to run away. This doesn't go so well, and the police quickly get hold of him. Finally, he gets violent with them. So he's charged for drink-driving, missing his court appearance and assaulting a police officer, and is given three months in prison.

Because it's George Best, the story is huge. It's all over the newspapers, TV and radio, and I, aged nearly four, realize what's going on and get upset. My mum finds it incredibly hard to explain things to me, because I can't understand why my dad won't be around for Christmas dressed up as Santa like he was the year before. He spends Christmas crying in prison.

My mum tries to protect me from most of it but somehow I hear the word 'prison' and am distraught, crying my eyes out at the thought of my dad in a place I imagine to be so terrible. He thinks I'm too young to understand, but I'm not and it hurts. My mum finds it really hard seeing me like this, and because it was all my dad's fault it's easy to imagine her getting angry with him, and me picking up on that and developing negative feelings towards him. But she doesn't get angry, and she doesn't say anything bad about him at all. So I carry on worshipping him and hoping that things will be better soon.

My dad had been good to us over the few months leading up to his jail sentence, and my mum knows him well enough to see how he gets himself into serious scrapes without meaning to – tricky situations arise and he doesn't handle them well, which makes things much worse. But most of all, she won't criticize him to me because he's my dad, even when he starts drinking again soon after he comes out of prison. No matter what he does, that's how she always reacts. My mum won't let herself put anything negative about him in my mind.

But this protective cloak won't last for ever, because I'm getting older and picking up on things more. A friend of mine says the time children spend with their parents when they're really young and which they don't remember later in life isn't wasted, because even though it's not at the front of their memories, it's in there somewhere, buried deep in the hard drive. That means it affects the child's relationship with the parent for ever, for good or bad. Aged three, I am developing feelings about my dad which are ones I will always have: I miss him badly, I am desperate to see him, and I don't understand why he's not around more. From then on, nothing ever really changes, no matter how much I want it to.

My mum makes sure I have a happy life. When I'm nearly four, at the start of 1985, we move to a little house near Maidenhead and I really like it there. My mum gets me a male nanny, Martin, so he can do things with me that other fathers might do with their sons. He plays football with me, takes me and my friends camping, we make tree houses, build forts, and play with bows and arrows.

We have a fireworks party that year, and my dad comes. I am so excited that he is there. By now it's so rare to have him around that I go crazy with joy every time I see him. There's no stability or consistency where he's concerned and that's reflected in how I feel about him – I'm either overjoyed to see him or desperately sad that he's not around. The trouble is, whenever I say goodbye I don't know when I'm going to see him next. His life is chaotic; he's floundering around drinking and trying to find a way to be happy without playing football. The result for me is that I get no security from him, just the hope that I'll see him again soon, and that at some point in the near future he's going to be around all the time. When I feel down about the situation, this hope always cheers me up.

I'm too young to look very deeply into what's going on. As I get older, though, I start to question things that went on at this time. Why wasn't he around? Where was he? Couldn't he have tried harder? And if he could, why didn't he? We were living in the same country, after all. Maybe it was because he didn't want to see me. Sometimes it's hard not to believe that's the answer.

Chapter 3

'Did he actually want to be a better father, but he couldn't do it? Or did he really not give a shit?'

Calum Best

In July 1986, my mum applies for a divorce from my dad and for sole custody of me. She wants to be able to take charge of my life on her own. My dad isn't up to much in the parenting stakes, so this is the sensible thing to do in every way. My mum knows my dad cares about me and that he's a proud guy, so she expects he will put up a fight at the court hearing and she isn't looking forward to it. She's sure he won't want to lose all custody of me. He is charming and clever, and she fears the judge will fall for the George Best charisma. But he doesn't even show up. The hearing goes ahead without him, the judge isn't impressed by his absence and my mum gets custody.

This is another example of one of those things he did

that I find out about when I get older and that make me wonder what must have been going through his head. Did he actually want to be a better father, but he couldn't do it? Or did he really not give a shit? Was he hungover after going on a huge bender to drown out the misery he felt because he knew my mum was going to get custody of me? Or did he stay away and deliberately lose custody because he knew I would be better off that way? That might mean he was drinking because he loved me, which would at least mean something. The idea of him out getting smashed for the hell of it, without a thought for me and the hearing, and missing it like he missed his appointment at the police station, doesn't feel great. I will find out a few years later that his girlfriend, Angie Lynn, is pregnant when the divorce hearing happens, which might well have affected him. His life is chaotic, and I'm sure he takes it really badly when Angie sadly loses the baby later in the year. It must have been a horrible time for both of them.

My relationship with my dad is about to enter a new phase, because the custody hearing is the start of my mum's plan to move us back to the States. My dad's life is in chaos and he's drinking more than ever, which means every little thing he does is all over the papers, radio and TV. My mum doesn't want me growing up with this around me, in the country where George Best is at his most famous. She thinks it will be awful for me when I go to school, with people knowing who my dad is and what crazy stuff he's been up to, and she wants to protect me from all that as much as she can. She has lined up a job working for Cher again as her trainer, and so we have something good to go to.

I wonder sometimes what my life would have been like if my mum hadn't made this decision, if we'd stayed in London instead of going back to LA. But no matter which way I look at it, I never doubt she made the right call.

Things are hard in the few months before we leave. My mum has a lot to do in London, organizing our move while also carrying on with her work to provide for us, so I'm sent to a school near Southend and live with my grandparents. They're warm, caring people who worry about my mum and me and desperately want our lives to be more secure and stable. Every morning my grandpa makes sure my uniform is perfect and my shoes are shined, and they do their best to look after me.

I'm furious that my mum isn't with me, but I do understand why. She visits every weekend and I love seeing her. We hang out and have dinner, and it's so lovely to have her around. And then it comes time for her to leave. She always parks in the same place – out of the door and up the road to the left – and every time she goes I chase her to her car, crying my eyes out, begging her not to leave me, screaming, 'Please don't leave! Please don't leave!' I'm desperate for her to stay, and I'm in pieces. She's crying too, but she has to leave. It's not that I don't love my grandparents; I just hate seeing my mum go. It's awful for everyone, including my poor grandma, because she has to pick up the pieces.

I go to Thorpe Hall School, a lovely little place, and every now and then parents are asked to come in for different events. Each time one of these is coming up, my mum tells my dad in plenty of time. He turns up once, for sports day. We go to meet him at the train station, and as always I'm buzzing, jumping around with excitement at the prospect of seeing him.

We go to the school and my dad is the star of the day. All the teachers and parents are thrilled to have George Best there, and I love that they're excited, even though I don't completely understand why. He wins the dads' race, takes part in the egg-and-spoon race and is brilliant with everyone. I am so unbelievably proud that this man who all the other parents are drawn to is my dad, and so incredibly happy that he is here with me, showing all the other kids, their parents and the teachers that we are a team. I think in that moment he is happy too, which makes me confused about why he doesn't come to see me more often. Every now and then he tries to do the father bit, but it only happens a couple of times. It's such a waste.

In January 1987, we finally go back to the US. We fly over with our stuff and move into Cher's guest house. She lives in a huge, beautiful place on the beach on Pacific Coast Highway, which must be one of the nicest places to live in the world. Her guest house is great, and Cher is the best godmother you could imagine. She buys me skateboards and is so sweet to me. She is lovely, warm, kind and caring.

Every now and then she picks me up from school in her limo and people notice, which means people notice me, which I am happy about. They want to know who is in the limo, and when word spreads that it's Cher and that we live with her, they think I'm cool. Kids can be very fickle, but this helps me fit in and make friends at school, and I suppose it gives me confidence.

My mum is working full time for Cher, and because she tours a lot my mum is often away with her for three weeks out of four. Much of the time I go with her, which means I'm on the road with Cher and her entourage. I find it a bit strange at first, but I settle in quite quickly. I have the best time with the backing singers and dancers, who are all gorgeous and kind of adopt me when we're away, so I get treated really well.

I make friends with the roadies too, who treat me like a little mascot. I guess I'm different to the usual crowd you get on tours – I'm the only kid around and I have a lot of fun. I see all the gigs, and stand in the crowd singing along with all Cher's fans.

While we're starting our new life in America, my dad has managed to get himself on to the public-speaking circuit in the UK and is earning good money. People are desperate to have him at their events because not only is he George Best the legend, but he's also funny and charming. He's so popular that he sometimes does two events in a day and can earn a few thousand for each one, so is bringing in great money. But there are two huge downsides to this: he's paid in cash, so the money goes out as quickly as it comes in, and there's alcohol at every event, so it's easy for him to drink. He starts gambling, and is still not paying his tax or his bills.

In August 1988, when I'm seven, my dad has a testimonial match at Windsor Park in Belfast. Before the game, I'm taken to my granddad's house. I see my dad's old bedroom and get shown the backyard, where my dad first played. I'm excited because I'm spending time with my dad and even though I don't understand what a testimonial is, I can tell something important is happening and I'm loving being with him for it.

I drive to the game with my dad and there are so many people around it's terrifying. I am beginning to understand that people love my dad, but I haven't seen this before and the sheer numbers do scare me. At the stadium, people are coming up to him, getting him to sign things or simply wanting to say hello to him. I walk along next to him holding his hand, loving that this man everyone wants to talk to is my dad and knowing that I'm safe if I stick close to him.

I go into the dressing room with him and the other players. There are legends here, like Pat Jennings and Ossie Ardiles, but I don't know who any of them are except for my dad. There's a really strong energy in the room and I don't know what to do, so my dad tells me to sit in the corner and wait. After a while, we walk out on to the pitch and I'm asked to do a pretend kick-off with him before the real one as a little show for the crowd. I'm so nervous because there are 25,000 people in the stadium and I've never seen anything like it. I'm terrified, but I slightly love the buzz of all the people cheering too. I do the kick-off and then watch the game. Every time my dad gets the ball the crowd goes nuts. At times it's so noisy I hide behind a chair and watch over the top of it.

At the end, I run out to my dad and we do a lap of honour together. I trot around the pitch next to him, trying my best to keep up. People are cheering him and I feel part of it and I'm so, so happy to be here with him. It's a special time for him and for all these people, and I'm right there next to him for the whole thing. It's a great, great day.

When I'm nine, my dad arranges to come over and visit me. I haven't seen him for ages and am even more excited than usual. My mum can see how desperately I want my dad to be around, to take an interest in me, and it upsets her because she knows how likely it is I'm going to be let down by him at some point.

On the day he arrives, we go to the airport to pick him up, but he's not there. My mum finds out that the flight has definitely arrived and that my dad was on it, but he is nowhere to be seen. She knows his habits, so we drive to Hermosa Beach, where he has his bar, Bestie's, to try to find him, but we can't see him anywhere. We check bar after bar, and eventually find someone who tells us he's in a hotel sleeping off all the drinks he had on the plane. In the end I don't see him at all on that visit and am heart-broken. I was looking forward to it so much, and I don't understand why my dad doesn't make the effort to see me. Then he goes home and life goes back to normal.

His is anything but normal, though. In 1990, when I'm nine, he makes his famous appearance on *Wogan*, where he has a lot to drink before going on to be inter-viewed. Terry Wogan himself later said he could see there was going to be trouble as soon as my dad walked on to the set: 'The eyes are glazed, and I knew the worst had happened . . . he's as drunk as a skunk.'

The most notorious part of the conversation – the part the newspapers went crazy about the next day – begins with my dad saying, 'Terry, I like screwing, all right?'

Wogan tries to make a joke of it, saying, 'So what do you do with your time these days?'

My dad replies, 'I screw.'

And then, with the audience making all sorts of shocked noises and a few of them laughing, the interview ends. It's funny, but also tragic.

The next year, in 1991, he is declared bankrupt again, this time owing around £100,000 in back taxes and interest. The following year he settles it for just £32,500. He's lucky to get away with so little.

For the years around this point, I don't see much of my dad. He is unstable, unreliable, and living on the other side of the world.

* * *

My mum is touring with Cher more and more now, and for the sake of my schooling I don't go with her as much. Instead, I stay in Malibu at Cher's house with her son Elijah, who's become a good friend of mine. I'm happy, but I really miss my mum and want her with me. I tell her how I feel; she agrees and decides to stop touring so much. She carries on working for Cher, but we move out of the guest house and into our own little place in Malibu.

Because of our move I start at a new school, Webster Elementary, in 1992 and I arrive with long, blonde hair. Having to leave my friends and make new ones again is a bit scary, but I've done OK before, so it doesn't worry me too much. I've got some confidence now, partly from the time spent on tour with the backing singers and the roadies, and I know that being a bit cheeky goes down well with people. When I go to new schools, I actually quite enjoy being the new kid. I stand out because I still have an English accent and I dress differently to the others, in a smart British style that my mum likes. The fact that I don't quite fit in means I can go and make friends with the coolest kid, or go straight up to talk to the prettiest girl (even at the age of eleven). Being a novelty gives you the freedom to do things like that, especially if, like me, you don't mind being the centre of attention. I soon learn that if I embrace the fact I'm different, and am comfortable with it, I get on well. I make friends I will be close to for ever.

I never mind moving to all these new places. I'm just

happy to be with my mum. As long as she's around, I think everything else will be fine. I'm constantly aware of how painful things are with my dad, but I cling to the hope that at some point it will be better and he'll want me around. But it doesn't work that way.

Soon after we arrive in Malibu, my mum meets a guy called Terry, and after a while they decide to get married. I like him and he's good to me – my mum wouldn't get serious with someone who isn't. She invites my dad to the wedding, and he says he'll come if she gets him a car from the airport to the ceremony. My mum agrees. She has invited him for me, really – she wants me to see that my dad is OK with her being with Terry, so I know not to worry, and she also wants me to spend time with him. I am delighted that he's going to be there and plan to hang out with him for the whole day. I won't leave his side, and he won't leave mine.

But again, he doesn't show up. And it's bad – he gets to the airport and instead of getting in the car my mum has arranged for him, he goes to Bestie's and gets stuck into some drinking. He doesn't even call to let me know he won't be there. He just doesn't appear. My mum is furious, and I am gutted. I burst into tears, and it casts a shadow over the whole day for everyone, which isn't fair. I feel like I don't matter to my dad, and I hate it.

Chapter 4

'I tell myself not to worry, and that things with my
dad will get better. This is just a temporary thing.'

Calum Best

Part of the agreement my parents made when my mum
and I moved back to the US was that when I was old
enough I would come to the UK every summer to spend
a couple of weeks with my dad. My mum is always
nervous about sending me away to be with him, but I'm
nothing but excited. I don't mind that I spend most of
the first couple of trips following him around London,
moving from pub to pub.

On my summer visit when I'm eleven, my dad
organizes my first visit to Manchester United. I'm going
to see the place where my dad did all those great things,
and I'm buzzing. I know what a great footballer he was,

and I'm so, so excited to be going there with him. Old Trafford is the place where he became a legend and by now I have seen enough videos, trophies, photographs and newspapers, and heard enough people talking about him to know exactly how important he was as a player. Here is where it all started; it's here that he became an idol. I'm so proud that he's my dad and that he wants to have me there with him. It feels like a huge deal to me, him taking me to Manchester United and wanting me to be part of a world that is so important to him.

We get to Old Trafford, and it's crazy. People are treating him like a god. It seems like every person we pass wants to stop him for an autograph or a photo, and he's happy to oblige. For me, it's weird seeing all this. I knew he was a star, but I had no idea he was treated this way. He's my dad, I keep thinking. Wow. This man who is everyone's hero is my dad, no one else's. Everyone can see me with him, they know I'm his son. I'm beaming with pride.

We go to the club shop and he gets me a red Manchester United shirt with the white collar, and he gets me a number 7 put on the back with BEST across the shoulders. I love it. I absolutely love it. I put it straight on and I'm so happy and proud to be walking round Old Trafford with his name and number on my back.

My dad buys me a football as well, and after the game the whole team sign it. We're in the VIP section and we talk to David Beckham's parents. They tell us about how he's just starting on his career and how exciting it is, and my dad turns to me and quietly says something about David Beckham being good, but he's no George Best. He's his usual cocky self and I love him for it.

There's an event after the game, and my dad does a speech with some other players. I love seeing him up on stage, being funny and relishing the attention. He's clearly loved by everyone. Afterwards we go to the Midland Hotel, where we're staying. I fall in love with the place because in the restaurant there are these hot plates where you cook your own food – steak or chicken or whatever you want. It's so much fun. We have dinner there, and I'm still buzzing. It's been a great day. I'm wearing my shirt and I have my new ball with me. I'm eating with my dad and a few other guys and everything is perfect.

After we've finished, I get a bit bored sitting there with my dad and his friends, so I take my ball and go and kick it around the lobby. Then I go outside the hotel, kicking it along the street and against walls. I don't think about how valuable this ball might be one day. I don't care how many trophies the players who signed it – Beckham, Giggs, Scholes, the Nevilles – might win one day. I just want to play football, so I kick it against anything I can find.

After a while I go back to my dad and his friends, and we end up in the big piano bar area. My dad is sitting there with some other guys. He's drinking brandy, and I can see him changing. His eyes are getting blurry, he's waving his hands around more when he's talking, and he looks much less like my dad than he did earlier in the day. I know he's like this because he's drinking.

The evening goes on, and I'm still running all over the place with my ball. Every now and then someone plays with me a bit, but basically I'm on my own.

At about 8pm I come back to the table from one of my little football runs and my dad isn't there. He's gone, and so has everyone else, and I don't know what to do. I'm standing there with my ball, staring at the chairs where they were all sitting and looking around the lobby for my dad, but I can't see him.

What do I do now? I don't have a room key. He'll be back for me soon, though, I'm sure of it. So I carry on kicking my ball around. An hour passes, no Dad. Another hour goes, and I'm getting upset. It's about 10pm now, and I don't like being here on my own. I don't know anyone, and I'm scared. I go up to the room to see if he's there. I knock on the door, but no one answers. I can't hear anyone inside.

Before my mum sent me over, she gave me a piece of paper with her number on and said if there's any kind of emergency, if I need anything at all, I should call her. Well, now I need something. I need someone to look after me.

One thing my dad did do was give me some cash. So I take one of my notes and change it for coins at the bar. Then I go out of the hotel to a red phone box, put in some money and call my mum. She's in the US, so my money doesn't last long. I end up going backwards and forwards from the phone box with notes and coins about five times because we keep getting cut off. Finally, we start talking properly. It's mid-afternoon in LA and my mum, who knows the time difference well, is seriously worried when I call. I am in tears.

'Mum,' I say, sobbing, 'I don't know where Dad is.'

'What? It's the middle of the night. Where are you?'

'I'm at a hotel in Manchester. He's gone, and I'm on my own. I don't know what to do.'

She tries to stay calm but I know she's upset. She asks for the name of the hotel and I give it to her.

'OK,' she says. 'Don't worry. Go back inside. Everything is fine. I can sort this out very easily. I'll call the hotel and everything will be fine, I promise.'

I go to the front desk and am peering over the top when my mum calls. She tells them to give me a burger, lots of chips, a drink and some ice cream, and then to put me in a new room, to show me how the TV works, and to charge everything to George Best.

They take me upstairs and put me in a room next to my dad's, with all my food. I think it's quite cool that I have my own room, but I'm traumatized that my dad has just left me. I eat and watch some TV, and am not happy at all. I feel alone and scared. I wish my dad was here with me. I'm still waiting for him, hoping he'll turn up. But he doesn't. It gets later and later, and eventually I fall asleep.

In the middle of the night, I wake up and try my dad's room again. There's no answer, so I go back into my own room and back to sleep.

The next day, I wake up early and I'm hungry, so I get out of bed and go down for some breakfast. My dad still isn't around, so I spend the morning hanging out in the hotel.

At lunchtime I get hungry, so I go for food. While I'm eating, my dad appears. He comes to the table, sits down and, in ways I don't quite understand at the time, he tells me he left me last night to go to see a hooker. He doesn't apologize or act like what he did was anything out of the ordinary, let alone wrong. He looks terrible, his hair is messy and greasy, and his eyes are bloodshot.

I don't know how to react, so I behave like this is normal. But I'm really hurt. I don't understand why he left me alone. Why didn't he want to be here with me? Why didn't he look after me? Eventually I tell myself not to worry, and that things with my dad will get better. This is just a temporary thing. I focus on what a great time we had before he left me and think that one day it will always be like that. I feel like shit now, but things between us will be so good. I know they will be.

The rest of the trip is spent in the pub. To me it feels like he tried hard at the start of my time with him, by arranging the visit to Manchester, but then lost interest or ran out of ideas and went back to his normal routine, which means the pub. I am still too young to link alcohol to the way he behaves, but in a few years I will come to see this as my first direct experience of something bad happening because my dad was drinking.

My eyes have been opened slightly, though, because I

now realize something isn't right with him. It can't be, if he can leave his eleven-year-old son alone like that. After this, things start to click together: I begin to notice newspaper stories about him and alcohol, and things people say seem to make sense in a different way. I begin to understand why he is the way he is – it's because he's a serious alcoholic.

Chapter 5

'I am about to start trying to go back to sleep when my dad rolls over, puts his face right in front of mine and kisses me.'

Calum Best

A few months later, my mum has to be in London for business. Luckily, this falls in one of the periods when my parents are still talking, so Dad invites us to stay with him in his flat on Oakley Street. It's a tiny, two-bedroom place, with a small front room and a really small second bedroom with a fold-out couch for a bed which my mum and I sleep on.

I am incredibly happy to be in town seeing my dad, as I am at any opportunity to spend time with him. To me it's as if Manchester never happened. I put it out of my mind and tell myself things will be better soon. This visit is the first opportunity for that to happen, but it doesn't work as I hope it will. My dad spends his days in the pub, possibly drinking even more than usual because of the pressure of having us around, and after a day or two of this my mum decides to take me out in London on her own. Since the incident in Manchester, I am starting to understand about Dad and the pub and drinking, and now know just enough to work out why we're not spending another day in his flat waiting for him.

My mum and I have a fun day, going around the sights and a few shops, and then we come back to Dad's flat. He's not there. After we've had dinner, it's time to go to bed and he still hasn't shown up. I decide to sleep in his room, partly because the sofa bed is so small and I'll be more comfortable there and partly because I just want to sleep in my dad's bed to feel close to him.

A few hours later, long after I fall asleep, my dad stumbles into the room and I wake up. He's obviously very drunk and he's noisy, and after a bit of rattling around by the door he gets into bed. I am about to start trying to go back to sleep when my dad rolls over, puts his face right in front of mine and kisses me – as in he sticks his tongue in my mouth. That kind of kiss.

I freeze. What is going on? What the hell is this? I have no idea what is happening, or why. I know what a French kiss is, so what the hell is my dad thinking of by doing it to me?

Years later, when I start drinking myself, I work out what happened here: he got home so out of his head that when he saw long, blonde hair in his bed he assumed it was a girl and did the obvious thing by kissing her, because he assumed that's what she was there for. But at the time, in the moment, all I know is that my stinking drunk dad just rolled over and put his wet, bearded mouth all over mine.

I scream, jump out of bed and run out of the room to my mum. I'm crying my eyes out. She looks after me, tells me it's all fine, everything is OK. The thing is, I don't actually think about why my dad might have kissed me; that never crosses my mind. This is just deeply weird, and it freaks me out more than anything that's ever happened. What kind of state must my dad be in to be able to do that, even if he has been drinking? In my mind, he becomes two people – the dad I love spending time with, the cool, fun guy, everyone's hero, and the drunk one, who's rarely around and does creepy things. I don't know how else to cope, so I split him up to preserve the good side.

I'm pretty sure my dad reacts to me screaming and running out of his room by passing out. He certainly doesn't come after me. The next morning, he goes to the pub as usual and we carry on like nothing happened. I don't know my dad well enough to bring it up with him, and I'm too young to understand the whole episode properly anyway. So I talk to my mum about it and that's all. She tells me to try not to worry, that my dad really loves me, and that sometimes when he's been drinking he does things that aren't the real him.

For a few days I'm confused and a little on edge, but,

as she always does, my mum calms me down and makes me focus on the positives. It would be so easy for her to show me how angry she is with him. She must have been furious, and I'm certain she gave him a proper telling-off at some point, but I don't see or hear it. She doesn't let how she feels about my dad's behaviour affect how I feel about him, and I will always love her for that. She knows there is good in him and wants me to believe in that. She also wants me to learn things for myself, which is why she continues to send me off to the UK on my own each summer, even after this. She's terrified, but I need to learn for myself.

My mum saw my dad when he was a great man, and she saw him when he was a dark man, and she wants me to know both sides of him. My mum believes that addiction is a choice at first, and as time goes by and the addiction gets deeper, it becomes harder and harder to fight it. Maybe she hopes seeing me will help my dad choose not to drink. Maybe I will give him something to fight for.

So later in the year, I still come over for my summer visit. I'm now beginning properly to understand alcohol's role in my dad's life. His routine is pub, food, home, every day. Pub all day, food in the evening, then home.

The Phene Arms in Chelsea is his favourite place. I spend my time there playing cribbage, watching football, and generally trying not to get too bored. Every time I'm here I think to myself, my dad doesn't seem too happy to have me around. I'm just fitting in with what he does every day. There's no, 'Right, what do you want to do today, son?' or 'Today I'm taking you here'. I know the trip we had to Manchester ended badly, but at least he wanted to take me somewhere. I'm starting to feel like I don't matter to him at all.

One evening, we're coming back from the pub and he's so drunk he's stumbling and has to lean on me to stay upright. We reach the front door, I get the keys out of his pocket and unlock the door because he can't. I take him into his room, flop him on to his bed and leave him to sleep. What am I supposed to do now? I go to bed and try to sleep. The next morning he's perfectly normal.

The trip isn't all bad, though. One morning I ask if we can go and play football together somewhere. I know how important football is to him and I play at home so I think it would be fun for us to play together. It's about 11am and he's only had a drink or two, which makes this the best time of day for him – I've already worked this out. My dad seems to think us playing football is a great idea and says yes immediately. It's such an obvious thing for us to do together, but for some reason it's never happened before. I am twelve.

We take a ball with us and walk from his flat in Oakley Street to a concrete pitch on Sydney Street a few blocks away, which has goals with no nets on and is in the middle of a really smart area. The sun is shining and we have the place to ourselves, just me, my dad and a ball.

Dad has his full beard and shaggy hair, and he's wearing that purple shell suit again. Over the next few years, as I come to understand what alcohol is to him and the effect it has on him, I learn that this version of my dad, messy and in that shell suit, is him when he's in a bad place. In the future, this is the image I will carry in my head of the man who will be in the middle of all the bad things that happen. But on this day, when I'm still young, he's just my dad, and we're playing football together.

We start by passing the ball between us. I'm trying hard to do my best, because I want him to think I can play his game too. After a while he starts giving me advice, telling me what I'm doing wrong when I pass the ball and how to do it better by using the inside of my foot. After the first few tips, our little game turns into a full-on training session. Dad teaches me how to drive a ball really hard by hitting it with my laces. Then he shows me how to take a corner kick properly by putting spin on the ball so it swerves into the goal. After that, it's sprints. He makes me run across the pitch, from one line to the other and back again, over and over, while he's telling me how important it is for a football player to be really quick and fit. I'm quite fast anyway – I win races at school – and I'm super-eager to show him.

We spend a few hours on the pitch, with him teaching me techniques I can use when I'm playing at school. All through it, I'm thinking how cool it is that I'm playing football with my dad. It's such a normal father-and-son thing to do, but this is the first time it's ever happened. I am loving it. And, of course, I'm getting a one-on-one private coaching session from one of the world's greatest players. I'm old enough to understand how awesome that is.

After we've finished and I can't run any more, we head to the pub. As soon as we get in, he starts telling people how fast I was and how well I played, which makes me feel great, because he's proud of me. Then he tells them I scored from a corner on my third try, which isn't actually true but I don't care because I love hearing him talk about me like this, with pride in his voice, boasting about how good I am at football.

There is no downside to this story, no violent, boozy end to the day. The only shadow over my memory of it is what happens the only other time we play football together, in Hyde Park a year later. I still have long blonde hair, and I'm wearing a Manchester United shirt which my dad gave me and black tracksuit trousers, with Reebok trainers. I know all this detail because there are photographs of us playing, and there are photographs of us playing because my dad set it up with the photographer so he could make some cash.

The photographer asks us to do a few things, posing and kicking the ball, and then at the end he gives my dad a brown paper bag full of cash, what looks to me like thousands of pounds. We go back to the Phene and he gives me some to spend, probably because he feels guilty about using me like that. At the time I am not bothered by what happened. But later it makes me sad to think such a precious moment was nothing more than a publicity stunt.

* * *

After I get home, I try not to think about my dad for a few months, until one day I hear he's coming over from London. Immediately I'm buzzing with excitement, counting down the days till he gets here. I know my mum is on speaking terms with my dad at the moment because the day of his arrival comes and we're going to the airport to pick him up. My mum wouldn't have offered to do that if they weren't talking. He's not staying with us, though. He wants to stay near Bestie's in Hermosa Beach, which is about an hour away down the coast from our place. It's a beautiful area, and if I could I'd live there for ever – it has a boardwalk along the front, a pier, lovely buildings. It's so pretty and I love the place. There are all these different beaches near Los Angeles, like Hermosa, Huntington, Newport, Santa Monica, Venice, all the way up to Malibu. It's a beautiful stretch of coast.

My dad is a partner in Bestie's with an old friend of his, Bobby McAlinden, and he takes great pride in it. We meet him at the airport and, as always, I'm thrilled to see him. I run towards him and hug him and he picks me up, and I'm just so excited he's here. He and my mum are happy to see each other too. My mum still loves him, but their relationship isn't always easy.

We drive to Hermosa Beach and my mum leaves me at Bestie's with my dad. I'll never forget the look on her face as she says goodbye – it's pure fear. She's obviously terrified about what might happen to me with him, but my dad is perfectly relaxed about it. He promises to look after me and I'm very happy to be with him. I don't think my mum finds either of our smiles very reassuring but she leaves me anyway. She doesn't really have a choice.

Bestie's doesn't look like much from the outside – it's all black and not very smart. You walk down three or four steps to a door and there's a big sign with Bestie's in red. I love the place – it's my dad's own bar and I feel like I run it with him.

We walk in and straight ahead is a big wall of memorabilia of my dad, most of which I've never seen before, such as a picture of him and Pelé which I will always remember. I'm so proud of him and this place because it means people in California, my home, know who my dad is, just like people back in the UK do. The bar is long and it's all made of old wood. It's not a clean-cut place, but not dirty or dingy either. On the right is a long, brown bar with all the drinks behind it and on the left is the seating area. At the far end, straight ahead, is my favourite bit, where the pool tables and dartboards are. There are three pool tables, and four dartboards, all with the rubber mats in front of them marking out the correct distances.

I am in heaven here. I can get a Coke and a burger whenever I want, play pool and darts all day, and I get treated like a prince because it's my dad's bar. We spend all day there, me playing pool and eating and meeting everyone – people who work at the bar, regulars, lots of them. They're all so happy that George is in town to do his thing and it's a great day. We're in there for three or four hours and then go to check into our hotel. It's a few blocks down and isn't the nicest hotel around, but it is the closest to Bestie's, which is what sells it to my dad.

We check into the hotel and I have my own room, which I'm thrilled about. It has adjoining doors to my dad's room but it is still my own room, and suddenly I feel very grown up. I'm loving this day. The hotel is blue and white and overlooks the beach. We leave our bags there and head back to Bestie's.

In the evenings the bar is really strict about the age of people they let in. It's a student area and lots of them are underage, so everyone who wants to come in has to show ID, which means they get lots of fakes. There's a bouncer called Martin, a really huge guy, with whom I hit it off straight away. Every night he collects fake IDs from all the people who fail to get in, and that night he gives them all to me for a laugh. This is brilliant – I'm thirteen years old and I have all these fake IDs, from Arizona, Florida, New York, all over the place.

I spend the evening playing pool and darts, doing the sorts of things I've been doing in pubs with my dad for years. He is a great, great pool player, and he's taking on anyone who'll challenge him and beating them, and he and I have games where he gives me tips about how to play better. I lap it up, being here with him, being George Best's son in George Best's bar. It's so much fun.

I don't really notice how much my dad is drinking. All I care about is that he's in California spending time with me, and everyone here is having a great time. There are a lot of older girls around who are being sweet to me because of my dad. The guys there are setting me up to go and talk to girls, which I'm very happy to do, and I play up to it, flirting with them. My dad knows what I'm doing and laughs too, in a kind of 'That's my boy' way.

The next day we go down to the beach. We swim in the ocean and walk down the pier. We go to the funfair and then something really special happens. Looking back, it's a bit corny, but I love this memory because it shows he was trying to be a good dad by doing things with me. That's why it is so special to me. It starts with my dad hiring a two-seater bicycle for us to ride together, a tandem. We ride it for ages, from Hermosa Beach all the way along the coast. He's at the front and I'm behind and we're laughing all the way because he's constantly joking around, telling me to start pulling my weight and pedal. Every time he looks round he catches me having a rest and we laugh even more.

I can never imagine him doing something like this in the UK. In the US he's free. Free from the fame and the fans. Free from the demons. On the beach, no one knows who he is. In the bar they do, but once we've cycled away from Hermosa Beach we're just another father and son cycling along together. No one is bothered by us. It's beautiful.

We ride for miles and miles, past a power station and off the road, where he shows off by taking us down little paths you're not supposed to be on. It's a real adventure and we feel like a team. That evening, it's back to the bar.

The next day I play up to Martin, my new friend the bouncer, by going down to a store to try to buy drinks using one of the fake IDs, just to see if it works. I fail, of course, and the guy in the store takes the ID. When I tell Martin what happened we have a good laugh. This is the kind of thing I do to show off, because I'm George's son. When I look back now I suppose I craved attention. I always have.

That's what it's like for the next couple of days. We eat ice cream, my dad asks me what I want for dinner, if I'd prefer Mexican or a burger, which means it's important to him that we eat what I want to eat. I've started to notice little things like that and they really matter to me. We hang out in the bar, at the beach and it's great, playing around, laughing and enjoying being together, making all these magical memories.

Until the third and last day, in the late afternoon, when my dad disappears.

We've been in the bar all day, enjoying ourselves all the way through. By now I've made friends with a woman who works behind the bar. She's in her forties and has been really caring towards me, always making sure I have what I need, drinks, food, coins for the pool table, anything. So when I start getting worried about where my dad is and am wondering whether or not I should call my mum, it's this lady who looks after me. She walks me back to the hotel, through the glass doors, along the blue-and-white hall, up the stairs, down the corridor and to my room. She gives me her number and says I should call if I need anything, and then leaves me in my room. I go to sleep, wondering where my dad is and why he left me.

When I wake up the sun is shining through my window. I notice the door between my room and my dad's is now slightly open, which it wasn't when I came in last night. That means my dad must be in there, and he must have checked up on me, which I'm very happy about. In just my boxer shorts, I get up and go over to it, so I can go and see him. I push it open, and there he is, standing by the bed. He's naked, hair wild and messy, eyes bloodshot, skin sweaty, and breathing heavily. And there's a blonde woman in the bed. She's lying on her front facing away from me so I can't see her face.

I'm looking at this scene, trying to take it all in and work out what it means. I see the blue carpets, the cream walls, the white sheets messed up on the bed, and then the two people in there. It's too much. I take a step back, pull the door shut and stand still, my mind frantically working to analyse the situation. My dad naked, this woman in the bed. Who is she? What's she doing here? I am thirteen, and I know about sex, but I've never seen anything up close and personal. As an introduction to it, this is probably not ideal.

My mind has jumped from a loving, fun few days with my dad, frolicking on the beach, eating nice food, riding a bicycle, playing pool and darts and hanging out with interesting people, to this – him naked with a random woman in his bed. So that's why he went missing.

Fucking hell, I think. I can't make any more sense of it than that. This whole scene is sordid and dirty. I'm in shock.

I don't know what to say, and I don't want to intrude, so I take a shower and go down to Bestie's on my own. I wait for my dad there and when he turns up after an hour or two, we don't talk about what I saw. It's another one of those situations that he doesn't know how to talk to me about and I certainly don't have a clue how to talk about it with him, so it's not spoken about at all.

Later that day, my mum comes to pick me up. She asks me if I had a good time, and I did. I had a great time. I'll never forget it, the good and the bad.

On the same trip – summer 1994 – my dad comes to coach my football team. I started playing properly a couple of years before, when a new local league started, probably as part of the build-up to the World Cup, which is being held in the US this year. My dad has been invited over for it, and I ask if he'll give us a training session. He says yes, he'd be happy to. I'm nervous about seeing him, but I'm still excited. He's doing this for me, after all.

By now, I love my football and I play for a team called Malibu Surf. We play in blue-and-white kit, and we're based on the Malibu Bluffs, this big, open grass area near the ocean, which is a beautiful place. The first time I came to training, a couple of years ago, there were about ten other kids playing, lots of mums and dads around, and someone had brought some cut-up oranges for us. I loved it immediately.

When we started playing, I was pretty good compared to the rest of the kids. I was fast, I had a good right foot, and I was tall, which helped. I didn't feel any pressure on me because of who my dad was – I was too young for that – so I just got on and played. It came naturally to me, and I started to enjoy myself, so wanted to play as much as possible.

As I played more, I began to put things together in my head – football and my dad, football and me – and that got me even more excited about the game and about being one of the best in my team. I would go home to my mum and say, 'I'm good at it! I'm good at it!' and it felt great because my dad was a footballer and now I was playing too. I didn't want to let him down. Obviously there's a difference between being the best player in Malibu Surf under-fourteens and being one of the best players in the world, but football became a link between us, something we had in common, and I was thrilled about it.

Inevitably, word got round the parents that my dad was that great player. The other players' dads started shouting, 'Give the ball to Bestie!' and I loved it, but it meant a lot to me that these people had got to know me before they found out about my dad. In their eyes, I was already good at football, so when they found out my dad was George Best, it wasn't the first thing they judged me on. They already knew me for other reasons, so finding out my dad was someone interesting didn't really alter their opinion of me. Here, I was me first, and George Best's son second, which meant a lot. They did start making a fuss though, and I enjoyed the attention.

For example, when a couple of the dads who were English found out who I was, they got all excited and said no wonder I was good at kicking the ball, my dad was George Best. The American dads said, 'Oh, who's George Best?' and when they found out he was one of the best footballers ever, they got excited and told the other parents, who told their kids, and then they got excited too. They already knew me, so learning that my dad was this amazing footballer just made me seem more interesting.

All this makes me seriously nervous on the day of my dad's training session. I have butterflies, but I'm not worried about the state he'll be in. I'm not quite at the stage of worrying whether or not he'll show up drunk or sober. It's the morning and the sun is shining, and I associate my drunk dad with the evenings and night-time, so I assume he'll be OK.

There are other things making me nervous, though. I don't know him very well, and I'm worried about him seeing me play. I want him to think I'm good at football, to be proud of me. I hope I'll be good enough. I'm also nervous about how good he'll be. Everyone is football mad at the moment. The World Cup is on, it's a big deal, and everyone knows I'm one of the best players in our team, but my dad is one of the best players ever, a legend.

I'm worried about whether or not he'll live up to everyone's expectations. He's older now, and I don't know how long it's been since he last played.

The day comes, and there are more people at training than ever before. That doesn't mean very many – probably fewer than fifty – but in our little football world there's quite a buzz to the occasion. At this point our team has been together for a few years and we're doing well, so word has spread a bit.

We're training as usual on the Bluffs. We do a few of our drills and then my dad shows up. He's wearing his full shell suit, light blue with black trim, and Reebok trainers. He has the usual long dark hair slicked back, and a full beard with flecks of grey in it. He has a watch on which was his gift from Fifa, football's governing body, for being at the 1994 World Cup tournament. It's engraved and looks expensive and clean and new, which means it stands out on him.

As soon as he arrives and people see him, I can feel them thinking, 'This is George Best? One of the best players ever? This little man? Is that really the guy with the skills?'

There's a tense moment, where everyone's wondering how this will go, but my dad smiles, says hello and cruises through it, and then he's just great. He's about forty, and can't be very fit, but he gets properly stuck in. He sends us over some crosses so we can practise heading the ball; he gives us some drills where we start at the goal line, run to him, he throws the ball at us, we head it back to him, then he throws it back over our heads, and we have to turn and shoot. We do a few different exercises and he gives us different bits of advice. He makes us do some sprints and by the end we're tired. He made us work hard, which meant he was taking it seriously, and I'm so happy about that.

At the end of training, all the kids want a picture with him, as do all the dads, especially the English ones, who are like excited little kids. Some of them shake my hand and thank me for bringing him along. The mums get that look on their faces I'm used to seeing on women when they're around my dad.

The whole day means a lot to me. I know he's not a young man any more and doesn't have the same magic moves he did when he was in his prime, so I'm really grateful to him for putting the effort in to show up, and being so good when he was here. He doesn't stay that long, but I don't mind. The time he was here was enough for me. It was short and sweet but a really meaningful moment. Here was my dad doing something for me, my dad here with me, us together, father and son. Everything I've ever wanted. We were together, and everyone saw us. I couldn't be happier.

Chapter 6

'Alcoholics don't operate on logic or reason, they work on impulse and once a drinking session has started, it has to run its course.'

George Best

Back at school, I dye my hair blue. It sounds dumb, I know, but I asked my mum first and she said sure, go ahead and do it if that's what you want. That's her way with me – she lets me do my own thing as long as I am honest with her and not getting into serious trouble. She lets me go my own way, so I can figure things out for myself and learn from my mistakes.

And the blue hair is definitely a mistake because it looks stupid and gets me kicked out of my school for a week. I have long hair, down past my chin, the same hair my dad mistook for a girl's, so there's no way I can hide it. I am only let into school again when I dye it back to its original colour, which isn't easy, because I have no idea how to turn blue hair blonde.

I know it was a stupid thing to do but I seem to do things to extremes, probably to get attention. At my school, I am the first kid to dye his hair, the first to get his tongue pierced, the first to get an ear pierced, and will be the first to get a tattoo, but my mum is cool about everything, absolutely everything. I think she knows that there's a reason for me being the way I am, for me needing to be cool and popular at school, and the ringleader when it comes to the naughty stuff. It's not her fault that I will go on to get myself into situations which could turn out far worse than they actually do, and which, when I think about them as an adult, I know I am lucky to get away with. My mum lets me be myself and gives me freedom. I suppose she doesn't want to restrict me in any way that I might rebel against. She saw what happened with my dad when anyone tried to impose rules on him. He would react by going wild, and she doesn't want me to do that. She wants me to be as grounded as possible and she thinks the best way for her to do this is to be a constant, calm, accepting presence in my life.

I'm enjoying being one of the popular kids when something happens that makes me even cooler: I get spotted by a model scout. My friends and I are really into skateboarding, and we dress like proper little skaters. One day we're skateboarding in Cross Creek, the local community centre in Malibu, when this older, seedy-looking guy stops me and asks if I've ever thought about modelling. I say no, and he says I should, and can he take my picture? Sure, go ahead, I say.

I go home later, tell my mum, and she's not impressed. She thinks he sounds like a creep, which, when I think about what happened, is understandable. But she does some research and it turns out he is the real thing. We get in touch and he takes me into an agency called LA Models, who send me out for my first audition. It's for Kraft Ketchup and will be shot by a well-known photographer called Peggy Sirota. I get the job. It pays me $2,500, and I am thrilled. I do Guess jeans next, which is another great job. I'm a pretty boy, with green eyes and long blonde hair, and I'm quite tall, which must be what they want at the moment.

The jobs come along every now and then. They're not constant, but when I do get one it's great. The work is fun, and the cash is very welcome, especially as I'm chasing after girls now.

I'm not doing very well at Malibu Middle School, where I go from the ages of thirteen to fifteen. I'm not a real troublemaker – one of the angry kids – but I'm not a good student either. I'm much more interested in girls, skateboarding, and something else I've started to spend a lot of time doing: getting high.

There's a side to Malibu which is much darker than people realize, and it's mostly down to the locals, who hate outsiders. There's a gang around called MLO, which stands for Malibu Locals Only, and they cause some trouble. It's mainly made up of guys who have left high school but still live in the area. They do things like sell drugs to the kids still at school, like me and my friends, and try to take out the high-school girls. I think they're sad and a bit grimy, but that doesn't stop me and my friends from buying weed from them when we first get into it. Some of these guys work as paparazzi photographers, and that kind of territorial surf-beach mentality is quite strong here.

Malibu is beautiful, and a great place for a family to live, which is why we have our home here. But when you see the underbelly, as I'm starting to, you see that drugs are everywhere. I'm the kind of kid who won't say no to anything, so I get caught up in some bad stuff.

By the time I turn fourteen, I've grown up a lot. I'm over six feet tall, and I think I know a lot about the world. But even after everything I see and do in Malibu, I'm still not prepared for what happens during my next visit to London, in summer 1995. I cherish these visits because I hardly ever see my dad, which is hard for me in the same way it would be for any other boy my age. He's busy at the moment, doing public speaking and media work. Still drinking, of course, but at least his days aren't empty.

Where he is concerned, little gestures and signs matter to me, like the huge empty champagne bottle he has in his flat, which is so big it's as high as the mantelpiece. Dad puts coins in it over the months before I come to visit and then we spend the money when I'm here. The more coins I see in the bottle when I arrive, the more it means he's been thinking about me when I wasn't around. This time there is a lot of money in the bottle, and I'm thrilled when I first see it. But that moment turns out to be the high point of my stay.

On my first day, we go to the Phene and my dad is drinking as normal. It feels like he doesn't want me here. But at the same time, people in the pub tell me how he's been talking about me coming over for the past few weeks, telling them how well my modelling is going, how tall I am, how well I'm doing with the girls, and how happy he was that he would be seeing me soon. But when I arrive, he just gets drunk and doesn't seem interested. Which version am I supposed to believe?

By now my dad has a new fiancée, Alex, a blonde air hostess he met in a nightclub and proposed to in the Phene. I really like her – she's quite young, is always sweet to me, and is fun to be around. She's also hot, which I'm very happy about, mainly because it shows that my dad can still be that charming, popular guy everyone loves. We get on well, and she looks out for me.

That afternoon, we're in the Phene – my dad, Alex and me, when this guy comes in and tries to sell us drugs. My dad hates drugs and he goes crazy at him: 'Who the fuck do you think you are? What the fuck do you think you're doing, coming in here and offering us that shit? I'm with my fucking family!' My dad is a small guy and he doesn't go looking for trouble, but he's not scared of people and he can be quite scary himself, which isn't something I've ever seen before.

A couple of days later, I'm in the Phene again with my dad, this time with an Irish friend of his. I don't know this guy, but to me he looks like a proper hard nut, the kind of Irishman you don't want to be messing with. He and my dad are having a lads' day out and doing some serious drinking.

After a lot of drinks we move on to the Rat and Carrot for a game of pool. We start playing and a really loud English guy notices my dad and starts talking to him: 'Hey, Bestie! Give us an autograph! Do you want a beer? What a legend!' Actually, it's more like shouting than talking, and that begins to piss off my dad, who says something back quite aggressively and they start arguing.

The next thing I know, my dad's mate drags this English guy out into the street and starts beating the living daylights out of him, in front of me and my dad. He stops after a few minutes and my dad says they need to get out of there, and they leg it back to the Phene.

I'm left standing there, on my own, and this guy is on the ground. I'm only fourteen and a bit naive, so I check he's OK. I start talking to him, he looks up, sees who I am, gets up and goes for me. He charges at me and I turn round and run. Luckily I'm quite fast and fit from football, so I get away pretty easily. I lose him in the streets of Chelsea, and then head to the Phene to find my dad, who's already there.

About twenty minutes after leaving the Rat and Carrot, I go to the loo in the Phene. When I come out, I see a white van pull up outside the pub. Five guys get out, come charging in and a massive ruck kicks off in the bar. Among the guys is the one from the Rat and Carrot, and they're all going for my dad and his mate. Almost immediately, my dad's mate gets hit round the head with a bar stool and is out cold on the floor. I can see my dad in the middle of all this, fighting away like the crazy, tough little dude he is.

I panic at the sight of him being attacked and start moving towards him. I swing at anything and anyone I see. I don't think I actually connect with anyone, but I'm giving it my best shot. I get hit in the back with a bar stool, then get pushed against the wall. Now I'm standing there with my back to the wall trying to protect myself from these guys. Out of the corner of my eye, I see my dad notice what's happening to me and he goes even more crazy, thinking I'm in real trouble. I see that the scary Irish dude is back on his feet, and all around me everyone seems to be hitting everyone.

Then it all stops, for no reason I can see, and the five guys run out of the pub, get into their van and drive off. We're standing there, looking at each other, and the ladies who work behind the bar immediately start checking I'm OK, which I am. I'm a bit bruised and upset, but there's no serious damage done. I'm also very shaken up and my heart is pumping. I sit down with a Coke and try to calm myself down.

A few minutes later the police turn up. They ask my dad what happened. 'Nothing,' he says. 'I didn't see anything.' They ask his mate what happened. Same answer: nothing happened, and if anything did happen, he didn't see it. They come to me next, and I say exactly the same. It's the first time I've been in a situation where the rule is you don't tell the cops anything. It's not great that my dad is the one teaching me to keep my mouth shut in front of the law, but I stand by him.

When things calm down, something pops into my memory from the middle of all the chaos, which I didn't register properly at the time. When the guys were running out, my dad yelled at them, 'Don't you ever fucking come to Belfast!' Even in this pub in the heart of Chelsea, with all his fame and notoriety, he's still a Belfast boy.

A few hours later, when things have quietened down and my dad has had a good few more drinks, we go for a Chinese and he's so drunk he eats his food with his hands. I am seeing him do this more and more – it happens when he's very pissed – and it's gross. What makes it even worse is that he carries on drinking. He can't seem to stop himself.

That's how my dad felt when he was drinking, as if he really couldn't stop. He described it like this: 'Alcoholics don't operate on logic or reason, they work on impulse and once a drinking session has started, it has to run its course, regardless of any other demands on your time which any normal person would react to.' I'm one of those other demands, and the drinking continues.

I phone my mum that evening, and when I start telling her about what happened I burst into tears. That's when

I realize just how messed up what happened was – a fourteen-year-old kid gets into a bar brawl with his dad in a Chelsea pub. It was pretty heavy stuff, and I wonder how often he gets into fights like that. It didn't happen because I was there – it kicked off because this guy recognized him and my drunk, angry dad didn't like the way he was spoken to.

The next day, we're at another bar, Henry J Bean's on the King's Road, at lunchtime. My dad is drinking dry white wine, and when I finish my Coke he tells me to go and get a proper drink. He gives me some cash and I walk up to the bar, feeling pretty cool about it. I don't know much about drinking anything other than beer, which I don't like all that much, but I like sweet things, so I decide to order something that sounds good to me. I choose a piña colada. I get back to the table carrying this huge glass topped with a chunk of pineapple, an umbrella and a straw. I'm pleased with my choice, but my dad is not impressed. 'If you're going to drink with me,' he says, 'you're not drinking that fucking thing.'

I get a beer after that.

My dad doesn't usually encourage me to drink, but he doesn't tell me not to either. I don't know if this is because he doesn't think I'll end up like him, or he doesn't care if I end up like him. Maybe he thinks he's not really in such a bad state after all, so showing me how he drinks and letting me drink too isn't a negative thing. Maybe it's an initiation of sorts. A rite of passage.

But to be honest, I don't think it is any of those things. He doesn't even think about it. He's too fixated on his own drinks, and me having one too barely registers. Does he think I'm too young? I'm not sure he even knows how old I am.

I end up leaving my dad in the pub that afternoon, because I don't want to sit around drinking all day, and I go back to his flat, where Alex is. We spend the evening hanging out, we eat dinner and play cribbage, and I enjoy myself. I don't get cosy nights in like this very often at my dad's place.

I already know that if I want to spend time with my dad I generally have to go to the pub. Most of the time, that's OK with me. I already know he has an alcohol problem, but I don't yet fully understand what that means, for him and for me, and I'm still young enough to think pubs and booze are more cool and fun than dangerous. But at the same time, it makes me sad when Dad chooses to go drinking instead of hanging out with me, especially when we've been apart for so long.

Tonight Alex and I are waiting for him to finish drinking and come home. We know he'll be back sooner or later because when the pub closes he'll have nowhere else to go.

Dad's flat is still the small, basic place on the ground floor of a townhouse on Oakley Street, the first door on the right as you walk in. He and Alex are sleeping in the bigger bedroom and I'm in the smaller one as usual, sleeping on the fold-out couch – a creaky piece of crap

– surrounded by my dad's clothes and trophies and various bits of memorabilia. There's more memorabilia in the living room, pictures of him with Matt Busby and Denis Law, a great big painting someone did of him, some family photos, a few CDs, a couch and a Native American rug. The kitchen and bathroom are tiny. It's all basic, nothing flamboyant or luxurious.

Alex is much younger than my dad, only twenty-three, which makes her just nine years older than me. When they first met I doubted her reasons for getting involved with him, but I don't any more. She loves him, that's obvious. And now I'm enjoying hanging out with her, enjoying her company and the reflected coolness of my old and broken dad getting married to this beautiful woman. She's drinking a glass of white wine and we're sitting on the floor playing cribbage, my dad's favourite pub game. He taught me how to play it in the pub. In fact, we've probably played cribbage in the pub more than anything else we've done together as father and son, definitely more than we've played football and probably more than we've even talked. I don't know enough about life to see the sadness in this. Not yet.

I am lying on the floor with my back to the living-room door and the TV is on. Alex seems a bit nervous. I'm not sure why. The later it gets, the more skittish she becomes. I don't know what's bothering her, but she's not comfortable. This is just a normal evening, I think; what's to worry about?

And then my dad arrives home.

We hear him try to put the key in the lock and Alex jumps up. 'Your dad's home,' she says, all nervous and agitated.

After a few tries he gets the door open and comes in. I turn and look, a smile ready for him when he appears.

The man I see shocks me. Dad is in a bad state. He has messy, shaggy hair and a full beard with lots of grey in it. His face is swollen and the skin on his hands and his cheeks and his forehead is red and peeling. He looks like he's been out drinking for three or four days.

Jesus, Dad, I think, you don't look so well.

There's a pause as he looks around. I see his eyes and they're blazing.

'What the fuck is going on here?' he snaps, raising his voice immediately. He's not just angry, he's raging.

He's leaning back against the wall for support and slurring his words, but he looks dangerous.

I look at Alex and she's terrified.

'I don't know what you mean, George,' she says. 'We've just been here, having a nice time.'

Like she thinks he would be happy his son and his fiancée are getting on. As he should be.

But that just sets him off. He's shouting now.

'What the fuck do you two think you're doing? What the fuck do you two think you're fucking doing?'

He repeats those words a few times, getting louder and louder. As he speaks he pushes himself away from the wall and starts waving his hands around like he always does when he talks and gets excited, only now they're going much faster than normal.

'Nothing, Bestie,' Alex says, looking at Dad with fear in her eyes. 'We're just playing cards, that's all.'

'Dad,' I say, trying to calm him down, 'we were just hanging out, playing cards and waiting for you to come home.'

'No you're fucking not,' he screams. 'I know what you two were doing. Who the fuck do you think you are? What the fuck do you think you're doing together?'

I realize what he must be thinking – that something is going on between me and Alex. Of course it's not. It never has and never will. But my dad, my drunk, old, alcohol-poisoned dad, is convinced his fourteen-year-old son and his young fiancée are getting it on behind his back. That's ridiculous. I might be taller than him, but I'm his son. He doesn't need to be threatened. He's my dad. How could I threaten him?

'It's not what you think,' Alex says, crying now. 'It's not what you think. There's nothing going on.'

Alex is pleading with him. I stand up and attempt to take control of the situation.

'Dad,' I speak calmly, 'chill out. This really is not what you think.'

I try to change the subject. I ask how his evening was, how he's doing. But instead of answering my questions he goes for me.

'Fuck off, you piece of shit. Fuck off. You're not my fucking son.'

91

The words make my whole body shiver. My chest tightens. I'm not his son? He's never spoken to me like this before. He's never hurt me like this before. My father, my idol, my hero, is telling me I'm not his son.

'Dad, what are you doing?' I say, trying to hide the shake in my voice. 'What are you talking about? What do you mean I'm not your son? What do you mean? Don't be so silly.'

I'm trying to keep calm – I'm the only one who hasn't lost it already – but I know I'm failing.

By now we've turned round and I'm standing with my back to the wall. Dad is staring at me with hatred in his eyes. I'm afraid of him.

'Don't you fucking lie to me,' he snarls, stepping closer. 'You're not my son, you fucking piece of shit.'

And boom – his right hand whips up to my throat. The back of my head hits the wall, I feel his hand tighten around my neck and then my feet lift up off the ground. I'm gasping for breath.

I'm already over six feet tall, much taller than my dad, and I think I'm pretty tough. I've looked at my dad before and thought, you're small and old, I don't need to be afraid of you. But right now, with him holding me by the neck off the ground up against the wall with one hand, screaming at me and telling me I'm not his son, I'm just a little boy. A terrified little boy.

'George, stop,' Alex screams. 'What are you doing? Please, George, stop.'

'Fuck off, you—' and he lets fly at her with a load of insults.

Alex is screaming and petrified; I'm terrified and I can hardly breathe with my dad's hand round my throat.

'You're not my fucking son,' he keeps shouting, again and again and again as he chokes me. 'You're not my son, you're not my fucking son.'

And then he lets me go. I drop down on to my feet and try to breathe. I'm rasping, coughing, trying to get air down my neck. I see his hand drop down to his side and then whack, up it comes and he backhands me across the right side of my head, knocking me over.

Now I'm on the ground, the side of my head is throbbing and I start crying, bawling my eyes out.

'Oh my God,' I say. 'Dad, how can you do this? What are you doing?'

'You're not my fucking son, you little shit,' he yells. 'I hate you. You're not even meant to be. You're not my fucking son.'

Over and over he says it: *you're not my son, you're not my fucking son, you're not even meant to be. I hate you.*

He doesn't say you're not meant to be here. He says you're not meant to be, as in I'm not meant to be at all. As in he didn't want a son in the first place and he definitely doesn't want me now.

I know what he's doing – he's telling me he hasn't seen me for so long because he doesn't want to see me. He lives on the other side of the world because he doesn't want me. He doesn't want me as his son. He hasn't paid me any attention for my entire life because he doesn't care about me. That's where I am with him. He's saying it now because he's drunk and the truth is coming out. I get the message, Dad. I am in pieces.

I'm crying hysterically and so is Alex and he's telling her to fuck off, and his face is full of so much rage and so much booze that his eyes are lost and to me it's as if this man is not even him any more. The alcohol has completely taken over.

And I think – I hope – maybe this really is just the alcohol talking. Maybe this monster who doesn't want me isn't my real dad. It's possible, I know it is, because a couple of days ago at the pub people were telling me how he'd been talking about me all week, how excited he was that I was coming over to see him and how he couldn't wait for me to get here.

But that was last week, before I got here. And now the alcohol demon has taken him over and that's why I'm in a ball at his feet, my face covered in tears while Alex screams. The booze has taken over and either he really does hate me or he really does love me and he started thinking about the guilt he feels for not being there for me and then all these things built up and the alcohol demon came out. Maybe this horrible drunk man isn't my real dad.

'Fuck you both, get the fuck out of here,' he says and storms off to his room, slamming the door behind him. His room is only a few feet away, so he doesn't have far to go. I get off the floor and follow him in. I am desperate for him to take back what he said, for him to tell me I am his son and he loves and wants me, anything to take the edge off what I'm feeling.

I open the door and stand at the end of his bed. 'I love you, Dad,' I say. 'I love you, I'm sorry. I love you.'

I'm still crying and Alex is in the doorway crying too. I keep repeating it – I love you, Dad, I'm sorry – although I don't know what I'm apologizing for. But it doesn't make any difference to him. He gets into bed fully clothed, turns his back to us and pulls the duvet over himself.

'Fuck you,' he shouts. 'You're not my son. Get the fuck out of my room. Fuck off.'

I look at him for a moment and feel small and alone. And beaten. He's won. I get the message. I leave it there.

Alex hugs me and is really apologetic. 'I'm so sorry,' she says. 'Please don't worry. He's had a lot to drink, he doesn't mean it.'

How can he not have meant it? He didn't say those things by accident. They must have come from some-where. I am upset, and now terrified of him. For the rest of my life, I will remember the feeling of him choking me, his fingers around my throat, that look in his eye, and the feeling that he doesn't want me to be his son. He doesn't want me, and he said it because he's drunk and that's when the truth comes out.

I call my mum and cry to her. I don't know what to do. I think I want to go home, but how? It's the middle of the night. I want to leave the flat but where would I go? For a walk? To see friends?

In the end I go to sleep on that shitty little couch, surrounded by my dad's clothes and his football memorabilia.

I wake up the next morning and my dad's not in the flat. What do I do now? I have no idea. Where do I go from here? I have two more weeks in town. Do I go and see him? Do I talk about it? Do I act like nothing happened? Should I just go home and try to forget all about him? Or is there something between us we can save? Can anything good be salvaged from last night's wreckage?

In the end, I decide to go to see my dad. I have to know where I stand with him. I can't just give up on him. I could never do that, so I'm hoping again, desperately telling myself it won't always be like it was last night, that one day things will be better. One day we'll be stronger. I know exactly where he'll be – the Phene. He's always there.

I get to the pub, compose myself, and walk in. He's sitting at the corner of the bar with a glass of white wine in front of him, in his usual morning state, as sober as he can be at this time of day.

I go straight over to him. I don't hesitate because right now I need more than anything in the world to talk to him, to know if we're OK.

He sees me coming and turns to look at me. 'Hi, son,' he says, as if things were totally normal.

And that's it. There's no conversation about what happened last night. No feelings discussed, no apologies offered. It is just left alone, swept under the rug, never to be talked about.

And over all the years that follow, over all the conversations we have, that night is never, ever mentioned. I'm not even sure he remembers any of it.

But I do, I remember it all, and I'm finding it hard to be around him now. I leave the pub and go to the Rat and Carrot. I've spent so much time in there with my dad that I've made friends with a few guys who work behind the bar, and I like the place because it has pool tables and is always full of girls. I come here on my own every now and then, to do something different, and sometimes my dad pops in while I'm here. If he does, I always shout out to him, 'Hi, Dad!' to make sure everyone in there knows I'm his son. I feel a need to claim him in some way. To show the world there's a connection between us, even if that's not how things really are. Despite everything, I'm proud of him. I'm not sure what I'll do if he comes in today, though.

I get in there, say hello to the guys I know, and immediately one of them says, 'Hey, Calum, what's that bruise on your neck?' I find a mirror and have a look. There's a handprint around my throat. You can actually see where my dad's fingers held on to me. It makes me feel sick. I'm so upset about what happened that I can't hide my feelings, and I end up telling the guys everything. They're shocked.

A few days later, a story appears in one of the papers about how George Best beat up his son. It must have been one of those guys who sold it. I thought they were my friends. Maybe I was naive to tell them what happened, but I didn't know any better. I'm fourteen, and I don't know anything at all about how the newspapers work.

That night messes me up for a long time. I'm shocked, ashamed and upset. Fundamentally, I don't know where I stand with my dad because he rejected me so viciously. I can't believe he could treat me like that. I'm in a daze for the next few days, and it carries on until I get back to the States and see my mum, who is so sad for me, which seems to happen every time I get home from London.

Chapter 7

'Imagine the life he could have lived if he'd never had a drink.'

Calum Best

I spend the rest of the summer hanging out with my friends. We fall in love with weed, and smoke it every day. That and skateboarding are how I fill my time off before I start in the ninth grade at Malibu High School in September. Once we're there, my friends and I quickly establish a routine: we wake up, meet up, smoke some weed before school, go to school, smoke weed at lunch-time and then at the end of the day, we go and smoke some more weed. This is every single day. We have friends who grow the stuff, and the older kids are more than happy to sell it to us, so it's incredibly easy to get. I've just been through a rough time with my dad, and drugs and the things that go with them – hours spent messing about with my friends, people I feel I belong with – are the best way I've found to block everything out. I don't really care if what we do is illegal or not. We aren't hurting anyone and no one is forcing us to do anything we don't want to, so I can't see much of a problem.

When I turn fifteen in February, one of the first things I do is get my licence and start driving around with my mum. She starts me off young, figuring that the sooner I learn and the more experience I get, the better at it and the safer I'll be. I love the freedom and can't wait to be driving around on my own.

The next drug we get into after weed is magic mushrooms. After school we often get some beers, mushrooms and weed and ride our BMX bikes down to a ravine by the beach, where we have a great time, drinking, smoking and taking drugs. Whenever a new drug comes along, we try it and, mostly, like it. And then one day someone brings acid to school.

None of us has seen it or taken it before, and we don't really know much about it except what we've heard from TV, magazines and stories. One other guy and I decide to take it straight away anyway. We don't stop to think about what might happen, we just take it as quickly as we can, even though we are at school and it's the middle of the day. This is how I am now – I don't hesitate to do things like this which aren't just dangerous to my health but could badly affect my education. I don't care about any of that. I am much more interested in cutting loose.

It doesn't take long until I'm sitting in class tripping

my head off, rubbing my desk with my hands, feeling like my eyes are popping out of my head, and looking at my friend, who is tripping as well. Both of us are giggling because we can't understand how the hell no one knows what we are doing. But we never get caught. We must be lucky.

My attitude to drugs has always been completely relaxed and easy – I like new experiences, new rushes, so whatever it is, I'll take it. I'm not worried, even though I know my dad hates drugs and would go crazy if he knew about any of it. I would hate to disappoint him, but it's possible another subconscious part of me wants to do these things to spite him. But what does it matter, if he's thousands of miles away? It's not as if he doesn't have his own vices. And I like weed and the other drugs I've tried so far. I don't have a worry in the world when I smoke it. I'm relaxed and happy and at peace with the world. My friends and I now always have some with us, and it's part of our lives whatever we are doing, every day.

I do worry about what my mum would think if she found out about all this, but not enough to stop. I don't ever want to upset her but she has given me the freedom to live how I want to and right now this is my choice. I figure that what she doesn't know can't hurt her.

After the mushrooms and acid come into our lives, we end up slipping into a really dark place with drugs, one I'll never forget.

We've worked out there are two challenges with our drug taking: getting hold of the drugs and finding somewhere to take them where we wouldn't get into any trouble for it. On the second challenge, we're lucky because the mum of one of my friends is a hippy and she lets us do whatever we want at their house. I mean anything.

On the first challenge, we get lucky too. We meet this kid out and about one day who is obviously not happy, in himself or his life. He's at a school for troubled kids, is goofy-looking and a bit slow and shy and awkward with us. But he obviously wants to be our friend, and he seems like a nice guy and is about our age, so we're happy for him to stick around.

Just after we meet and he is trying to get in with us, one of the first things he says is that he has this friend called Jerry who he can get free acid from. After we get to know the kid better, we quickly find out that he's one of a group known as Jerry's Kids. Jerry is a guy in his late thirties who lives at Point Dume, the most prestigious part of Malibu. His parents live in a big house and Jerry lives in a smaller place at the end of the garden. There are beaten-up, battered cars around, and even though his parents are rich it's all quite seedy and run down.

Jerry's Kids hang out at his house, and he gives them drugs and lets them do what they want in there. This sounds good to us. But before we're invited to go there too, we have to get to know Jerry and, of course, it falls on me to go and see him first. So the goofy kid gets Jerry to come and pick me up. My friends wait at the hippy mum's house and I skateboard down to the bottom of the hill next to it. After I've waited for a while, Jerry comes by in his blue Chevy pick-up and takes me to his house.

The place is a really dingy, seventies-style shithole, with brown carpet and foam furniture, and everywhere is dark and dirty. And Jerry is a strange man. He has a weird limp, long shaggy hair and a beard. When we get into the house, he asks what I want. I say acid, please, and he gives me a sheet of acid tabs. A whole sheet, for free. I think this is very cool.

Some of Jerry's friends are there and he invites me to hang out for a while, which makes me feel even cooler because I'm sitting there with all these older guys when I'm still only fifteen. After a while, Jerry takes me back to my friends with the acid, which he never asks us to pay for.

A week or two later, I ask Jerry if I can bring some of my friends to his house because I think it's cool there and I think they would like it too. I'm getting to know Jerry better and he says that would be fine. So two friends and I go round to his house one day and the goofy kid is there, the kid we know nothing about other than he seems nice, but is obviously a bit troubled. We talk to him and he says to us, 'Do you want to try this other stuff?'

As I've already said, I always seem to be the first to try anything, so I say, sure, let's do it. We'll try whatever. We go with the kid into one of the bedrooms and it's dark, damp, depressing and nasty in there. When I get older, I really don't like the idea of being somewhere like this, but when I'm fifteen I'm not scared or nervous. I just think it's exciting.

We go into the room and the goofy kid sits on the bed. He has a spoon in one hand and a lighter burning under it in the other hand, and he's cooking something up. On the table in front of him he has a Coke can which is bent in half and has a hole in it, with bits of ash on it. I don't really know what's going on, so I just sit and watch.

Next the kid scrapes the spoon and this little rock drops on to the table. He breaks off a small piece and puts it on the pile of ash, then breathes it in through the can. Then he goes, 'Who's next?'

Fuck it, I think. I'll do it.

I don't know it at the time, but we're smoking freebase. This guy had got some cocaine, put it in with some baking powder and water and some other stuff, and then cooked up the rock. It's serious stuff, part of a much darker scene than we've been into until now.

The drug makes me feel good. After I've taken the hit, I blow out the smoke and say to my friends, 'Someone ask me a question!' And someone says, 'What's 242 times 399?' and I throw this number back at them, sure I know what the answer is because I'm so high I think I'm a genius. I have an answer for everything.

For the next few weeks, we keep going to Jerry's house to take acid and smoke freebase. One day Jerry puts us in the back of his truck and drives all the way out to East LA, which is the scariest part of town, to pick up a batch of coke the size of a basketball. We sit in the back, happy as anything for the whole journey, with no idea of the danger we could be in. East LA is where the serious gangsters are, and we are a bunch of young white boys who don't really know anything about anything.

My mum doesn't suspect anything dodgy is going on because I lie to her. I tell her we're going to Jerry's house to work on cars and dirt bikes, and generally mess around, because I don't want her to worry. I don't like lying to her, but I would rather feel guilty for doing that than tell her the truth. I find out a few years later she's gone to see Jerry's parents to make sure he's OK, and they've told her I'm being truthful and nothing bad is going on. Apparently the parents are nice, so my mum doesn't worry. But the truth is, Jerry's parents have no idea what is really going on down in that house.

About four weeks after the trip to East LA, I'm sitting in class in school and I get called to the principal's office. On the way there I'm trying to work out what I might be in trouble for. I come up with a couple of ideas, but when I get into the office I find out I'm a long way off. Instead of an angry principal, there are two police detectives waiting for me. I am terrified. I sit down and decide I should say I know nothing about anything, like I did with my dad at the Phene after that fight.

'Calum,' one of the cops says, 'we have some questions for you about a man called Jerry, who lives in Point Dume. Do you know him?'

'No,' I say, 'I have no idea what you're talking about.'

My first thought is that I don't want them to know what I've been doing at Jerry's house.

But the policeman ignores what I say and tells me they've had a complaint from the goofy kid about cocaine and acid being taken there. I say I know absolutely nothing whatsoever about anything like that, but they carry on asking me questions, and eventually I admit smoking some weed there, but no more than that.

Word spreads quickly among my friends and, because the school is involved, to their parents, which includes my mum. She's quite relaxed about it, though, because she thinks nothing all that bad has been going on. A few days later I am at home in my room talking on the phone to one of my friends. We're terrified about how much trouble we are potentially in and I'm saying to him, 'What are we going to do? The cops are involved, so we need to come up with a plan. How are we going to get out of this?' We talk through the whole story, trying to work out a way of getting us into the clear, and we think we're making progress.

In the middle of the conversation I turn and look at my door, and there's my mum. She's heard every word. My stomach starts turning somersaults. Shit. We can't hide anything now. I put the phone down and look at my mum's face. From her expression, I realize how serious the situation is, and I get really upset and start apologizing and crying because I don't want my mum to be angry or disappointed in me. I don't want to let her down.

But she doesn't get angry. Instead, she is completely

calm. She sits me down and says, 'Calum, you have to tell me what's been going on so we can deal with it and everything can get sorted out.'

She says it in a way that is so kind and gentle that I have absolutely no choice other than to tell her everything, which I do. The whole lot, every last detail.

This is obviously a serious situation, so a meeting is then set up at someone's house with me and my mum, my friends and their parents. We go along to it and are told that there is more to what has been going on than just drugs. It turns out that when we were smoking the freebase and needed more, the goofy kid would go to Jerry to get it for us, and Jerry would get the kid to touch him in return for the drugs.

We all feel so, so awful. We had no idea that was going on, no idea at all. We thought Jerry was just a nice older dude who was hip and cool and rich enough to give out free drugs. To find out he was molesting the weak boy of the group was terrible. I know that sounds naive, but we were teenagers. We didn't know any better. Jerry knew the kid was the vulnerable one and I guess that's why he picked on him.

As soon as I hear what has been happening I own up to everything. I end up giving a witness statement and going to court for Jerry's trial, which my mum is really proud of because no one else does that. I don't actually have to get on the stand and be cross-examined because I'm too young, but my statement is used. At the trial Jerry's parents are screaming and shouting about all us kids being liars, but that doesn't help him, and he goes to jail for abusing the goofy kid.

He gets out of jail a couple of years later and I see him driving around the place. I'm terrified he's going to come and get me. But nothing ever happens. As I said, Malibu can be a dark place.

But this whole episode doesn't stop us taking drugs. I feel like I let down my mum with everything that happened with Jerry, but that doesn't keep me away from drugs. I know she will support me no matter what and so I carry on living how I want to. This includes us having scares, because one day we're at the house of my friend with the hippy mum, taking acid. Her son suddenly starts flipping out, shaking and being all weird and disturbed. He starts saying, 'I'm here, I'm here,' in an odd voice and generally being very strange.

None of us has had a bad trip before and we have no idea what to do. We are worried about him. So what else can we do except ring his mum? He is the only guy I know whose mum is available for this kind of emergency and, when we call her, she is totally cool and calm. She tells us exactly what is going on and what to do.

She says, 'He's having an out-of-body experience. It's nothing to worry about because he's had one before while he's tripping. What you need to do is put him in a cold shower to give him a shock and slap him round the face until he calms down.'

This is the guy's mum talking. And she isn't worried because she's seen it all before with him. Unbelievable. So we start slapping him round the face, and because we're all tripping too we find it funny. The mum comes home an hour later and by then her son is OK. We are fifteen at the time, and this is the weird side of growing up in Malibu.

Not long after, I get my first tattoo. I have already had my ear and my tongue pierced, so it seems like the obvious next thing to do. I bug my mum for weeks about it, going on and on about how much I want one. In the end, I wear her down, and she drives me to a tattoo place on Melrose Boulevard to get it done. Because I'm so young, I need my mum to sign a form giving me permission, and right before she signs it she says, 'Promise me that's the only one you'll ever get.' I make the promise, she signs the forms and I get the tattoo, a Chinese symbol meaning strength. I love it, but it's not long before I break my promise, and I go on to get lots more tattoos over the years, but my mum never complains. She's happy to let me find my own way.

In May, I go over to London for my dad's fiftieth birthday party, which is at Stringfellows. People have been planning it for months, and it's going to be a big deal with lots of press invited. I'm not bothered about that; I'm more excited that it's a big birthday for my dad and I'm going to be there with him. I've heard of Stringfellows before, so I have an idea of what the place is about, but I'm not really prepared for the reality.

It's a short trip, and I don't see that much of my dad.

I'm wary of him after last summer, and he seems to have reacted the same way he usually does to difficult situations, which is by drinking more. I hate that I present a problem for him, but at the same time I'm just happy to be around him, and this party is another opportunity for us to build the bond I want so much. We're going to be together as father and son on his birthday, and I'm optimistic about what might happen between us.

My dad has started working on Sky Sports' Saturday-afternoon football show, where a few ex-players sit in a studio watching games and talking about the live action. The matches themselves aren't on screen; it's just the former players telling viewers what's been going on. He's good at it – he loves talking football, and is clever and funny – but, typically, he's messing up the opportunity by sometimes not showing up because he's been out drinking. I love seeing him on TV and I wish he would make the most of this chance.

I spend the day of his party out and about in London, and I don't know where my dad is, so I arrive on my own. I walk into the club at about 8pm and am blown away. It's overwhelming – just so much going on.

The first thing I notice is the security guards, who are the biggest men I've ever seen. Then I walk in, past the cloakroom, through a door, and there's a long bar, which is where I first see the girls. They're beautiful, they're everywhere, and they're pretty much naked. For a teenage boy, it's like walking into heaven. Finally, there's Peter Stringfellow himself. He looks like no one I've met before. He has long blonde hair, and he's wearing a bright suit, a leopard-skin shirt and earrings. He's unbelievably flamboyant. And I look at him and think, he is definitely not cool. But he wins me over in seconds because of his personality. He throws his arms around me, tells me what great friends he is with my dad, how happy he is to have me there, and I can't help but like him. He's a warm, charming guy who's enjoying his life. If this was my place, I think to myself, I'd be pretty happy too.

Peter sits me down and gets me a drink. I ask for a whisky – I know better than to order a piña colada when my dad's around – and everything's good. I chat with Peter, there's a big cake, and I'm looking around at the photographers who are waiting for my dad, and, of course, I look at the girls. Being so young, I have no idea what you're supposed to do with them, other than just look.

'Where's your dad?' Peter asks.

'I don't know,' I say.

Alarm bells don't ring immediately. But gradually, as more and more minutes pass, and then it's an hour, and then longer, it becomes obvious something is wrong. People begin to realize he's not going to show up. I'm embarrassed, and annoyed. I'm with Peter and he's disappointed, but even so, he says to me, 'Son, treat this place like your own,' and hands me a wad of the cash they use in there – they call it angel money. I look up and there are two dancers right by me, there's lobster and chips on the table, plenty of drinks around, and I still have this

111

money to spend. At this moment, I love this man, and I love this place. I could get so used to this. I spend the rest of the night having as many dances and drinks as I want, and I actually manage to forget about my dad.

Much later, Peter asks how old I am. He's not too pleased when I say I'm fifteen. But he's still nice to me. He says I'm always welcome back, and if ever I need anything to give him a call. He really is a sweet guy.

Years later, when I move to London, I go in and reintroduce myself to Peter. He's even more pleased to see me. I start to go to Stringfellows all the time, and I even go and stay at his villa in Menorca. We end up being friends for a long time and that's something I really value. He is one of a handful of my dad's friends who really take me under their wing, and I'll always be grateful.

I'm upset about my dad not showing up, but the night ends up being so crazy and so much fun that I don't worry about it too much. I expect Peter was annoyed, after going to so much trouble to set it up, but maybe, like I am, he is used to my dad letting him down. I certainly already know that my dad has a habit of not turning up to important things.

As the years go by I hear stories about other events he's missed, such as the time he was apparently meant to be in the photo for the cover of the Beatles' *Abbey Road* album, the fifth person crossing the street, but he didn't make it. That is one of the most iconic photographs ever taken. And I've been told he was meant to be in the film *Escape to Victory*, with Michael Caine, Sylvester Stallone,

Pelé, Bobby Moore and all those other great players, but again, he didn't show up. If those stories are true – and I don't know for sure if they are, but they certainly sound like they might be – his failure to appear must have been down to alcohol. Imagine the life he could have lived if he'd never had a drink.

Chapter 8

'Alcoholics will always take the line of expediency,
telling loved ones what they want to hear.'

George Best

That summer, I take a friend with me to London. I do
this because I don't want a repeat of what happened the
previous year, which is why my mum is happy for him to
go with me. The trip becomes something completely
different – instead of me trailing around after my dad,
getting upset because he's ignoring me, I'm hanging out
with a friend in a city where we have total freedom and
can have as much fun as we want.

As it turns out, we have a brilliant couple of weeks. My
dad gives us lots of spending money, but I don't see much
of him. I think giving me cash to go and do what I like,
and then letting me have all the freedom I want, perhaps
makes him feel less guilty about everything. And for those

two weeks my friend and I work the freedom for everything we can. We spend the whole fortnight going out
and doing whatever we want. We go to clubs like the
Ministry of Sound, and take ecstasy. We buy weed, and
hang out on the King's Road.

My dad's agent and best mate, Phil Hughes, who is a
lovely guy, sees exactly what is going on. He says, 'Every
time you come over, your dad gives you a pocket full of
money and leaves you to wander along the King's Road.
George always has great plans for what you're going to do
together, and is always excited about seeing you, but by
the time you arrive, he's on another bender. You never
spend any quality time together.'

This year is no different. But for once, I don't mind so
much. I'm at an age where the world is opening up for
me, and freedom is exciting. In previous years, my dad's
attitude during my visits has left me devastated, and in
the future I will be hurt again. But this year, just once,
I'm having too much fun with my friend to care.

We go shopping, which is something I do every
summer. Every year I make sure I go back to the US with
the latest Manchester United shirt with my name on the
back, and Kappa tracksuits. Malibu hasn't seen this gear
before, and when I bring a bit of England back with me,
my friends always love it.

It's not such an obvious one, but I also bring back a
Newcastle United shirt. For some reason, my friends and
I love Newcastle Brown Ale. It's our favourite drink. It
makes for a funny image – us suntanned, skateboarding

California kids drinking this stuff made in the cold north-east of England – but we really do love it. So when I go to England, I always get a Newcastle United shirt, with the black and white stripes and the Newcastle Brown Ale logo on the front, and that's the thing my friends are always jealous of. They like the Manchester United kit and the Kappa tracksuits, but the Newcastle United shirt with my name on the back is the thing that always gets talked about. This year, we both get one.

My dad isn't in a great place. He and Alex have been fighting, and there's a legal problem with the ownership of their flat – almost definitely down to my dad being bad with money. He and Alex are married now and he tells her he'll change for her, but the words are hollow because, as he confesses years later in his autobiography, 'Alcoholics will always take the line of expediency, telling loved ones what they want to hear . . . I had been going on benders to escape all the hassles in my life.'

Remembering Phil's words about how he behaves while I'm over here, I come to realize that I was one of those hassles. I was just another form of pressure on him. Most normal people would be happy to see their only son, to have the opportunity to bond with him. But, as my dad said, alcoholics don't do things in the same way normal people do.

One day we're in the Phene, and one of the people my dad drinks with every day makes a passing reference to my dad having a daughter who's a few years older than me. My reaction is simply that it's not true. I don't give it a second thought, because I think it's simply not possible. I'm my dad's only child. No one has ever mentioned this other child to me, so she can't exist.

Back in California, I ask my mum about the possibility that I might have a sister. She says there is absolutely no chance, and explains where the story has come from. When she was with my dad before I was born, an old girlfriend of his got in touch to say she was pregnant and that if my dad went back to her she would have the baby, but if he didn't, she wouldn't keep it.

My dad didn't reply to the letter, stayed with my mum, and he never heard from this woman again. My mum thinks the whole thing was a hoax anyway and is convinced there is no other child. She says my dad brings up the story every now and then when he needs an excuse for his drinking. It's a convenient thing to come out with, a little tactic he uses to manipulate people into talking about something other than his alcoholism, to make them feel sorry for him so they let him carry on drowning his sorrows. I don't really understand this side of him yet, but I trust my mum, so I put the possibility out of my mind, and it stays out for a long time.

Now I'm home, I spend my time in the usual way: hanging out with my friends and smoking a lot. It doesn't sound great, but we're not complete reprobates. We aren't the kind of bad kids who get arrested and go to jail. We're naughty kids on the beach, who spend their days in the sunshine skateboarding around some of the most expensive shops in the world, trying to find little corners to smoke weed or trip out on acid, like little vagrants.

My friends are very important to me. I have a close group from my class at school who I hang out with all the time. We think we're much older than we are, and run around with a lot of freedom and enough cash to get most of what we want. My mum and I are the poorest family among all my friends, but we live near the beach, so we're blessed.

Maybe it's because of what my friends and I go through together in these years, trying all that stuff and learning about life together, but those guys will always be my best, best friends, the ones I would trust with anything and who are the same whenever I see them, even if it's been a couple of years or even longer.

For most of this year, I'm counting down the days until I turn sixteen and can drive on my own. I've had a BMX for a few years and I can't wait to upgrade. Just before my birthday, I decide I want a car. And not just a car, I want a big truck. My mum's marriage to Terry didn't last long, certainly not long enough for me really to bond with him. She has a new boyfriend now, Mark, and he has a Ford F350, which is the biggest truck you've ever seen in your life. I want an F150, which is still huge, but looks small next to Mark's. He's a cool guy, an ex-ice-hockey player who's also into boxing, and I like him. We don't have any kind of father–son relationship, though. I don't go looking for that with him, and he doesn't push it with me either. But we get on perfectly well. I'm glad he's around for my mum.

I find out how much the F150 costs and my mum isn't happy. It's something like $27,000, and she doesn't want me to get into all that debt, but one day the three of us go to a Ford dealership to have a look at it anyway. The truck is black and it's incredible. It has the open bit at the back where I can put my skateboards and snowboards, and an extension on the cab with a second row of seats and doors for them. It's perfect. But none of us has the kind of cash needed to buy it. I have enough from my modelling work to pay a good deposit, but nowhere near all of it. I'm starting to think it's not going to happen, when Mark, who I suspect is trying to impress my mum, says he'll take the debt on in his name and I can work out how to pay him as we go along. I am thrilled.

The day I pass my test I drive off in my massive truck, leaving my terrified mum behind, and pick up all my friends so we can go off on an overnight camping trip. It's awesome. I am so grateful to Mark. I'm the first one in my school year to turn up in a car, and what a car it is. You can't miss it.

For the next few months, Mark and I talk about how to make it even better. Eventually, we go over to the San Fernando Valley – usually just known as the Valley – and find this place run by some Spanish guys who do improvements cheaply. They raise it by three inches, so it can have thirty-three-inch wheels, and it goes from being a cool truck to an absolute beast. I love driving this thing.

Mark's happy too, because he loves my mum, and if he makes me happy he knows that'll please her.

A few weeks later, I've started playing with the truck, doing wheel spins and seeing how fast I can go. One day I drive out of school with a friend in the truck with me and put my foot down. A little way up the road we pass a police car. I slow right down, but it's too late. The car pulls a U-turn and follows me home. I get my first driving violation ticket aged sixteen.

I'm smoking a lot of weed at the moment, so am lucky I wasn't tested because it was almost certainly in my system. The habit is constant through the day: before I go to school, at lunchtime, after school, in the evenings before and after whatever it is I do that night. I even smoke before I go to the cinema. My friends and I all do it and I expect my mum knows what's going on, but she doesn't say anything, as is her way.

At the time I don't pick up on the similarity between what my dad and I are doing. He's drinking all day, I'm smoking weed all day. He's drunk most of the time, I'm stoned most of the time. As I get older, I see the sad irony in this. I also come to think that if we were together more and had a good relationship, it's likely neither of us would be living like this.

At the moment my mum is working at a place called Malibu Gym, and one day I go to see her with a friend. I park the car, go and talk to my mum, then come back to the car to my friend. We're planning to go to Coffee Bean next because it's always full of girls. I turn the car on, turn right to pull out, and there's a horrible grinding sound. Because I'm so high up in my car I didn't see a concrete bollard by the space I'm parked in. I've scratched and dented the whole of one side of the truck. It's ruined. And it's only just been done up. I'm gutted, close to tears.

I have to go back to Mark and tell him, which is horrible. We have just spent so much money doing it up that we can't afford to have it fixed, so I spend the next year and a half driving around with the dents and scratches. I'm devastated. It's turned a beauty of a car into a nightmare.

But the car is still useful. We have moved to Point Dume, a different part of Malibu, and my friends and I start to get to know some Valley girls from over the hill. There's a big rivalry between the two areas and it's fun for us to head over there every now and then to see how well we get on with them. One Friday night my friend and I drive out to the Valley, talk to some girls, drink and smoke and drive back along the Pacific Coast Highway at about four in the morning. There are no other cars around, but there is only one road in and out of Malibu and the cops know this, so they sit and wait for some silly young guy to drive by going too fast. Everyone from Malibu knows that's what the cops do, so I'm driving along at fifty miles an hour and no more.

I come down this stretch called Es Candido and a cop appears in the road behind us. He follows us for a few miles, and just when we're getting close to where I live in Point Dume, he pulls me over. He takes me out of the car and makes me walk the line and touch my nose. I am shaking with nerves. He asks me if there's anything in the car and I realize I can't lie to the cops any more. I can't do what my dad did in that pub – I tried it once after the Jerry thing and it didn't get me far, so I say yes, there's a pipe in the back seat. It's a glass thing which we use for smoking weed. He goes in and of course he finds the pipe. I'm arrested, he takes the keys to the car and lets my friend go. I ask my friend to go and tell my mum. I feel horrible, absolutely sick.

The police take me over the hill to another part of LA, called Agora, because there isn't a station in Malibu. It's about 5am on Saturday morning and, because it's a small station, they don't have enough staff to be able to release people at the weekend, which means I'm going to have to stay there until Monday morning. When they tell me this, I am terrified. I'm a kid, and I'm going to jail for the weekend. I know the stories about what goes on in places like this – they're full of gangsters and crackheads and all kinds of bad people I don't ever want to meet. I'm sixteen – what are they going to do to me? I'm shaking with fear.

We go to the station and the cop takes me into a booth so he can ask me some questions. He asks me to pee in a cup so it can be tested, but I can't do it. I can't pee. I'm so nervous I can't do anything. The cop is standing behind me, which doesn't help.

'What's the problem?' he asks.

'I'm too nervous,' I say. 'I can't do it.'

He gives me a look that says he's not impressed, and then goes and turns on the tap in the sink on the wall. But it doesn't help. I still can't pee. I try to slow down my breathing to help me relax and, eventually, after what feels like hours, I manage to produce a bit, just enough. Then the cop says it's time to go into my cell. This is the moment I've been dreading, like I've never dreaded anything in my life. My stomach drops. He leads me down a corridor and to a door. I feel like a condemned man, walking to his death. My life is never going to be the same.

The cop opens the door, and . . . I breathe a huge sigh of relief. The room couldn't be further from what I expected, which was based on the prison cells I've seen on TV. For one thing, there's no one else in it. No crackheads or gangsters. For another, it's clean. There's a metal toilet in the corner, which I did expect, a bed with a blue mattress – no sheets or anything like that, but comfortable enough to sleep on, especially when you're as tired and hungover as I am. It's not luxurious by most people's standards, but for me, right now, when I was expecting to walk into hell, it's the best, most comfortable and welcoming room I've ever seen.

The next morning they bring me eggs, toast and orange juice for breakfast. The eggs are slightly blue, so I don't eat them. They bring sandwiches for lunch and they're gross too. I remember thinking, all the food is disgusting, but at least there are no murderers around.

I spend the next two days and nights hungry and bored

out of my mind. All I can do is sleep and stare into space. But I'm safe. And now I know I'm safe, part of me begins to enjoy it, spending the weekend in jail. I'm actually quite excited to tell my mates about it when I get out.

But during these long hours on my own, I start going over some pretty deep stuff. I know my mum is going to come and pick me up on Monday morning and I can't help thinking about how this looks and feels for her. It must remind her of my dad. I know how he behaves, I understand drinking and what it does to you and she must have been to a good few police stations to get him the morning after the night before. I feel terrible about doing this to her, about history repeating itself, and I also understand that it doesn't bode well for me that I'm imitating his example already, aged just sixteen. This can't be a good sign.

But I tell myself I'm fine. I'm not going to do this again, and it's not like I was totally wasted. I was a little bit over the limit, that's all. I don't drink like my dad does; there's no need for Mum to worry about me. But I don't see this situation through my mum's eyes. I might well be right about my drinking, that I don't do it like my dad does, but that doesn't mean there's nothing for her to worry about. At the moment I don't understand what must be on her mind – wondering if this is how it starts, and if I'm going the same way my dad did. It must be terrifying for her.

On Monday morning, when I'm waiting for her, I'm nervous. I'm confident I'm not on the way to becoming an alcoholic like my dad, but I'm still ashamed of myself for this and feel bad for putting my mum through it. But at the same time she's a pretty cool mum, and in general doesn't tell me off for much, so when I see her I can't help smirking. I think the fact I do that takes the edge off her anger, because when she sees me grinning, she knows I'm OK. She might not be angry, but it's obvious she was worried. 'What the hell were you thinking?' she says. 'I had no idea what was happening to you all weekend.'

She tells me my friend went straight to her house after I was arrested, woke her up and told her what had happened. She immediately called the station and they said yes, we've got him, but there's nothing you can do until Monday morning. Just be here then and you can have him back. So she spent the weekend worrying about me, probably replaying the same prison scenes I was before I got to my cell. With everything that's gone on with my dad, I feel awful.

As we're leaving, I ask for my licence back and they give it to me. A court date is set for a few weeks' time and I am desperately worried about losing my licence. That would be a disaster – no truck, no independence, no freedom. Luckily Mum has a friend who is a lawyer so she sends me to see him. He asks where my licence is and I say it's right here, and show him. And that's it, game over, charges dropped. The police aren't supposed to give you your licence back and because of that procedural mistake, I get off. The lawyer costs a few thousand dollars, which comes out of my modelling earnings, but it's worth every cent.

* * *

Soon after this, I'm hanging out with my friends at this little square in Malibu where we go to skateboard. There are a few shops and things around it – a karate school, an alcohol shop, a pet store and a pizza place. I see a friend of mine come out of the pizza place carrying a pile of pizza boxes. I talk to him and he tells me he has a job delivering pizza, and he's earning about $200 dollars a night. That sounds good to me, so I go straight in and get myself a job. For six months I deliver pizzas in my black truck and it's great. Most nights I make at least $100.

I'm still modelling, but the jobs don't come along all that often, so I have time to do something else. To me, the job delivering pizzas is about freedom as well as cash. I have my truck, and I already spend my evenings driving around in it, loving my new freedom. I always have a friend or two along with me, and we smoke weed and have a laugh, so now I'm just delivering pizzas at the same time as doing pretty well exactly what I'd be doing anyway. I just have to follow a route set out by someone else.

Aside from the cash, another perk is that I end up delivering pizzas to some of the hottest Malibu mums you can imagine. Some of them flirt with me, I flirt back, and it's fun. Then one becomes more than just a flirt. She's in her late thirties and is married with kids, but gives me her phone number anyway. I pluck up the courage to call her, and we end up having an affair for a few months. It's purely sexual: she calls me when her house is empty and I go round, or she gets us hotel rooms, or just jumps in my truck with me if I'm nearby. These are crazy times and a lot of fun.

My mum lets me have all this freedom because she knows that if she gives me too many rules and regulations I'll rebel even harder and, knowing what my dad has become, going down that road terrifies her. We don't discuss it, but I'm sure she knows what I'm doing and also believes that the best thing she can do for me is to allow me to grow into my own person. To find my own way. And I know now that she made the right decision. I am not an unhappy guy – I enjoy my life, and appreciate my mum, my friends and the beautiful place where we live – but because of my dad, on some level I carry a kind of painful anger with me all the time. It doesn't make me a bad, mean kid, but it does make me reckless.

I expect my mum hoped I wouldn't make all these mistakes and would learn my lessons quicker, but she knows me well enough to understand that trying to stop me, or to force me to live a certain way, wouldn't work. She knows that I need stability from her more than anything, to know that she's there for me always, no matter what. And I do know that. It hasn't been easy for her, raising me as a single mum. She works hard, training people at the gym as much as she can, and we've lived in seven or eight different places in Malibu, but she's always there for me, no matter what I do. If things were better with my dad it wouldn't be like this, but they're not, so this is our life, and it's a pretty good one.

I feel guilty for all the things I put my mum through, for all the worry I cause her, but I'm too young really to understand how hard it must be for her, so it's not enough to make me change. As I get older and grow up, I begin to have more of an idea of how she must have felt and I start to wish I had done things differently for her sake. My mum put up with a lot from me.

Chapter 9

'I'm sure that if I keep trying, keep coming to him, keep reminding him I'm his son and I'm here, the relationship I dream of having with him will happen.'

Calum Best

My visit to London in the summer of 1998 goes better than the last few, mainly because I'm not so dependent on my dad. I suppose I've come to know his drinking, and have learned to expect less of him. I'm seventeen now, I made some friends last time I was here, and know the city better, so I do my own thing quite a lot. This means when I get depressed sitting in the pub with my dad, I can go off and do something else. But that doesn't mean I don't go to the pub at all – I want to be with him, so I spend as much time there as I can stand, and because I'm used to pubs now, I'm more comfortable. We play cribbage together, or games of pool, talk about Manchester United and generally pass the time. We don't talk about anything serious or deep. We never have, but I hope we will one day. I want to tell my dad I love him, and for him to say it back to me, because he never does. But it doesn't happen.

We go out for a few meals at places which have started to mean a lot to me, even though I only visit them a couple of times a year. There's Choy's, a Chinese place, and the Big Easy, where we go for ribs, and I've even started to get a soft spot for the Phene, and the Rat and Carrot, my dad's other regular pub. Despite everything that's happened on my visits over the past few years, I don't let myself feel traumatized or worried. I focus on just being happy to spend time with my dad, and I can do that because I'm sure things are going to be better. I'm sure that if I keep trying, keep coming to him, keep reminding him I'm his son and I'm here, the relationship I dream of having with him will happen.

No matter what he's done, or how drunk he gets (and he does get drunk, every day), there are still things that make me think he's cool. For example, one day we're playing pool in the Rat and Carrot, hanging out in the pub like we always do, when this beautiful girl roller-blades into the room, comes right up to my dad and says hi, like they're friends. She is stunning, and I don't think I've ever seen anyone so unbelievably gorgeous. I'm wondering how it can be possible for my dad to know someone like this – he must be cool.

He introduces me, and her name is Sienna Miller. Sienna sits on the pool table and starts talking to my dad, and she's sparky and funny as well as being hot. We're about the same age, so we start chatting and make friends. Over the next few days I start hanging out with her a bit. I go to her house and meet her mum and her friends, and I fall completely and utterly in love with her. She's the first girl I feel like this about. We 'date' as much as you can at that age, but it fizzles out because I have to go back to the US so quickly.

Back home, I have a nasty reality check. For the past couple of years I haven't been doing well at school, spending far too much time focusing on girls and getting high instead of studying. At the end of the summer term, when I finished eleventh grade, it had got really bad and I was told I had failed so many classes I was going to have to repeat eleventh grade. I can't bear the thought of an extra year, but at the same time I need to graduate from high school. Fortunately, my mum manages to find this place called Olympic Continuation School up in Santa Monica, where I can go for six weeks over the summer and make up the credits I need without the extra year in school.

I go over there on the first day, and it's full of Mexicans and black guys. I'm the only white guy in my class, and the only one from Malibu, which makes me realize just how polarized LA is. But I have never minded standing out, and I get on well with the other guys there. I crack on and work as hard as I can, I get my courses back to where I need to be, and make some good new friends as well. I actually have a pretty good time, even though I'm working all summer.

For my final year, instead of going back to Malibu High, I go to a private school called Colin McEwen High School. It's full of students whose parents have money and who want to make sure their kids finish school with the best possible education. But we are all pretty deviant. Every morning we sit in our cars and smoke weed before class. Then, at lunchtime, we get sandwiches and go back to our cars and smoke weed again. After that, we spend most of the afternoon laughing, and then when school finishes we smoke more weed. Things are so chaotic that we call the school Colin McClueless and it fits in well with the kind of student I've been all the way through school. Somehow, despite all this, I manage to graduate, which I'm thrilled about.

Even before graduation, I'd started thinking seriously about my future. For a while I had fantasies of being a footballer, like my dad, but it's become clear that even though I'm one of the best players in my team, and our team is top of its league, I'm not actually that good. If I was, someone would have said something to me by now. I've been going to football camps in Long Beach every summer for the past few years, where we do nothing but play and train for two weeks. All the coaches love that I'm George Best's son and they must be waiting for a sudden burst of genius. But it doesn't come. No one ever asks me to go to play for any other teams above where I am already playing.

Sixteen was the age when I was at my athletic peak. We played a tournament against teams from around the world then and won it. I scored lots of goals and someone told me scouts were there from Manchester United. I didn't know if that was true, or if it was a lie or a rumour, and I never found out for sure. All I know is that no one got in touch with me. I thought I played well, so maybe I'm just not good enough. My dad was scouted when he was young, and if there were scouts at the tournament then I'm sure they would have come to have a look at me simply because of who my dad is. So if they were there, they must have thought I don't have what it takes.

I also see footage of kids around my age playing in other countries, like Michael Owen in England, and I realize I'm nowhere near as good as they are. If I'd had the same upbringing as the guys who play in the Premiership, who did nothing but kick a ball around all day every day from when they could stand up, who were in youth teams and being coached before they started school, then I might have had a chance. Maybe. Who knows? But that wasn't my life. When I was growing up I had skate-boarding, snowboarding, the beach, basketball, so many different things to do other than play football. I love playing, play a lot, and play to win, but my team's coach is someone's dad. Here football just isn't serious in that way. But I'm happy. Being good in my own little circle is enough for me.

College doesn't interest me. I'm not academic, so I won't enjoy the studying, and the college guys I know seem to spend all their time drinking, which is enough to convince my mum it's not a good idea for me to go.

That leaves me one option: modelling, and it seems like a positive move. I've done some good jobs and am still with LA Models. Kraft Ketchup earned me $12,000 dollars, so I figure that now I'm older and can start working full time there might be great opportunities for me out there. LA Models agree, and we start putting serious effort in. Things go well and I get a few good jobs. My dad only comes into it very rarely, when foreign clients are impressed that I'm George Best's son, but it doesn't happen much, and it doesn't get me work. Far more often it happens that clients think I look like Jude Law and book me because of the resemblance they think they can see.

By now, around the time I finish school, I'm loving LA. A few months ago, a friend of mine took me to a club in Hollywood and, by a stroke of pure good luck, I made friends with two girls who work on the door, Sarah and Jen. I didn't know this at the time, but Sarah and Jen are known in nightclubs all across Hollywood, and so now I have friends who can get me into a cool club any time I want. I'm way underage – you have to be twenty-one in the States – but that doesn't matter. I get on well with the girls, and they think I'm cute, and because I'm a cheeky, cocky kid I get on with the bouncers too, so I am let into all the clubs and start making a lot of new friends. None of these people know who my dad is. They just know me, doing my own thing. That might seem like a strange thing to pick up on, but at this point I'm old enough to realize one thing: my dad casts a big shadow. I love my dad, but I don't want to be treated differently because of who he is. I want people to take me for me.

LA is a place where strange but brilliant things can happen. I make friends with a girl called Sarah Foster, whose dad is David Foster, Michael Jackson's producer. One day we're hanging out with some other friends when her dad rings and says we should all come over because Michael is there. So we go to his house, which is spectacular even compared to the biggest LA mansions, and meet Michael. We all say hello, he says hello, we have a little chat, and that's it. There is no screaming or craziness, because in LA this is normal. Or at least everyone pretends it's normal. He's just a famous guy who's at Sarah's dad's house. LA is just different to anywhere else.

When I start hanging out with Sarah and Jen, more of this stuff happens. One night I end up playing ping-pong with a few people back at Leonardo DiCaprio's house. Then on another night Sarah introduces me to a friend of hers, a sweet, pretty, blonde girl called Britney Spears, who is about my age. We get on well and agree to meet for a drink the next night, but nothing sparkles between us and we don't see each other again.

I have already decided that commitment isn't for me. I'm no good at it. There are so many things going on in my life, and so many gorgeous girls around, that I get distracted. Even now, a pattern has emerged which sees me like a girl, start seeing her, and then lose interest quickly, because someone else catches my eye. Some people might see this as a deep-rooted thing, to do with my dad and his commitment issues. But it doesn't feel like that to me. It feels far less complicated than that.

After I graduate, I move out of my mum's place and into a flat in Brentwood, a cool, studenty area on the west side of LA, with my friend Travis Fimmel, who's a model for Calvin Klein. We have a great time, driving round together, going out, meeting girls, and because we're young, we can live this life at night and still look good enough to work during the days. I'm doing some good work – not on the same scale as Travis, who's all over billboards in his underwear – but it's going well.

One day a scout from an Italian modelling agency flies in to see some of the models from my agency. Her name is Carlotta and we hit it off. Not romantically, but we have a good buzz together. We go to a seventies-themed night at a club called Las Palmas, and while we're there she says to me, 'I'm definitely taking you back to Italy with me. They'll love you there.'

Milan's the centre of the world for fashion, so this is exciting stuff. I'm not sure I believe her at first, but a week later a firm offer comes through. They want me in Milan. It so happens that at the same time I get a call from my dad telling me that his great friend Milan Mandarić has offered me the chance to have a trial at his football club in England – Portsmouth. I don't get calls from my dad very often, so I'm really happy, especially because this one means he's been thinking about me and trying to do something for me. But no matter how I feel about what my dad has done, my choice is still this: do I want to go to Milan to model, to the fashion capital of the world where I'll be with beautiful women and earning great money, or do I want to go to Portsmouth for a trial to be a footballer, when I already know I'm not good enough?

Carlotta says she wants me there for six months to a year, to see if I can really make it big in the modelling world. I love my life in LA, but I can't say no to that. It'll be a great adventure, as well as an incredible work opportunity. I talk to my mum and she agrees. Chances like this don't come along very often. The decision is easy: I'm going to Milan.

I pack up my stuff, move out of the flat, give up my rent, leave some things with my mum, and go off with two bags, more excited than nervous.

I land at Milan airport at about 4am the next day with an address written on a bit of paper in my pocket. I get a cab to the address, get dropped off and find myself standing outside this house in the darkness on a deserted street. I knock, but no one answers. I knock again, but still nothing. I yell up at the windows; same reaction. I wonder what the hell I'm doing here, and how much trouble it will cause if I go home as soon as possible.

Finally, a woman comes down and lets me in. On the way up, she tells me it's an apartment especially for models who are working in the city, and when I see the place I know what she means. There's hardly any furniture, nothing decorative, just a lot of small cot beds for all the models. It's a dormitory. I'm sharing a room with guys from Yugoslavia, Russia, Italy and Canada, and I get into bed as soon as I can. These guys are all strangers to me, and I can't believe I left everything back home for this. This isn't the glamorous modelling world I was expecting.

The next morning I call my mum and tell her I think I've made a huge mistake. This isn't what I thought I was coming over for. Talking to her calms me down, and she tells me to stick at it for a while and see how things go. It's too early to give up. As usual, she is right, and I jump straight into a very different kind of life.

Two days later I'm on a plane to China for my first job – a week's catwalk work. The trip turns into one of the best times of my life. On the flight out, there are about twenty of us models sitting at the back of the plane smoking and drinking (in those days you could smoke on planes) and for me, aged eighteen, to be sitting there with all these beautiful girls on this adventure is amazing. We have a party on the way out there and I hit it off with a Brazilian girl who can barely speak a word of English. Despite the language barrier, we spend the week together. We hold hands a lot, but conversation is zero. We still have a connection, though, and have a great time together.

During the days we all work hard, because it's a huge

fashion show in Beijing. In the evenings, whoever we've been working for during the day takes us to different restaurants. It's madly busy, especially backstage when all the dressing and undressing is going on, and it's a lot of fun. I try to be as polite as possible to all the Chinese people we're working with, so I learn the words for 'hello' and 'thank you' and use them as often as I can. I do things like ask what the best beer in China is – Tsingtao – and drink that when we go out. We go to local nightclubs and the Brazilian girl and I have these crazy moments where we're trying to work out where the club is or how to get back to our hotel with only our room keys with the name of the hotel on to help us. Neither of us speaks Chinese and we can't talk to each other either, but somehow we get by. It's a mad experience, one of the best times ever.

Back in Milan, for a while I'm the only one of the male models getting work. I'm doing jobs for all sorts of big names – Canali, Bally, L'Uomo, Vogue. I'm really smashing it and earning great money. And no one, not the bookers or the clients, has a clue who my dad is. This modelling career is all me, on my own.

Unfortunately, as is typical with me, I'm spending the cash as quickly as it comes in, not saving anything. I can't do quiet nights in. I'm not that kind of guy. I want to go out in the evening, and I want people I know to come with me, but the only people I know are the other models and they have no money. So I pay. We're all having such a great time I don't stop to think about the consequences of letting all this cash slip away. This is a habit it will take a long time for me to break out of.

I don't realize it at the time, but my way with money is the same as my dad's. As fast as it comes in, it goes out. Neither of us plans very far ahead.

A couple of months in, I meet a stunning Swiss girl who's a bit older than me, and she totally blows my mind. I've never been with a girl who does this to me. One day she says to me, 'Calum, come with me to Lake Como.' Of course I say yes, immediately. I'd go anywhere with her.

We drive there and we stay in a five-star hotel overlooking the lake. I'm young, but I'm not too young to appreciate how gorgeous this place is and how beautiful she is. We spend a couple of days there, and it's amazing.

When we get back to Milan and park the car, she pops open the boot and I see it's full of weed. Huge parcels of the stuff. My insides shake when I see it all, and I know instantly what must have happened. Someone smuggled it into Italy from Switzerland and at some point must have dropped the weed into the car, because she was never out of my sight, unless she sneaked off while I was asleep. I figure someone paid her to do this, paid her hotel bill and she brought me along so she could pretend I was her boyfriend and no one would get suspicious.

I can't believe she's done this, nor how close we must have come to being caught. If we'd been busted, I don't know how many years I'd have spent in jail. It's terrifying, and I can't trust her any more, so it's over between us very quickly.

Afterwards, I wonder how I got caught up in this. How could I have been so clueless? Why didn't I notice what was going on? Back in LA this wouldn't have happened to me. I've spent almost my entire life there and I like to think I have a bit of street sense. But I never suspected this girl was dodgy. It didn't even occur to me to be suspicious. She played me well.

Being in Milan means I am closer to London, and my dad. But I'm beginning to see things slightly differently. I've put so much effort into trying to have a proper relationship and he's given me nothing back. We hardly ever talk, because he's virtually impossible to get hold of on the phone, and he almost never calls me. The years of feeling like he's pushing me away are hardening me. I feel like getting on with my life, and waiting for him to reach out to me.

I'm not aware of how ill he is. He doesn't realize it himself, as he would later write in his autobiography, 'I know this may sound ridiculous, but it didn't cross my mind that the drink was doing me any physical damage – well, not of a life-threatening kind,' but these are actually the early stages of his liver failing. And it's getting worse. It so happens he's around the same age his mother was when she died. This must make him feel awful, and I wonder if he is scared he's heading the same way. But knowing my dad, drinking will be the only way he can cope with the sadness he feels about his mother dying because of alcohol and his fears for his own future. It's another vicious circle.

In early 2000 I hear he's been in hospital. I'm on a job at the time, but as soon as it's finished I go over to London. I head straight to his flat, but there's no one in so I sit on the doorstep and wait. Eventually, my dad and Alex show up. I am shocked by what I see. I haven't seen him for a while, but he looks years older. He's thin and frail, and his face is pale and drawn. As he's walking towards the door he sees me from a distance, and then stops looking at me. He doesn't say hello, doesn't hug me, nothing. I thought he'd be pleased to see me, maybe even touched that I'd made the effort to be here for him. But there's nothing. I stay for a few days and try to get through to him, but it doesn't work. He's the same as always. I head back to Milan with a heavy heart. With hindsight, I think now that he must have been ashamed. He didn't want me to see him like this. He wanted to be my hero, not the sick, weakened man he was when he came out of hospital. This was part of the tragedy of our relationship. I just wanted to know him for what and who he was. I wasn't interested in the legend, just him. But he thought George Best the man and father wasn't good enough, so he drank to hide away.

My dad doesn't tell me that Professor Roger Williams, the liver specialist at the Cromwell Hospital in west London, a man who will become a huge part of our lives, has told him that one more drink could kill him. There's no middle ground – he must stop, or his life is in danger. But he doesn't listen and, in the summer, starts drinking again after an argument with Alex.

After a year in Milan, aged nineteen, I go back to LA. My agency is really pleased with the work I did over there. I've made some great contacts, done shoots with big names and, professionally, the trip was a huge success. They line up more work for me, so things are looking very positive on that front, and it's good to be back with my friends, up to our old tricks.

One of the first things we do is try to break into the Playboy Midsummer Night's Dream party. It's a huge deal – the dream party for young guys like us. The previous year, a friend and I bribed our way in, paying the security guys $500 to let us through, and had an awesome night which saw us both in a jacuzzi with a load of naked girls.

This year, we want to go again, but we know the people in charge are getting wise to tactics like ours the previous year, so we make a plan, and we take it seriously because of what's at stake. We look at a map and work out what we think will be the easiest way to break in – a spot right at the far edge of the Playboy Mansion's grounds. Then we map out a route to that spot via the gardens of the houses next door. They're massive mansions, so the gardens are huge.

On the night, in our party kit, we park close to the house, sneak into the first garden, and go for it. We have to stick to the darkest parts of the gardens so no one sees us, so we scale fences, we climb over rocks, we crawl through dirt and cobwebs, and finally we get to the back-yard of the house right next to the Playboy Mansion. There's a bit of grass to cross, then we go round a corner, and at that point we're at the part of the mansion's perimeter we think is weak, because it's far enough away from the main entrances for security not to be interested.

It's looking good so far. We just have this one bit left to deal with. We do a *Mission Impossible*-style sprint across the grass, get there safely, go round the corner with the finishing line in sight – and see about fifty other guys standing by the mansion fence, all trying exactly the same thing we are. They're all dressed in different kinds of underwear, and some have their shirts off. Every single one is covered in dirt.

These guys are standing there, waiting and watching, and I'm not in the mood for that. We know the fence is electric and set up so that if anyone touches it an alarm goes off telling security exactly where it's happened. But we've come this far. I run up, climb over the fence, land on the other side and get ready to sprint for the party. But as soon as my feet hit the ground, boom! I'm tackled to the floor from behind. I mean dropped instantly, just wiped out, in the way a normal guy like me would be if he was hit by a professional American football player.

The security guys pick me up and lead me to the security room, where there are six other guys in exactly the same situation I am, bruised and disappointed. We sit there looking pathetic, and the security guys take our photos so they can put them on the wall for next year, in case we try again. They say they're feeling kind so won't call the police this time, but we should never, ever come back. We're then taken to the back entrance and kicked out. I get in a cab and go home, gutted I'm missing the party.

The next day, my friend calls me and is laughing down the phone as he tells me what happened. He saw me jump over the fence and get tackled by the security guys. As soon as they started leading me away, with their backs to the fence, he jumped over and ran for it. Because security was busy with me, they didn't see him. He got in and partied all night.

Chapter 10

'My dad is still a stranger to me, but it's too late to be bitter.'

Calum Best

Soon after, I'm living back in Brentwood, this time with my friend Pascal and we're having a great time. Modelling is going well, and I'm loving life in LA. I've become friends with Pascal and another guy called Trevor, who are a little older than me and are well known around the city and the clubs, and have a good group of friends. They're both good-looking, chilled-out beach guys from Malibu, and I like hanging out with them. The three of us go into town a lot, and thanks to Jennifer and Sarah, my friends who run the club doors, we get into all the best places. The city girls start to know who we are, and the three of us get noticed when we arrive somewhere. We're pretty boys from the beach, basically, so we stand out among the city people.

I'm hanging out with people older than me, so I'm dating girls who are older than me, even though sometimes they intimidate me. One night I go out with one of these older girls and my friends. We meet up with some of her friends at a place on Sunset Boulevard called Dublin's, the current hotspot, which is an Irish whiskey bar and nightclub, and the scene at the table is like something out of a music video: girls with bleached blonde hair, huge chests and big red lips. All the women are probably in their mid-thirties, so are dressed a little young for their ages. But that doesn't bother me – they're cool and we have fun.

I get on particularly well with one of them, a woman called Bobbie Brown, who was in a famous video for a song by the band Warrant called 'Cherry Pie' (which came out when I was nine), and she asks me if I want to go with her to a pyjama party at the Playboy Mansion. I can't say yes quickly enough. This will be the first time I've actually been to one of their parties legitimately. I won't need to bribe anyone, or try to break in, and the security guys won't hammer me. I say yes, for sure. I'd love to.

A few days later, she comes to my place in Brentwood and picks me up. I'm wearing pyjama bottoms, normal house slippers and a white vest. I get in the car with this hot, *Baywatch*-type blonde who's a bit older than me but still gorgeous and I think I'm living the dream.

We get to the mansion, park, get our wristbands, get

on the shuttle buses they put on to take guests from the car park to the party, and go to the mansion. Compared to my last two visits, the process is unbelievably easy. When we get to the main gate – which is the last and most important security barrier – and get through, I'm so excited I want to burst out laughing. I can't believe I've got in, aged nineteen and with my photo on the wall of banned people from last year. But I'm in, and I'm in legitimately, so I'm going to enjoy it.

The party is massive. There are thousands of people here. We go in, and pretty quickly go our separate ways, as we're not really that interested in each other. I run into friends and hang out with them. As you walk in, there's a bar to the right where you can get tequila shots, a jacuzzi to the left, and the grotto is down below. There's a tent further in where there's the dance floor and tables and chairs, there's the zoo, there are girls walking round in body paint, some in bikinis, and there are couples making out all over the place.

There are stunning women everywhere. One stands out immediately. She has dark hair, and looks so young and pretty compared to the others, who seem to have a bit of a hard edge about them, which happens to a lot of girls in LA. This brunette is the only one who really blows me away. She doesn't have to make an effort to look beautiful in this crowd.

I start talking to her, and we go to the bar to do some shots. We lose each other after that; I start hanging out with my friends again, feeling like a kid in a candy store, but later, about 1am, I find her again back by the bar. I ask where she stays, and she tells me it's in a building near the tennis courts. We take our drinks and she walks me down there, past the pinball machines and the pool table, and on to her building. We go and sit on the tennis courts.

Her name is Nicole Lenz and she's Miss March 2000. She's twenty, and I lie to her about my age. I tell her I'm twenty-two, not nineteen. It's only three years, but in LA being on the wrong side of twenty-one is a big deal. It means if you want to take a girl out to a club or for dinner, there's always the possibility that you won't get in, or you won't be allowed to buy a bottle of wine. It's one of those things girls just don't like here, the idea of a guy not getting in somewhere. It doesn't matter so much if the girl is under twenty-one, because girls don't get asked for ID as much as guys.

So we're on the tennis court and are getting on brilliantly, laughing our backsides off, kissing and flirting. I'm nineteen, I'm in the Playboy Mansion, I've had plenty to drink, I'm with this beautiful girl, and my heart's beating hard. I'm not in love, but I'm definitely in raptures. The party is everything I hoped for.

We get a bit lost in the moment, then suddenly there's a security guy shouting at us. 'Who's over there?' he yells into the courts.

'It's only me, Nicole,' she says.

'Who's with you?'

'Only my friend Calum.'

They tell us the party ended an hour ago and I have to leave. I ask if there are any buses left? No, all gone.

So that's it, the party's over. Security walk me away from the mansion and open the main gate just for me. This is a moment I'll remember for ever. I'm in my vest, my pyjamas and my slippers, and I live about an hour's walk away down Sunset Boulevard. But do I care? No. I've just had the best night ever. I have Nicole's number, and life couldn't be better. I walk home happy.

The next day, I call Nicole. She's only in town for another couple of days before she heads home, which is miles away. I want to impress her, but my truck still has that huge dent down the side, so I call my friend Trevor and ask to borrow his car. He has a Yukon, a big beast of a truck with tinted windows, rims, everything. He has a house on the beach, and always has people round for barbecues.

'If I pick her up and bring her round,' I say, 'you absolutely can't tell her it's your car, OK?'

'Sure, no problem,' he says.

I set off to pick up Nicole, and I'm thrilled to bits. I'm going to the Playboy Mansion in this awesome truck to pick up an actual Playmate, a real-life *Playboy* centrefold. Life is good.

I pull up to the gates, say it's Calum here to pick up Nicole Lenz, and they let me in. I drive up to the house, Nicole comes out, and she is even more stunning than I remember. I cannot believe how lucky I am. She hops in the car, says hello, and then, 'Nice car.'

'Thanks,' I say. 'I appreciate it.'

I drive her down to Trevor's house in Malibu, introduce her to everyone and we're having a great day. She's lovely and we laugh all the time.

A few hours in, Trevor asks me for the keys to the car. He doesn't do it on purpose – he just needs the keys – but he asks in a way which can only mean it's his car. Nicole is a bright girl, and this doesn't pass her by, though I don't realize it at the time.

Later, as we're getting in the car to leave, she says, 'This isn't your car, is it?'

'No,' I admit, 'it's not.'

'Why would you feel like you need to lie to me?'

I tell her about my truck with the scratch down the side, and that I wanted to impress her, but it doesn't make up for the lie. As we drive back to the mansion, I know the bubble has burst. I drop her off and we say a just-friends goodbye.

I try to see her again, but she isn't interested. Somehow she finds out my real age and calls me out for that too. And so my relationship with a Playmate ends before it really even began. It was a great night and a great day, and makes for wonderful memories, but I'll always think it could have been more. It's my fault that it wasn't. I should never have lied about my age in the first place, and shouldn't have lied about the car either. Instead of trying to seem older and impress her, I should have been honest, and just been myself.

* * *

A few months later, a model agent from London gets in touch and says she thinks she can get me some great work in the UK because I'm George Best's son. I'm already doing well, and she thinks my dad's profile will give me an extra-special edge. She asks me to come over for a couple of weeks and see how it goes. I think, why the hell not? And I decide to go for it. At this point I have absolutely no idea at all about what is going to happen when people make the connection between my career and my dad's name in the UK. The possibility of being on the receiving end of criticism and judgement does not even enter my head.

A week later, I land in London and go to the agent's office to pick up the keys to the place she's arranged for me. It's out in east London, and when I get to the place I know immediately that I can't stay there. It's a studio apartment in a grotty building with a single bed and no TV. I know what I'm like, and I'll go crazy in a place like this, on my own with nothing to do. I'll be miserable. I go outside and call the agent to say I need to find some-where else to stay. They put me up in a hotel near my dad's flat, a little bedsit, which isn't luxurious but that's not what I want anyway. This place is near my dad, so in a part of London I know. That's all I need.

I put my stuff in there and go for something to eat at Pucci Pizza, somewhere I have been lots of times with my dad. In there, I meet a girl called Hannah, who is a friend of Sienna Miller. Hannah is into fashion and knows lots of people. I tell her about my modelling, what I'm doing, why I'm in London, and she says I'd be perfect for Select Models, a big, really good agency in London. She takes me in to meet them the next day, and they sign me up on the spot. I will finish the work I'm doing for the other agent then join Select.

While I'm there, I do jobs for Burberry, and one for Monsoon with Elizabeth Jagger and Leah Wood, so I'm really happy with how things are working out. The agent who brought me over also gets me a job as the face of a new Marks & Spencer range. I'll be doing photo shoots and interviews for it, and it's a really big deal. The shoots don't begin for a few weeks, so I go back to LA for a while and arrange to fly back for them.

The first part of the job is a shoot for *The Times*. It doesn't get off to a great start when I miss my flight to London because I'm out partying, which, ironically, is the kind of thing my dad would do. I end up being a day late, which means they lose a day's shooting. It also means that after I am flown business class from LA to London, there's a helicopter waiting to take me to the Isle of Wight so that I get there as quickly as possible. Although I feel guilty at the trouble I've caused, flying from London to the Isle of Wight in a chopper is a great experience. It's a tiny two-seater thing, and the pilot lets me have a go with the controls. I apologize to everyone when I finally arrive, and we get down to work right away.

The shots are great, some of the best I'll ever do. The theme is James Bond, and there's one of me getting out of the helicopter, one of me jumping over a fence, another in a jacuzzi. It's a really stylish, brilliantly done shoot.

The photos, along with an interview, appear in *The Times*'s Saturday Magazine in November 2001. The cover is me in a white shirt and black suit, holding a martini on a beach with my hair slicked back. The photograph is black and white and it's really cool. The headline is 'Sins of the father – Calum Best on George, women and drink'.

The interview that accompanies it is funny. They play up the bad boy, womanizer angle, and I'm happy to go with it. I talk about flirting, and how flattering women and paying them little compliments works. Even in print I come across as cheeky and a bit cocky, which is probably fair. But then the interview turns serious. This is how a chunk near the end goes:

> Somehow the conversation always drifts back to his father. Calum's attitude to Best senior seems to sway violently between the unconditional love of a child and something closer to disgust. You have to understand that Calum has never seen his father sober.
>
> 'It's not your typical father–son relationship,' he says, inhaling deeply. 'The problem is, my whole life, every time I've come to England to see him he's always been drunk. Being sober is a recent thing. The last time I saw him was in December, three months after he got out of hospital and he was really ill. It's almost a year later and he claims he's still sober, so we'll see.
>
> 'Alex used to tell me that when I'd come to see him,

he'd go on benders; putting it all on to me that he was getting drunk because he didn't know how to handle things. For the first couple of years I thought, "God! That's horrible. I do that to him?" and then I just thought, "Fuck! It's not my fault." But it takes a while to figure that out.

'My dad is still a stranger to me, but it's too late to be bitter. I just want to be able to sit down with him and talk to him about his life, his background, anything. I just know what I've read or watched on video or been told; he's never explained it to me himself.

'I can't even label what I'd like to hear. I just want to have a father–son relationship. Not something fake, like when he's had a few drinks in the pub; it shouldn't be like that. That's why he needed to have this little life-threatening scare. So that he could snap out of it. I'm glad it's happened now, because if it was to happen any later I would be so over him, it wouldn't be funny.'

This is an accurate version of how I feel; I'm just doing what I always do and trying to sound like it doesn't bother me all that much, or make a joke about it. The truth is, I'm not speaking to my dad much at the moment, and I'm upset about it. I've had enough of making an effort with him and getting nothing back. I feel like it's up to him to reach out to me now. I'm angry with him, and hurt by what's happened over the years.

He's not helping either, because he's still drinking. In February 2001 he had been hospitalized with pneumonia and by this time his immune system is getting weaker and weaker. I don't know how many 'one more drink could kill you' warnings he's had from the professor now, but they haven't made any difference, and it makes me very sad. The same is true for the warning his sister Carol has given him. She's told my dad she doesn't want to lose him the way they lost their mother, but he's just carried on drinking. The defiant face I put on for the interview is my way of coping with knowing what he's doing to himself.

This shoot and interview were supposed to be my introduction to the UK, and in that sense it couldn't have gone better. For now, over here I'm Calum Best, the model who happens to be George Best's son. The same month as *The Times* piece, I appear on the cover of the *Evening Standard*'s fashion magazine, *ES*, with a headline 'Calum Best, Superstar – George's son hits the premier league'. The shot is just me with my long hair, and it's another proper bit of modelling work. At the moment I don't mind being mentioned with my dad in the press. I figure it's good for my career and it's nice that the world knows there's that bond between us. It's like the time I shouted out his name in the pub a few years ago – it's almost as if I need reassurance from outside us that he really is my dad because I get so little from him.

Without seeing my dad, I go back to LA, where I'm living with Travis Fimmel again, in a flat in Hollywood. We're having a great time, both doing well at work and going out together. Our flat has the basic necessities: a couple of beds, one couch and a TV. I'm still driving around in my Ford truck, which is a bit beaten up now, and Travis has a Bronco. We're known in all the clubs, and life is good. Not long after, Travis's career takes off and he moves into a house up in the hills. It's a beautiful place, and when I visit I stay in his guest room. I have a friend from London, Tim, who comes to stay with me in LA in early 2002. One day we're driving along and he says to me, 'Why don't you move to London?'

I'm tempted, but I'm having such a great time in LA at the moment that I just don't want to leave. I'm twenty, so am in no rush to go. But then my mum says we need to have a talk. We meet up and she tells me my dad is very ill, and a bit lost, so now might be good for me to go to London and get to know him a bit better while there's still time. She says I might be old enough to deal with it properly now, and to find out things for myself as a man, rather than a kid.

The things she says – 'very ill' and 'while there's still time' – knock me sideways. My mum doesn't need to spell things out for me. My dad isn't young, but he's not an old man either – he's in his fifties and he's George Best, he's bulletproof. Or he's supposed to be, anyway. But after hearing what my mum has to say, I realize he's not. He's an alcoholic who has drunk so much over the years that his health is deteriorating. That's the situation right now and it terrifies me. I always thought he'd be around for ever and it was just a matter of time until we had the relationship I always wanted. Now I'm being told time might be running out. I feel sick.

Suddenly going to London makes sense. My career is going well, but it's not taking off like Travis's, so I figure, why not? I did well in London last time, so it's fair to think that might continue, or even get better. But the point is, I have a good career and taking it to London is definitely not a step back. Because of the way fashion works, the chances are I would do well over there even without the link to my dad, because of the work I've already done. This is how I look at it, because at this point I still don't fully appreciate how powerful my dad's name is in the UK. I'm not at all prepared for what's going to happen. All I think is, going to London will be good for my career and, most importantly, I'll get to spend time with my dad. I'm barely talking to him at the moment because he's so unresponsive to me, but it doesn't take much to reignite my hope for what our relationship might become. The more I think about it, the more excited I get. This could be the opportunity I've been waiting for, a chance to live near my dad and to be part of his life properly, not just for a couple of weeks a year or the occasional visit.

I decide to pack up my life in LA, where I have great friends, as well as my mum, and head to London. I have absolutely no idea how crazy things will get over the next few years. All I think about is spending time with my dad, and working.

The next thing I do is call my dad and tell him I'm

moving over there. I catch him in the morning UK time. We talk, and immediately I can hear there's something different about him – he's sober. I realize I've never actually had a proper conversation with him when he hadn't had a drink. Or at least I can't remember ever having one.

I'm excited, and he seems happy too. I remind him of things we've done together, and he says he's looking forward to taking me to Pucci for pizza and to us playing pool and cribbage together. He says I must come and stay with him, and that we'll be going to Manchester United games and down to Portsmouth to see his old friend Milan Mandarić. We give each other banter about who's going to win our pool games. We remember times together at Hermosa Beach (the good ones), and as always, I say, 'I love you' at the end, with a hopeful tone in my voice, wanting him to say it back to me. But he never does. 'OK, son, see you at the airport,' is the most I get from him.

The conversation ends, and I feel good. This really could be it for us, where it all starts going right. There was nothing earth-shattering about it, and we didn't talk about anything deep. But we had a nice chat, and he's obviously happy that I've reached out to him and am coming over to see him. I don't know how or if he'll be drinking, but hearing him excited about my move pleases me anyway. In the past, when we've spoken, our phone conversations have only been a few minutes long. This one was different. My dad has never been good at showing his feelings, but in his own way it feels like today he was trying to tell me something, like he wanted me to know he is looking forward to having me in London.

Chapter 11

'My real regret in life is not seeing my son growing
up. It's something that really hurts.'

George Best

A couple of weeks later, in spring 2002, I pack a suitcase,
fly to London, and go to my friend Tim's flat in north
London, where he's said I can stay. I don't know until I
arrive just how small his flat is: it's a one-bedroom place
with bunk beds. Seriously, bunk beds. What have I done?
I think to myself: LA was all sunshine and open spaces,
the beach, views, big houses, and now I'm here, in a tiny
flat, in a cold city. But I know from my time in Milan
that things aren't always perfect immediately, so I stick
with it.

I go in for a meeting with Select in their office in north
London to discuss where they think I'm going. They're
really excited, and list these great jobs they have lined up

for me, so I say I need a new place to live. Tim is a great friend, and kind for letting me stay, but his flat is too small for the two of us. Select arrange a room for me at the Gore Hotel in Kensington. I'm paying for it out of my earnings, so it's not free, and they warn me how much it costs, but they've told me how much I'll be earning and I don't care. I want to live somewhere nice and this place, a smart hotel on Queensgate, will do very nicely.

I end up spending a few months in the Gore Hotel. I'm working non-stop, so paying for it isn't a problem. I'm not interested in saving, or being sensible with my money. I just want to have a good time, and the Gore fits right into that. I book some more great modelling jobs, on the catwalk for Versace and Giorgio Armani, and for Ermenegildo Zegna in China, and when you add those to the campaigns I've done in the US for Tommy Hilfiger and Skechers, plus a shoot with Mario Testino, my modelling CV looks really good. For a twenty-year-old model, I'm doing well.

During this time, I see my dad every now and then. I realize I was too optimistic after our talk on the phone, because now I'm here he doesn't seem ready to have me around, so all I get is random, small visits. He doesn't call me or try to see me, so if I want to see him I have to go and find him. So we're back to how things have always been, with me always reaching out to him. That means going to his flat, or to the Phene, or one of the other pubs and restaurants where he hangs out. He doesn't have a mobile phone, but he doesn't go to many different places, so it's never hard to track him down. But I don't do it often. I don't want to try too hard, because I worry that if I am in his face all the time I will push him away. And I also stay away because I feel like he doesn't want to see me, and I don't want to keep reminding myself of that. I hoped he would be pleased to have me over here, and maybe on some deep level he is; he's just not showing it to me at the moment.

It takes me ages to get anything from him. I see him a bit at his flat, we go to a health club once, but mainly I see him in the Phene. If I want to spend time with him, I have to go to the pub, that's just the way it is. From eleven in the morning till ten at night. Doesn't matter how bad his liver is.

Sometimes I wake up in the morning and go and join him, which isn't healthy for me either, but if I want to see him that's what I have to do. We have the odd meal together, a Chinese or at Pucci Pizza, but it's not often, and it's not deep in any real way because he's always drunk. I'm worried about his health now, and I try to speak to him about it. But no matter what I do, I can't tell him off. I don't know him well enough, and any time I do try it he tells me to fuck off.

He's writing a column now for the *Mail on Sunday*, and in his first one he says this: 'My real regret in life is not seeing my son growing up. It's something that really hurts. But now I look at Calum and how he's turned out. He's such an amazing person. Every time we talk on the phone he finishes it off by saying, "I love you, Dad", which considering I wasn't around is a great compliment.'

But I don't mean it as a compliment. I tell him I love him because I want him to know how I feel, and because I hope he feels the same and will tell me he loves me too. But he never does. I'm glad he wrote those things about me, but how much can it really mean if he doesn't actually show me how he feels? Or change how he acts? Are those things real, or are they just sweet words he thinks will make him look good if he puts them in a newspaper? I don't know what to believe.

Luckily I'm busy with my own stuff at the moment, so I don't have too much time to dwell on things concerning my dad. I have appointments and jobs every day because of these magazine shoots, modelling jobs, appearances, interviews, meetings. I'm not on drugs, I'm not drinking heavily, I'm healthy, staying in a nice hotel, and I feel good.

But it's not all perfect. For the first month, I work during the day, but in the evenings I don't do anything, and I'm getting more and more bored. I'm not good at being on my own, which is possibly something I get from my dad. I like going out, having fun with my friends, talking and messing around, but I don't have any friends here who I can do that with. Virtually every evening I'm alone in the hotel, and I don't like it. I know that I'll get really miserable if I let this go on for too long, so I decide to do something about it.

I call my agency and say I want to go to a party, I want

to go out. I'm bored. They say fine, but I have to be careful. I must go to the right kind of party, and be seen with the right kind of people, or else my career will suffer. No problem, I say, I know what I'm doing.

I get invited to the GQ Fashion Awards, and I love it. This is what I wanted. It's cool, it's glamorous, and the people are interesting. I meet Caprice, the model, and we get on well. The next morning there's a photo of the two of us on the front page of the *Sun*. The papers love it – George Best's son with this beautiful blonde – and I am shocked. I had no idea this would happen; I don't know anything about the UK press and their thirst for a story.

Not long after that, I go to another event and the next day the *Evening Standard* mentions three people who were there: Mick Jagger, Kate Moss, and me. I can't believe my name is up there with people so famous. Me, listed alongside them? It's very weird, crazy even, but I enjoy it. I like that people are interested in me. I'm new to fame, and to the press too, and I think it's exciting, being in the papers and having people know who I am. For a twenty-one-year-old guy, it's great fun. At first.

The stories make me realize I could have a lot of good times in London, and I'm bored of sitting at home alone in the evenings. But where do I start? I need a way in. Then I have an idea. I've been reading the papers and I've noticed that the hottest person around at the moment seems to be this girl called Jordan, or Katie Price. I'll get in touch with her, I decide, and she can show me around the city's nightlife.

I get in touch with someone I know for her number and I send her a text saying it's Calum Best here, I'm in town, where's the best place to go out tonight? I have no reservations about doing this; I'm not shy at all. She replies and tells me to meet her at Chinawhite that night. I don't realize at the time how big a moment this is, and how much this decision will affect the next few years of my life. For me, it's simply about having fun.

I arrive at Chinawhite at 10.30 pm and tell the bouncers I'm there to meet Katie Price. Sure you are, they say, so is everyone else, and then they point at a very long queue.

I don't know what to do, but I certainly don't want to be stuck out in the cold all night. I think of one option, and for the first and only time in my life I say these words to get myself into a club: 'I'm George Best's son.' I say them like a question because I'm begging, and the second they hear my dad's name the bouncers' faces change and the doors are suddenly wide open.

I get taken through to the VIP section, and someone introduces me to Katie Price. She's not remotely interested in me, says hello and that's it. I'm a long-haired surfer dude, and that's clearly not her thing.

I'm not bothered, though, because I'm in the club so I can enjoy myself. There's a bar, I get a drink and think, right, let's see what's going on. Someone recognizes me and says, 'Come and meet the Chelsea boys,' and I'm taken over to a table of footballers. There's Celestine Babayaro, John Terry, Frank Lampard and Wayne Bridge. They're all high-fiving me, going on about what a legend my dad is. They invite me to sit at their table and have a drink, and then they start introducing me to girls. I can't lie, I love it all. This is brilliant. Drinks, good lads to talk to, girls around. This is what I like.

I hit it off best with Celestine Babayaro, and we're friends for the next few years. I also meet a guy called Jake Panayiotou, who tells me he was friends with my dad and that he's opening a new club called the Wellington next week, and please come down. I go back to my hotel excited about what's happening, about making friends and not being lonely any more.

The next day I call Maxine at Select and tell her about my night out. She goes all serious and says, 'Calum, I have to warn you, don't get caught up in this nightclub stuff. It'll ruin your career and you're doing so well. It happens to so many of my clients. Please, don't get sucked into that world.'

Select want me to stay at the high end of fashion, doing more shoots with Mario Testino and Leah Wood and Elizabeth Jagger. The *Sun*, Caprice and Jordan are not the scene they have in mind for me. But I don't care. I like modelling, but I want to have fun too.

'Don't worry,' I say to Maxine, 'it's cool. I can handle it. I just want to go out and enjoy myself a bit. I'll be fine.'

I go to the Wellington club for the launch night and the press go nuts. I take the model Victoria Silvstedt with me; I met her at the GQ awards the same night I met

Caprice, and when I called and asked her to come along to the Wellington with me she was very happy to agree. The next day we're all over the papers.

A few days later, I read a piece in *The Times* by Simon Mills talking about the Wellington being the cool new hotspot in London. It mentions Kate Moss, Jude Law, and me. Maxine's words of warning seem ridiculous. How can being mentioned in the same article as those two be a bad thing?

I start hitting it hard, going out and making the most of the London scene. Until now I've been getting great modelling jobs, but, although I don't recognize it, Maxine's forebodings begin to play out and this is the start of the downward spiral. During this period, I'm introduced to cocaine. I've taken it before, back in LA, but it's different there. Back home it's occasional, just popping up every now and then. But in London it's everywhere, every night. I'm offered lines all the time, and I end up taking much, much more than I ever did in the US. It makes a good night even better and longer lasting, and I think fuck it, why not? I do line after line in nightclub toilets, with people I barely know. I'm not very good at moderation. People want me in their clubs, people in the clubs want to talk to me, they give me coke, and I can't get enough of it. I cannot see the parallels with my dad's life.

At first it's OK. I can still work the next day. I'm twenty-one and I'm still taking my modelling pretty seriously, so I don't miss jobs or get to work really messed up. I think I'm being careful, but the truth is, this is just the start. Over the next few months work keeps coming in, but it slows down, partly because of the name I'm getting in the papers, but also because of my physical condition. I'm not looking after myself like I should, and for a model that's the most important thing.

During this period contact with my dad is rare. He doesn't seem interested, and I try not to think about him too much, but one day he calls me, completely out of the blue. 'Bestie,' he says, 'I'm feeling down and I want to see you. Let's have a drink.'

I've never had a call like this from him before, where he's so openly said he wants to see me. This is what fathers and sons should do, right? He's having a bad moment so wants me with him – maybe now he finally gets that we're there for each other? I don't like the fact he's feeling down, and I don't like him wanting to drink, for obvious reasons, but I absolutely love that he wants me to be with him. I immediately drop everything. 'I'll be right there,' I say. 'Where are you?'

He's at PJ's, a bar on the Fulham Road, and I get there as quickly as I can. The first thing I notice is that he looks good, wearing dress trousers, a white shirt, a nice jacket and nice shoes. At least he's not in his eighties shell suit, so things might not be all that bad. I've rushed there in a tracksuit, and with my long hair pulled back in a pony-tail, so it's me that doesn't look great.

He's drinking a white wine and I decide to try to cheer him up, to try to make this a good day, so I have a brandy.

There's no point worrying today, I reason. Just go with it, don't fight him. And things start to go well. We talk, we laugh, we discuss a hot waitress, he relaxes and we just hang out together having a straightforward good time. Sure, we're drinking, so there's a bit of a shadow hanging over us, but he's happy, which is better than usual.

A couple of hours later we're still having a really good time. He's on the ball, we're chatting and it's great. We decide to leave PJ's for food, so we walk down the road to Pucci Pizza.

The ten minutes or so it takes to get there become one of the happiest times I ever spend with him. We are joking and joking, laughing all the way, bantering with each other in a lovely, relaxed manner. Those minutes might have been drunken minutes, but they were hilarious, a really special time. A few days later a photo appears in a paper of us on that walk and we're both laughing. Obviously drunk too, but happy. Really happy.

Pucci's is one of my dad's regular haunts. He has his own table at the front and there is a plaque from him signed to Signor Pucci himself on the wall. They used to make the pizza dough right in front of you, and when I was younger I'd go behind the counter and the chef would teach me how to do it so I could make my own. I am happy here.

We sit down at a round table, continue drinking, order margarita pizza and our usual bresaola completa, which is something my dad introduced me to. It's dried beef with mozzarella, tomatoes and basil, and we put it together with garlic bread and it's delicious. It will always be one of my absolute favourite meals.

People are coming over to say hello, there are girls around, and we're having a great day. Drunk, but great. We're having such a good time I don't want it to end.

And then I crack a joke and go to slap my dad on the chest. Not hard, but playfully. We've been bantering all afternoon and it's a continuation of that.

But, as always happens with my dad, a moment comes where a happy story turns dark, and this is it. He always has his reading glasses hanging on a string round his neck and my slap breaks them. They're not expensive glasses, and they're probably easy to fix, so it's no big deal, but me breaking them by accident is enough to make him switch. He explodes.

'You cunt,' he snaps. 'You stupid fucking cunt. You fucking idiot. What are you doing? I can't take you any-where. What the hell is the matter with you?'

'Dad, I'm sorry,' I say. 'I didn't mean to.'

'That's not good enough, you stupid little shit.'

My dad gets up and storms out of the restaurant. I'm left sitting there on my own. My first thought is that I hope everyone else in the restaurant doesn't think my dad hates me. I don't want anyone thinking that. Because he doesn't hate me. I know he doesn't, it's the drink that makes him like this. That wasn't the real George. I sit there and look around and feel like everyone's looking at me thinking what a stupid kid I am for pissing off George

Best so badly that he got up and left. What a prize idiot I must be to annoy him that much – that must be what's going through their minds.

I don't know what to do, so I sit as casually as I can, almost waving to him as he goes, pretending there's nothing wrong and hoping no one notices anything. I feel pathetic.

I decide to have another beer and carry on as normal, pretending everything is OK. Maybe he'll come back. A few minutes later he hasn't reappeared, so I go outside to see if I can find him. I can't see him anywhere, so I come back in, call a friend and he comes to join me. We end up doing lines of coke and I push my dad out of my thoughts.

The story doesn't end there. A few weeks later my dad tells me what happened. He went home, got in his Mini Cooper and tried to drive to the house in the country where he now lives with Alex. He quickly got pulled over, arrested and taken into the station, where the police take pictures with him.

When it comes to court, his lawyer says he was drink-driving because he had an argument with me and so the newspapers write stories about my drunken row with my dad. They have a field day with that: George gets arrested for drink-driving and blames the 'blazing row' he just had with Calum.

Chapter 12

'We were almost there, almost at that place I've been searching for all my life. But I hated it because all that, everything I've dreamed about for so long, was gone in an instant.'

Calum Best

In August 2002, a few months later, I'm in a cab on the way to a meeting with my agency, Select, in north London. My relationship with them is getting rocky. I arrived in London with a great modelling career ahead of me, but since I got here things have changed. I'm drinking too much, taking drugs and being seen with the wrong people in the wrong places. I'm out every single night and have got myself a party-boy reputation in the newspapers. I suppose I deserve it, but the papers certainly enjoy making the 'like father, like son' connection. I shut my mind to comparisons between us. I don't stop to think about it, possibly because I don't want to acknowledge that I might be behaving as self-destructively as he did.

I'm certainly damaging myself professionally, because my new reputation doesn't support the high-fashion image Select were hoping for, and now my lifestyle is having a negative effect on my appearance. I've put on weight, I'm pale, my skin is puffy and pallid and I don't look healthy. I was a sporty, fresh-faced California kid with a suntan and a six-pack when I got here. That was what got me my modelling jobs. I don't look like that any more.

But I don't mind too much. I came to London to get to know my dad and I was happy to give up my career to do that. I've lived on the other side of the world from him for my whole life, only seeing him for a couple of weeks a year and I spent most of those trips in the pub watching him drink. All my life, I've been trying to find a way to get to know him and coming to London was my chance to make that happen. But so far it hasn't been great. In fact, it's been like all those holidays when I was younger, only longer.

As I've got older, I've come to believe that me being around makes him drink more, not less. Why? Well, I think deep down my dad is a good man who knows how much his drinking has hurt people he cares about. He knows alcohol has stopped me from knowing him, because for me drink is like the thick glass windows you get at zoos. I can see my dad but I can't get to him because of what's in the way. I'm sure he knows this, and perhaps feels the same. Seeing me reminds him of it, which hurts him, and to deal with the pain he drinks. The more he drinks, the worse he feels, and the worse he feels, the more he drinks. He's stuck in a vicious circle and I don't know what to do about it.

Today, I expect Select are going to tell me I need to get my life in order. Lose weight, make myself look better, get my face out of the papers, stop the crazy nightlife. The usual.

In the cab, the radio is on. I'm not really paying attention to it, just staring out of the window at the world, when I hear a name. My father's name.

'We have some breaking news,' the radio says. 'Soccer legend George Best will undergo a liver transplant today. A matching liver has been found and he has been admitted to Cromwell Hospital in west London.'

I freeze. I didn't know this was happening. No one told me. I didn't know he was having this major surgery today. We had an argument recently but it was the kind of thing that happens all the time. Nowhere near enough to keep me in the dark about something this huge. I know he's not been looking healthy recently. His face is red, his skin is peeling and he always has dandruff in his hair. You can tell his body is run down because on the outside there are all the signs that it's not doing the right things on the inside. I'm gutted I didn't know how bad things had got. But at least I've found out now. My meeting with Select doesn't matter any more. I need to be with my dad.

'Change of plan,' I say to the driver. 'Take me to Cromwell Hospital.'

* * *

I get to the hospital and go to my dad's room. Already there are Alex and Denis Law, his old friend from Manchester United and another legendary player. I speak to the doctor in charge, who's a lovely guy, and he says my dad's in surgery. I ask when he'll be out. Could be two hours, could be ten, the doctor says. It depends how it goes.

I know how significant a new liver is to an alcoholic – that it is, effectively, a second chance at life. I hope more than I've ever hoped for anything that my dad's transplant will be a new start, for him and for us. He'll be healthier and happier and we will start to get to know each other properly. We'll have time together, time to be father and son. He won't drink any more, so I'll be with my real dad, not the twisted version of himself he becomes when he's drunk.

At the same time, I know it will be tough for him to see me when he's sober after the operation, because I'm a reminder of the things he sacrificed for alcohol. It'll be hard for him not to start drinking again. But as always with him, I hope for the best, because it's all I can do.

A few hours later, Dad wakes up. He's thin and jaundiced, his cheeks are sunken, his eyes are yellow and he looks twenty years older than he is, but the doctor says he's recovered much quicker than expected. It's sad to see him like this, but it's a great moment. Our new life is starting now, today. I think how lucky my dad has been, that the liver has come in and he's now doing so well.

Above: My parents in the early part of their relationship.

Below left: They had some great times together and were very happy, although alcohol was beginning to play a larger role in their lives.

Below right: At their wedding in Las Vegas in 1978.

Above: My dad was very excited about my mum getting pregnant with me, and in the early weeks of my life he was a doting father.

Below: He looks very content.

Above: I wish this picture was the story of our whole relationship.

Below: Learning to play football – I hadn't figured out how to kick just yet.

Above: My mum is very into fitness and has always encouraged me to be the same way.

Right: At my dad's testimonial in 1988. I am far too big to be carried but it made a nice photo!

Below: Playing football in the park – a set-up with a photographer who had paid my dad.

Above: Practising my skills on the beach in LA.

Right: Enjoying the attention we got at the airport.

Below: The skateboarding teenager, at my dad's flat in London.

If I wanted to see my dad it was either at the pub or on the way to one.

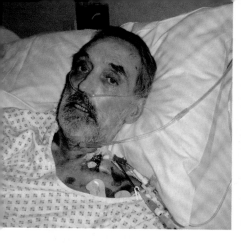

The end of my dad's life. The last photo of him is a shocking image. I wish he could have seen how much love there was for him at his funeral and the tributes to him at Old Trafford.

Left: During the filming of *Brought Up By Booze*.

Below: Returning to Belfast for some filming in 2014. The beard was fun for a while, but I'm glad I got rid of it!

Typical George, is what people will say, he has the luck of the devil.

When he starts talking, I see a sparkle in his eyes.

'Calum,' he says, smiling at me, 'I feel like this is a new start for us. A new time for us. I can't wait for us to go on holiday together, to spend time together. To start again.'

I'm thinking, this is it, it's really happening. He's never spoken to me like that before. He's never said anything so deep and real. This is the new start I'd dreamt of. A new George, a new dad. As long as I've known him he's been tainted by drink, but from now on he's going to have a clear head. He'll be the real him. He's going to recognize me, to want to be with me. He's not going to be ill any more. We can make up for all the time we've missed out on. This is what I left my career, my mum and my friends in America for. This moment is what I did it for. I'm in tears, thinking yes, great, finally, I've waited so long for this and here it is. I don't want things to ever go back.

Over the next few weeks I see Dad at his house and at a health farm where he stays a lot. I'm not with him all the time, because he's recovering. He's slowly getting better, looking healthier and getting stronger, and when I do see him we have an incredible time, talking about football, laughing about girls, about old times, such as how he taught me to play cribbage in the pub when I was a kid. Most importantly, he's sober, which means it's all real.

Then he says, 'Calum, we're going on holiday to Corfu

and I'd love it if you come. I want to go to the sunshine, I feel better there, and I want you with me.'

I am overwhelmed. This is all my dreams come true. All I've ever wanted. This is our time to bond, to be together properly, our new life made real. He says he and Alex and her parents will fly out to a villa they've rented together the next day and I should join them as soon as possible.

I get there as quickly as I can, which means taking off in the middle of the night and waiting six hours for a connecting flight from somewhere in the middle of Europe. It's the fastest way, so I don't mind. I'd swim there if Dad asked me to.

I get to Corfu and take a cab to the villa. As soon as I arrive I see Dad. He's lying in the sun and looking better now that he's got a bit of colour. He's walking around, doing things, and he seems really pleased to see me. We're laughing together immediately. He asks what I've been up to, what's going on in my life, and we talk about Manchester United – the kind of normal conversation fathers and sons have, but which we haven't had before. This is my new dad, my sober dad, and I love it. For the next four days we're going to bond like we never have before.

Then I see that Alex and her mum and dad are drinking alcohol. I'm furious. How can they drink in front of my dad? He's a recovering alcoholic. They should be supporting him, like I'm trying to. I feel bad because I like Alex, I always have, and I know how much she's supported my dad and how much she cares about him. Even so, I can't help being angry with her and her parents for drinking in front of him. I'm furious with them. But I put my feelings to one side. I don't want arguments to spoil these few days.

On my second day, we get a boat taxi to go out for lunch because my dad says he wants to take me to this restaurant where he promises I'll have the best lobster I've ever eaten. I'm so happy that he wants to show me this place and tell me these things. I've been dying for this to happen, for him to be like this. At the restaurant, Alex and her parents are drinking wine but Dad is drinking Coke. Inside I'm not happy about it, but I don't want to ruin the atmosphere so I say nothing. I make a point of having Coke too. We have a great time.

The next day we get up and go straight down to swim in the sea. We're relaxing in the water, laughing and talking in the sunshine. The sea is warm, Dad is happy and all I can think is how good this feels, how it's been worth all the waiting and the pain to get to this point with him. He's looking better all the time. His skin has stopped flaking and he's got a tan. He still looks frail, but that's nothing new because he's always been a small guy. He has power when he walks into a room because of who he is and how he carries himself, not because he's a big, strapping man. If you watch videos of him playing football, he looks small and skinny compared to the other players. So now, he's built as he always was. He's not wasting away.

A couple of days later and I'm still having the time of my life. It's perfect. I'm with my dad, we've been sunbathing together and laughing and talking in a new way. The new start he promised is happening. I am unbelievably, ecstatically happy.

On my last day, I go for a nap after lunch. I wake up and walk down to the kitchen, still blurry-eyed and sleepy. From the doorway I see my dad putting something in the door of the fridge really quickly, like he doesn't want to be seen, and then leaving the kitchen through the doorway opposite the one where I am. He couldn't know I was here.

I didn't see what he put in the fridge but I heard something. My dozy brain takes a couple of seconds to register what the noise was. It sounded like the soft splash wine makes falling back to the bottom of the bottle when it's turned upright again after you've been pouring it. But I know it can't be that. Dad is sober now. It can't be wine.

I rush over to the fridge because I need to be sure. There's one thing in the door: a half-empty bottle of dry white wine, with no cork in it. That must be what he was drinking. There's no other possibility. He wouldn't have swigged the milk or the cranberry juice because both are sealed shut. And dry white wine is his drink.

The realization hits me like a punch in the guts. He's drinking again. He's fucking drinking again.

My mind starts whirring with questions and options. How am I going to deal with this? Should I call him out? No way – I know how badly he reacts when I do that. I'm terrified of what he might do. What other options do I have? I'm on holiday with him and we're having a great time, so maybe I should just try to make it better. Maybe I can help him. Maybe that drink was just a quick mistake, one small slip, and really we're going to be fine. Maybe I should ignore it and carry on being positive.

So I decide to say nothing, to just push on through and enjoy the holiday and my time with my dad as much as I can, in the hope that the good memories we create get him off the drink again. For the next few hours I seek out as many moments with him as I possibly can: if he pulls up a chair to sunbathe, I pull up a chair next to him. If he goes for a swim, I'm there too. I do that, and the rest of the day is OK. I keep telling myself, one swig of a bottle doesn't make him a drunk. It's just one mistake.

I leave the villa to head back to London later that afternoon and on my way home I have time to process what has happened. I decide to try not to be angry or sad that my dad might be drinking again. Instead I focus on the fact I just spent four lovely days with him, for the first time ever. I'm grateful because I now have the memories of those days, which I will always cherish. I loved them and I hope Dad feels the same. I hope him swigging from that bottle was just a quick mistake and that he's going to come home and get back on track and be the dad I've always wanted him to be and which I think he's always wanted to be too.

At the same time, I realize that happy ending is unlikely

to happen. The swig I saw him take was a reality check, because deep down I know it's going to take some sort of miracle for him to stay off the drink. I'm twenty-one and I've known my dad sober for three weeks of my life, and I'm beginning to think that short period is the aberration. Maybe him drunk is normal, and those four days of clear-headed, happy, sober Dad on holiday are all I'll ever get. Those four days were great, but they're over and maybe we're fucked again.

When I get back to London I deal with things the only way I know how: I go straight out on the town. I have no one to talk to about my dad, no one I can spend a quiet evening with, getting things off my chest. My only friends here are the ones I know through clubs, and if I don't want to spend an evening alone I have to go out. So I do what I've been doing since I moved to London. I drink through it, and try my best to get on with my life. I don't know what else to do. I'm not conscious of the irony of this – that drinking is the only way I can cope with my dad's drinking, and that he drinks because he can't cope with his own problems. Also, I don't see myself as the same kind of drinker as my dad. I drink socially, not on my own and not all day, every day. To me, that makes it OK.

After the holiday, we don't see each other for a while. I don't go looking for him, and he doesn't call me. During this time word gets out that he's drinking again. It becomes accepted knowledge in the press and among his friends and family that he's back on the booze. I'm gutted.

* * *

In early 2004 I read in the papers that Dad and Alex are on the verge of breaking up, or might even already be separated. I wouldn't blame Alex for wanting their relationship to end. There's only so much one person can take, no matter how much she loves him.

My dad, no matter how ill or messed up he is, can't be on his own. He always needs someone to take care of him and now, even though they're splitting up, he turns to Alex. A few weeks after we get back from Corfu I want to know how he's doing, so one day I go to see Alex at their house out in the country and ask. She tells me it's got so bad she's caught my dad drinking brandy out of Lucozade bottles. That means he's drinking properly again, hiding booze away and drinking all the time. This is terrible news.

I see now that it didn't matter if Alex and her parents drank in front of him in Corfu. It wouldn't make any difference. He wants to drink, so he will. There's nothing anyone can do to stop him.

But part of me still hopes he'll decide to stop. I can't help myself. Ever since I was a kid, all I hoped for was my dad. His love, his acceptance, his conversation, just being with him. No matter how much he hurt me or disappointed me, I always hoped there would come a time when he really would change, and the hope always seemed to cover up the pain. I started to hope again as soon as I got back from Corfu. I couldn't help it, and even now, knowing he really is drinking again, I'm trying to hang on to that hope. I go over and over what happened between us during those weeks. We were so close when he woke up after the operation. He said things to me I'd never heard before and those days in Corfu were magical. We were almost there, almost at that place I've been searching for all my life. But I hated it because all that, everything I've dreamed about for so long, was gone in an instant.

The great memories are what get my hope going again. I hope my dad sees things the way I do and decides he wants to change, to recapture what we had and to make it last. I want to see him the way everyone else does, because all my life, just about everybody I've ever met has had a nice thing to say about my dad. What a legend, what a gentleman, what a classy guy. I'm sure to them he is, but to me he is always tainted by booze and is a really shitty dad. He is at his funniest at nine in the morning when he's having his first glass of wine. By 11am he's a bit moody. By 2pm, when he's on the brandies, he is a disaster and usually stays that way for the rest of the day. That's the dad I have known all my life, except for the weeks after the liver transplant and for those few days in Corfu.

Chapter 13

'Even after everything he went through before that,
he's still drinking. I can't see how he'll ever stop.'

Calum Best

My dad doesn't confide in me, but I hear about what's
going on between them from Alex, and from mutual
friends. In spring 2004 he moves out of their house and
goes to stay at Champneys Health Spa near Liphook in
Hampshire, a really lovely place. He is good friends with
the owner, Stephen Purdew, and goes there quite often,
especially at moments like this.

I haven't seen my dad for a while, I know he's in a bad
way because of the drink, and his marriage is in trouble
– he and Alex divorce in April 2004 – so this is a good
moment for me to go and spend some time with him. He
doesn't ask me to; it's my idea, and I suggest it. I figure he
might need someone close to him at the moment, even if

it just means he isn't drinking alone all day every day. But I hope for more than that. I want him to know that his son is by his side at a difficult moment in his life. I hope that might bring us closer together. He might see me differently, he might want me around him more.

I'm in a pretty bad way at the moment too. Work isn't great, I'm not modelling any more, and I'm out a lot. Some time in a health spa might be good for me physically too. I've met Stephen a few times and he's always invited me to visit. I haven't said yes before, but now I call him to ask if I can come and stay with my dad. He says yes, of course I can.

I check in for two weeks, hoping my dad and I will both come out in better shape. But I quickly see that my dad's idea of staying in a health spa doesn't match up with mine. He drinks as he usually does, only in nicer surroundings and wearing a Champneys white towel robe. The media reports that he's staying here, and the angle every time is that he's here trying to clean himself up. But the truth is very different.

We have good, healthy breakfasts and good dinners too, and we swim and have massages and so on, but he's drinking as much as always, from first thing in the morning right through until he goes to bed. So he's still on that downward spiral.

As for our relationship, nothing changes. Our conversations aren't meaningful in any way at all. Sometimes we struggle to find things to talk about. It's actually awkward between us. I've always hoped for a relationship with him where silences are comfortable, where we can just sit there and be together with no pressure, like a normal father and son would. But our relationship is far more complicated than that, and silences aren't comfortable. They're tense, and while we're sitting there I imagine he's thinking the same things I am: what should I say? What can we talk about? What does he think of me? How can we get past everything that has happened over the years?

And the thing is, the more you worry about what to say, and the harder you try to think of things to talk about, the more difficult it gets and the less conversation there is. I want to tell him how I feel, how I want things to be between us, and that I love him no matter what went on in the past, but I don't. I can't say things like that to him. He'd run away. He's an alcoholic full of regrets, and an old-school Irishman who keeps his emotions hidden away. I can't communicate with him. It's tough, completely different to Corfu.

One morning at Champneys he says to me, 'We're going out today. I'm meeting a girl in town.'

I'm surprised by this, but say OK, and off we go. We might not say much, but at least we're together. I have no idea who this girl we're going to see is, how he's met her or what the story is, and I know I can't ask either, so I keep quiet and go with it. We head to a village close by and into the local pub. It's a nice area but a dingy little bar. This blonde girl turns up and is all over my dad. I'm confused by this. She's young, in her twenties, possibly

187

even younger than me, and she's come to see my dad? I'm not sure I like it.

This girl is bubbly, and not too bright, and after a while my dad gets her sitting on his knee. They're flirting and kissing a bit, and I can't help feeling this is really weird. Maybe I'm a bit jealous and competitive, and I think she should be going after me, not my dad. But mostly I just don't like seeing this girl and my dad all over each other. It's seriously uncomfortable. I came here to bond with my dad, not watch him perving over a girl. It's the same old story, the same thing that happened at that hotel in Manchester, and back at Hermosa Beach: he'd rather spend time with some random girl than with his son. I hate it. As I sit there in this dingy bar, so many bad memories are coming back.

I realize nothing has changed. Everything I hoped for with him is as far away as it's ever been. I don't know how to handle the situation, sitting here with him and this girl. I've seen my dad with many women in the past, but it's never felt like this. These two weeks were supposed to be my time with him, just the two of us. But he doesn't want that.

I can't stand it for long, and I go back to Champneys on my own. The first thing I do is call my mum and we have one of those conversations that begin with me saying, 'You're not going to believe what he's done . . .', the kind we've had countless times over the years when I've called her from England. And of all the people I could say that to, my mum is probably the only one in the world who actually would believe whatever it is he's been up to. Nothing about my dad would surprise her.

So I'm on the phone ranting to my mum about my dad and this girl. I'm really upset, and it's fucking this and fucking that, and he's such an asshole, and who did this girl think she was? I'm really letting rip, going on and on, and my language is pretty offensive. Suddenly this woman comes up from the pool area and taps me on the shoulder. I tell my mum to hang on a minute while I see what she wants. 'You might want to keep your voice down,' the woman says. 'We can all hear every word you're saying.' She gestures down to the pool, and there are about twenty people lying around it sunbathing.

I don't see my dad again until the evening, when he acts like nothing out of the ordinary happened. We carry on in our awkward little routine until a few days later, when my dad wants to go out again. Not to meet a girl this time, but just to go to a bar. We go to a different place, another quiet little pub, and sit down with our drinks. We're having the same kind of superficial conversation we've been having since I got here, when this guy walks into the pub, sees my dad and says, 'George, if I knew you were here, I'd have brought my camera!' My dad looks at him and says, 'If I knew you were here, I wouldn't have come.'

I can't help laughing at this, and I think my dad is pretty cool for being quick enough and brave enough to come back with that line. I realize that's the part of my dad's character that gives him his charm, and is the reason why people want to talk to him, because he has this sharp wit, this glint in his eye. That's why he can come out with phrases like, 'I spent my money on booze, birds and fast cars. I wasted the rest,' or 'I gave up drinking in 1979. It was the worst twenty minutes of my life.' They're dark subjects, especially to me because I lost him to those things, but I still admire him for his ability to be so sharp.

This is the first of two moments during that fortnight when I look at my dad and think maybe you're not such a bad guy after all. Telling the guy in the pub where to go makes me respect him in a laddish way; the second incident makes me actually like him. It happens a couple of days later, when we go to another pub near Liphook. We both have a few drinks, and some fish and chips, and the conversation is typically tense and awkward. It's time to leave, so we order a cab back to Champneys. The taxi comes and I go to get in the back with my dad. But he stops me, and says, 'No, son, someone has to sit in the front with him,' pointing at the driver. It is a respect thing – my dad wants it to be clear that we don't think we are better than the driver. He wants our behaviour to reflect the fact that we believe this man driving the car is no less than us. I sit in the front, but if I wasn't there my dad would've done, which is exactly what happens on the next taxi ride we take.

This little lesson stays with me for ever. Whenever I get into a taxi, I always think about it. Sometimes I can't sit in the front, and sometimes I really don't want to, but that principle, and the knowledge I should show good manners to everyone, never leaves me.

This is the side of my dad that I love, the good man that he can be, the old-school Irish gentleman, and the man I want to get to know better. But it doesn't happen. As always, alcohol gets in the way. He starts drinking even more heavily towards the end of our time at Champneys, and I leave knowing my father is in a really bad way. It might have been a health farm, but he wasn't there on a health kick. It's another blow in the guts for me, another stark demonstration that he's not getting back on the straight and narrow, and I can really see the hold alcohol has over him.

After Corfu, I hoped the drink I saw him have there was just a slip, and when I heard he was at a health farm I thought great, he's trying to get better, I'll go and help him. But he's not trying to get better. Even after everything he went through before that, he's still drinking. I can't see how he'll ever stop.

Back in London, one day my dad calls and invites me to go and watch a Portsmouth match with him. He tells me to meet him at the basement flat he still has on Cheyne Walk in Chelsea – which is where he moved to a couple of years ago after financial problems meant he had to sell his home on Oakley Street – and we'll go down there in the car Milan Mandarić sends. And dress smartly, he says. I don't really know what dressing smartly is, so I turn up looking like I always do, which means trainers, some slacks and a jacket. My dad looks smart; he's made an effort.

As long as I've known him, he's looked OK. But he's never really taken care of himself. He always has a shaggy beard and shaggy hair that hasn't been washed for a while. He looks his worst when he's been in the same shell suit for three days in a row, which happens quite often. But then he'll clean himself up, put on a suit, and he looks fine again, which is how he appears today. I'm pleased, and think maybe he's getting better. Even now, I'm still capable of telling myself he really might have turned a corner.

We drive down to Portsmouth, and in the car the conversation is the same superficial stuff as always. We get to the stadium and I meet Milan. He's lovely to me, a charming, friendly guy who obviously adores my dad. My dad obviously admires him too, because my middle name is Milan. They first met in the seventies when my dad played for his team in the US, the San Jose Earthquakes, and have been friends ever since.

My dad asks me if I want to bet on the game, and that is my introduction to gambling. I say yes, sure, anything you're doing I want to do too. My bet is simply Portsmouth to win, but my dad, who clearly knows a lot more about gambling than I do, has all kinds of bets on corners, first goalscorer, how many corner kicks, how many yellow cards, who'll get the first one and so on.

We sit down for lunch with Milan. My dad is drinking,

but it's fine for now. We watch the game, and my dad is drinking more and more, and doing it quickly. He seems less and less interested in me, so I start thinking about what I might do tonight.

As the second half starts, I get a call from a friend in London, who says he's watching the game and has just seen me on TV. The camera has obviously been panning round the crowd during the break and picked out the legend George Best, and there I am sitting next to him. I am thrilled. Not because I'm on TV, but because it shows me and my dad having a bonding moment together, it shows the world we're a unit, father and son. After what we've been through and what's been written about both of us, such as the 'blazing row' we had before my dad was caught drink-driving, this is really important to me. No matter what else happens today, I have that.

We go back into the bar after the game, and by now my dad is three sheets to the wind, properly pissed. I'm always really defensive of him, especially when he's drunk. I'm on edge, looking around at what people are saying, what kind of looks they're giving each other. I'm paranoid about what people think of him, basically. I know he's in bad shape, I hate the fact and I can't stand it when other people notice it. I want him to be immortal, not this messed-up, drunk little man. And now, in the bar at Portsmouth, he's drunk and I'm twitchy.

I see one of the Portsmouth players do something which sets me off. He says something about my dad being a legend; I only half-hear him, but he says it in a way that sounds sarcastic to me, like, '*That's* the legend George Best?'

I get right in his face and start shouting. And he puts his hands up and says, 'Whoa, whoa, mate, who are you?' 'I'm George's son,' I say, 'and I heard what you said.'

We have a bit of a confrontation because I think I'm trying to protect my dad from an insult. But looking back, I'm not sure he meant it the way I thought he did. I turned it into an insult in my mind because I was paranoid, because the truth is, at this stage my dad doesn't look great. Right now he is very obviously drunk, and I know how bad his health is and that it's getting worse. So I reacted like that out of my frustration and embarrassment. That player didn't insult my dad. That pissed, dishevelled little man really was the legend George Best.

We get the car back, my dad so drunk he can hardly talk. We park up in Chelsea and I say thank you for a good one today. He barely notices and goes off to the Phene, and I go to watch *Match of the Day* to see us on screen.

Did we bond? Did we have a good day? I'm not sure. It wasn't a bad day – there were fun moments – but it was fraught and tense, and my dad and I didn't say anything of any depth or importance to each other. Just the same old story.

I get lost in my own life in order to stop thinking so much about my dad, which means going out constantly, drink and drugs and bad food and no sleep. I realize that my dad is on his own path to wherever he's going, and nothing I can do will make any difference. It's painful, and my mum says to me that he's going to have to fix himself. I can't help him. No one can. We've all tried.

I'm seeing Sarah Harding now, the singer from Girls Aloud. She's a lovely girl, and this relationship is the closest I have ever got to something really serious. She's cool, beautiful and we really connect. But I'm not a good boyfriend. I'm out every night, hitting it harder than I ever have before, and I don't take our relationship as seriously as I should. I treat her badly, I take her for granted, I cheat, all those things that my dad did to my mum. And, sure enough, I lose her. I'm upset, but I don't let myself dwell on it for too long – I go out even more to take my mind off her. I don't realize how unwise this is. Going out too much cost me my relationship with Sarah, and now I'm going out more. That's not clever. Luckily Sarah and I stay friends.

Chapter 14

'His skin has gone a bit yellow and his eyes are weird, yellow and bloodshot. He's never been yellow before. He's looked frail, with flaky skin, but not like this. I'm scared, but I can't say anything.'

Calum Best

It's early 2005, and I'm twenty-four now. My dad is still drinking, still living between his little flat and the pub, and still not doing anything about his failing health. I have no ideas about what I can do to help him and living with this knowledge is hard. It doesn't help that my years of going out too much are having an effect on my appearance and, consequently, my modelling. I'm getting a double chin, I've put on weight, my hair is short and thinning and my tan has gone. And so Select drop me, because if I can't get any modelling work, what's the point of having me as a client? I'm gutted, and realize what I've thrown away since I got here. I should have changed my lifestyle, but the truth is I didn't want to. I don't have much of a life away from my nights out.

I move into a flat on Weymouth Street in the West End, the centre of town, with a friend of mine, Adee Phelan, a top hairdresser. This means I'm within walking distance of the nightclubs, which is dangerous. We're out every night at different events, and things are getting more and more out of hand.

A few weeks later, I'm out one night and I meet an agent who tells me I'm like a golden ticket that hasn't been cashed in, and he'd like to represent me, so how about it? I can't think of a reason to say no. I'm not with Select any more, so I don't have anything to lose. I decide to join the agent and see where it takes me. Some people warn me off him, saying he uses people and falls out with his clients once he's milked them as much as he can. But I like him, and I could really do with earning some money, so I go for it.

I tell the agent I want to be an actor, which has been my ambition for a long time, but he says no actors in this country are getting paid £3,000 a time to do personal appearances in nightclubs, which is what I could be on, and I start to get interested. He tells me he works with reality TV stars and says he already knows of a show which would be interested in me. He says it would be a great launch pad into that world for me. It's called *Celebrity Love Island*. I think, why not? I haven't been on TV before and it might be fun. So I go into ITV for the audition, meet the producers, and it goes well. I'm still out every night, but I'm young enough to have the energy not to be hungover the next day. I can have a big night, go and do well in a meeting the next morning, and then be ready to go out again that night. My body can work with this lifestyle for now.

At least I think it can. Later, when I get into healthy living and start taking proper care of myself, I look back at my pictures from this time and I can see how fucked up I was. My eyes are a mess, my face is puffy, my skin is bad and, just to top it off, I wear fake tan. Overall, it's a gross look. I don't realize it at the time, but I look terrible. It's no wonder Select weren't interested in me any more. The fresh-faced boy from California who did those awesome shoots for *The Times* and *ES* is long gone.

The audition goes well, and I like the producers, but I'm not sure about *Celebrity Love Island*. The show basically puts twelve people, six guys and six girls, on an island together for a few weeks, and the entertainment comes from seeing who gets together and who doesn't. It sounds fun, but I don't think I want to do reality TV. It's not the career I want for myself. I want to be an actor, and I can't see how this will help me. I tell my agent this, and he replies by telling me, 'They're offering you fifty thousand.'

I'm shocked. I don't think I can resist that kind of money, but I want to talk to my mum before I make a decision. I call her, and she tells me I'm still a young man and I should take opportunities like this – interesting, fun things that might lead to more in the future. We both know I've let the situation with my dad dominate my life, overpower me, and she says it would be good for me to go out and do something like this, away from London and away from my dad. I've come to realize that my mum is right about most things, and that settles it. A fee of £50,000 and my mum's backing? I'm in.

Before I go, I tell my dad I'm doing the show and he gives me one piece of advice about the media. At this point in my life I'm not yet on the bad side of the papers – I'm still the fun playboy – but my dad warns me, 'Be careful of the press. They're ruthless.' I haven't learned my lessons yet, so I don't really know what to do with his advice. I just carry on as before.

And so a few weeks later, I pack for Fiji. I'm flown out first class to an island that is one of the most beautiful places I have ever seen. It's amazing, jaw-droppingly gorgeous, and I'm so happy I'm here. It ends up being one of the best times of my life.

The first thing that happens is I land on the mainland and am put in a hotel, where I'm supposed to stay on my own for a few days. They take away everyone's phones so we can't contact each other, but I have two and hide one. A couple of friends of mine, Fran Cosgrave and Abi Titmuss, are doing the show too, and I call Fran. Luckily he answers – he did the same thing with his phone – and we're in different bungalows in the same hotel. I get in a golf buggy and drive over to see him and he tells me he's met this local tourist guide who's invited him to a party tonight that is being thrown by the locals. I think that's an awesome idea, so we go down.

We get to the party, and there's a bonfire, all these Fijian women and big Fijian guys, and we sit down with them. They're all in their traditional kit and chilling out. We have a great night with them. It's hot, there's a band playing, and a big bucket of kava, a traditional local drink that they make from ground-up roots of the kava plant plus water and this brown stuff that looks like mud. You scoop it out with half a coconut, sip it and it's supposed to make you trip. I start drinking the stuff like it's going out of fashion, and Fran does the same. The Fijians tell us to slow down because we don't know what we're doing, but we carry on. Luckily it doesn't have too much of an effect in the end, and by the end of the night the Fijian guys just think we're crazy. Fran goes back to his bungalow, I drive my golf cart back to mine, and the next morning we're good to go.

We spend the next few days learning how to jet-ski and scuba dive, and about all the health and safety things we need to know for the show. I'm so excited to be in Fiji, it's such a beautiful place.

On day five, the show starts. I meet the other guys. There's Du'aine Ladejo, the athlete; Paul Danan and Michael Greco, both actors; and Lee Sharpe, the ex-footballer, as well as Fran, who's billed as a nightclub owner. We all have our own jet-skis and the show opens with our entrance – we cruise up to the beach on these things in an arrow formation with me at the front.

Waiting for us are the girls, standing in bikinis outside this beautiful mansion, and I think wow, this is fantasy land. There's a helicopter with a camera hanging out of it, a boat with a cameraman on board, and a crew on the beach. It seems big time to me.

There's Abi, whom I know; the model Rebecca Loos; two others I know, Jayne Middlemiss, the TV presenter, and model Lady Isabella Hervey; and then Liz McClarnon from Atomic Kitten, and the actress Judi Shekoni. I run on to the beach and say hi to them, and then that's us on the island for the next six weeks. It feels like hanging out with my friends.

We're given different tasks to do each day to make the show entertaining, and when I win one they make it to do with my dad. I'm invited in to talk to the camera, which is basically me in a room with an earpiece in, and they say your prize for winning this task is that you can fly out anyone you want to visit you. I ask for my dad, and go back out. A day later I get a message from Phil Hughes on behalf of my dad: your dad is really proud of you but unfortunately he can't make it at the moment. I'm disappointed he can't come, but I'm not really surprised. I just hope he's watching and really is proud of me and happy with what I'm doing.

During another chat, I'm asked if my dad would do this show. I say of course he would – it's all about booze, sunshine and girls. They ask me about my dad three or four times and I go along with it. In fact, it makes me happy, because I think if my dad is watching this and he knows they're talking to me about him, he'll like it.

I end up having one of the best times of my life. I get on really well with Rebecca Loos, who's a cool girl, and I think I'm coming across OK, until one day she farts at the dinner table and I react with disgust. The camera shows a shot of me screwing up my face just after she farts, and not long after that I'm voted out while she stays. I guess the girls watching the show didn't approve of my reaction.

I leave the show two weeks before the end, so I ask my agent to call ITV and tell them that if I can stay here until the end of the show I'll do a little piece to camera every day, talking about what's happened on the island. And they agree to this, so I stay. I have two weeks by myself, and have fun with the people working behind the scenes. At the end, we have a big party, and all in all the experience was brilliant.

I come back to London and things are full on. The show has done well and we're all in the limelight. My agent talks me through a long list of things I'm wanted for – appearances and interviews, meetings and auditions. And six months' worth of personal appearances in night-clubs at £3,000 a pop, two or three a week.

I spend the next months attending event after event after event, and doing interviews with all the magazines. I do PAs every Friday and Saturday, and often Thursdays too, so that's three nights out in each week. But I also go out in London on Mondays, Wednesdays and, if I'm around, Thursdays. So it's a long year of drink, drugs and girls.

I'm making good money, but spending it as fast as it comes in. The trouble is, I don't know how to save. I don't know about tax, or any of that stuff, which is probably exactly how my dad got into financial trouble so much. One day I look at my bank account and I have £70,000 in there, but a week or two later it's almost all gone. My problem is, I like being the guy who stands up and says, 'I'll take care of this,' and buys everyone dinner, or pays for the round of drinks. And the next round, and the one after that. I even do it in places I can get everything for free. I don't know what makes me behave like this – I probably just want to be popular, like whenever I started a new school and tried to make friends with the cool kids – and at the time I don't even realize I'm being irresponsible. I'm just enjoying myself.

I'm also buying stupid stuff – diamonds for girls, £900 bracelets for myself, clothes I don't need, like a chinchilla jacket for £3,000. Three grand on a chinchilla jacket? What am I thinking? Later, when I have less than nothing, I'll come to understand the value of three grand, but at this point in my life it's a night's work, so it's easy come, easy go. I think to myself, I'll earn six grand this weekend, so I can pay for it out of that, and then next week I'm doing three nights, so that's another nine grand. With money like that coming in, I can easily live like this.

Over the years, all this stuff disappears, and I don't know where it goes. I give some things away, or lend them, and gradually it all vanishes.

I have no accountant, no management skills and no

idea about financial rules or regulations. I like to think I'm quite clued into the ways of the world, because I've travelled a lot and have been working and supporting myself for years, and I think my mum raised me well, but none of that helps me now. My life is one long blur of nights out. I'm not from London, and I'm not grounded here in any way at all. My life in this city almost doesn't feel real, and that means I don't even think of putting money away for the future, or what kind of tax responsibilities I might have because of the money I'm earning. It doesn't occur to me. I'm too caught up in this insane existence.

People mention things like tax, VAT and National Insurance to me every now and then, but so much money is coming in I figure I don't have to worry about it, because if ever I do need to pay some, I'll quickly earn what I need. So I put that kind of stuff out of my mind and carry on with my life. PAs, nights out, a tiny flat with no furniture apart from a bed, girls, drink and drugs. That's my world. It's probably pretty similar to my dad's. We're both lonely guys. But we can't help each other.

I don't have much to do with my dad at the moment. We never talk on the phone, and if I want to see him I have to go to the Phene, or suggest we go out for dinner. We go to the Big Easy a couple of times, a place on the King's Road where we've eaten ribs together more than once over the years. I have good memories of that place, so that's where I suggest we go. But I don't see him much.

Every time I think about him, I am reminded that he doesn't want to see me, and that even though I've been in London for years now, what I wanted us to become hasn't happened. I know that if my dad wanted it to happen, it would have happened, and that does not feel good. He comes into my head when I'm feeling low and makes me feel even worse, which makes me want to go out even more to help myself forget, and that only drags me down even further. I'm on a horrible downward spiral and I don't know what to do about it. My only solution is to go out and hide from reality, just like my dad.

I'm in touch more with Phil Hughes, my dad's agent, than I am with my dad. Phil and he have been close for years, and I've known him for as long as I can remember. I can't imagine the shit Phil has had to put up with from my dad over the years, but no matter what happens he's always there for him. My dad is so lucky to have him. Phil is good-hearted, a really decent guy, and he looks out for me too. He gives me regular updates about where he and my dad are, and what my dad is doing, where he is that day, if he's doing interviews and so on. One day, in April 2005, just after I've made *Celebrity Love Island*, he calls and says he has a new office in Fulham, and would I like to come and see it?

When Phil and I talk without my dad around, we discuss everything except my dad's health. It's too upsetting for us. Phil's an emotional guy who loves my dad to bits, so it's hard for him to speak about the state he's in. They've worked together, travelled together, made money together, been friends and close to each other's families for a long, long time.

For me, I don't want to accept how sick my dad is. At the back of my mind I realize that because he's back drinking again no one's going to give him a second liver transplant, which means there's only one place he's headed. But I can't accept this properly. Part of me still thinks he's invincible, he's George Best, he'll get through this, when deep down I know he won't.

I go into Phil's office and my dad is there, so we don't even have to dance around the subject of his health – it's just not mentioned at all. But I'm shocked at the state he's in. I haven't seen him for a couple of months, since before I went to Fiji for *Love Island*, and he's clearly taken a turn for the worse. His skin has gone a bit yellow and his eyes are weird, yellow and bloodshot. He's never been yellow before. He's looked frail, with flaky skin, but not like this. I'm scared, but I can't say anything.

Phil asks what I think of the place, and I snap out of it. I'm really proud of what I see. On the wall there's a picture of my dad and Pelé, my dad's footprints, and around the place there's all this stuff and memorabilia which looks really impressive. I'm delighted to see it all, but at the same time I can't help but think I want some of this. Some memories. I have nothing of my dad's, literally nothing at all. I would love to have some of these things. Just to have, for me, so some part of him is mine, no matter how tiny.

I speak up and say exactly that – I would love to have

some of this myself. Well, says Phil, that's why we've asked you to come in today. My dad tells me they're about to start a memorabilia business, and they would like me to be involved. They're going to set up a company, and they want me to be the director and Phil to be the company secretary. I ask why? My dad says it's because he wants to leave me with something.

Looking at the state he's in, I assume this must have happened because he's had a moment where he's realized he is getting to the end. He must have felt it somehow, and been keen to get this signed and sealed before it's too late. My dad is an intelligent man, and he must understand what the physical consequences of his drinking are, and that he's running out of time, so this is his way of trying to look after me and Phil. The only thing on my mind is a question: how much longer does he have? I try hard not to choke up.

They put a document on the table for me to sign, which distracts me. I don't read it, I don't look at the fine print, I don't do anything except put my signature where they want it. I am thrilled about this – knowing my dad wants me to sign it, knowing Phil wants me to sign it, and knowing that it means I am part of this business with them.

They explain the venture is going to be selling things like moulds of my dad's boots and his feet, and they are going to have George Best plates made. They say anything with George Best's signature or brand on will be part of this business, and that I'm part of it too.

This feels like a huge moment in my life. An opportunity to be part of something with my dad, which will last, which I can help build, and which he wants me to have. It's a huge thing he's giving me and Phil – his name. And I'm not even excited about the money we might make. That doesn't cross my mind. It's the feeling that I am properly part of my dad's life. He wants me involved. I'm not someone he sees occasionally because he has to, a person he would prefer had never existed. I'm his son, his only child, and because of that he's giving me this, his legacy.

I think I can make something of it, too. It's true that I'm spending money stupidly at the moment, but I'm making it too, and I understand how money is made and how important it is to get along with people. I think I'm good at that; I like socializing and talking, and I'm confident I can make a success of this. I'll be serious about it, I'll do it properly. Phil will make sure the business side is done right – he's a clever, straight guy – and we will make it a success. I'm excited about what we can do, but more than anything else it feels great that I'm now part of the bigger picture of my dad's life.

But it's serious, too. Phil says this could be a lifelong business for me, and my dad says it's something he wants to leave me for my future. The new company is called George Best Direct Limited, and I can't sign the forms quickly enough.

I leave the meeting feeling confused. I am so, so happy because of what this means for me and my dad, how this means he really does care about me, and how he must have been thinking about me and my future in order for this business to happen, and how he wants me to be properly part of his life. It feels amazing. But I am also terrified about his health. I mean deeply, genuinely terrified, because for the first time I realize I don't know how much longer he's going to be around.

I call my mum and tell her how he is, how he's looking yellow. She tells me it's jaundice, and it's what happens to alcoholics. How ill is he? I ask. Very, she says.

This underlines what I already thought: now he knows the end is coming, he's trying to make sure I'm looked after when he's gone.

Chapter 15

'My dad turns to my mum as she walks in, she sits down, takes his hand, and that's the moment where I have to get out. Looking at the two of them is too much for me. I can't take it.'

Calum Best

My dad and I do start spending more time together after this, because not long after we sign the papers he starts going into hospital for treatments to his liver, and Phil and I go with him to make sure he's not on his own while he does his blood dialysis. The Cromwell Hospital becomes like a second home. There's a roundabout at the front where cars pull in and out. In the main entrance is a lobby, and if you go straight through two sets of double doors and then turn right, you get to the place where serious emergencies go. We're not there yet. At the moment my dad is in the ward upstairs, and to get there

I turn right just before the second double doors, then up three flights of stairs. Soon I'll be able to do this with my eyes closed.

The Cromwell Hospital is a smart place, but I hate it. I hate the smell, the feel of it, the environment, and most of all I hate the thought that my dad is in here, ill. All these thoughts rush through my head: he's seriously sick, but he's George Best, he always pulls through, he'll be all right. I tell myself that over and over – Bestie gets away with murder, he'll get through this. He's been blagging things for years, he's had one new liver, he's got all these great people looking after him, such as Professor Roger Williams. He's got away with so many things, he always comes out on top. He's a blessed individual. He'll get through this. He has to.

I'm constantly telling myself these things, trying over and over again to convince myself that I don't need to worry too much, doing all I can to keep the faith alive. I'm praying he'll live longer and that we'll be able to do and say all the things I've always wanted us to. I know now that I can't change him. I've accepted that. He has to want to change himself, and if he lives long enough I hope he'll get there. If he decides he wants to change, everything will get better.

This treatment routine goes on for a few months, and I'm uncomfortable every time. My dad and I don't have a very talkative relationship, so very often he'll be lying on the bed hooked up to a machine watching TV, and I'll be sitting in a chair next to him, either on my phone or watching too. We don't talk about anything, we don't say a word about what's happening to him. Sometimes I'll go out to get us food, to pass the time. We're not ignoring each other, it's just neither of us knows how to bond with the other at a moment like this, or how to bring some closeness and relaxation to the atmosphere.

Neither of us will discuss the long-term reason he's in hospital – his bad liver. So we sit there, talking about nothing of any consequence, day after day. It's so ridiculous it could be one of those funny but painful movie scenes, where two men with so much to say to each other fail miserably to talk about their feelings.

We chat a bit, but it's superficial stuff. How are Manchester United doing? I can't wait to go down to Portsmouth again. Did you see their result at the weekend? How's Alex? I'd love some barbecue ribs from Choi's right now, how about you? Wouldn't you kill for a duck pancake? That kind of thing, just general chit-chat, both of us carefully avoiding the big things that are happening, trying to lighten the mood by talking about things like Choi's and our meals there, which are some of my best memories with my dad, looking for things we can connect over in some way.

I have no idea how messed up my dad's head must be at the moment, how it must feel to be him. He's only recently gone through a divorce, he's seriously ill, and he knows it's all down to his drinking, so it's his own fault. How must that feel for him? I know he's put me through some terrible shit, but I feel sorry for him, truly sorry. He must know that he hasn't got much longer, and that's why he gave me and Phil the business to work on. He's never done anything like that before, yet here he is now, lining up something for me and Phil which he hopes will look after us for the rest of our days. He must know he's dying. Poor guy.

I'm getting more and more worried about him every day. I'm still out and about, doing my thing, my PAs at the weekends and going on my nights out. I'm trying to get on with my life, but I am constantly worrying about my dad. He's on my mind all the time. Where is he? How is he? I keep myself busy, which means going out a lot, because if I didn't I'd just be sitting at home getting myself into a state. I know what I'm like and I'd drive myself crazy.

I talk to my mum a lot. She tells me I need to realize that a point is coming where I will have to face the fact that my dad's life is going to end. I'll have to deal with it. I'm trying to figure out how I'll cope, and I can't. I don't know what I'll do. I feel pretty lost at the moment, but my dad is still alive. We can still fight this. No matter what anyone says, I refuse to accept it's over.

In late summer 2005, I get a call from Phil. He's in tears. 'Your dad's not well,' he says. 'He was complaining of stomach pains, and then he keeled over, so I brought him in. I've spoken to the professor and he says it's not looking good. His insides are a mess.'

I get to the hospital and walk into my dad's room. Phil is in there with him, and is crying as he tells me my dad's blood is worse than it's ever been, his stomach is bad, and they're really worried. All the doctors can do is take him down into intensive care. They're doing everything they can.

I sit down in a chair, and Phil and I wait, with the TV on. I doze off at one point, only for a few minutes, and when I open my eyes it's still just me and Phil in the room. A few hours later, when my dad is still not back, we decide it's best for me to head home to get some sleep and then take Phil's place in a few hours.

I wake up in the morning and immediately call Phil. He tells me my dad is OK. Not brilliant, but he's OK. Is it still an emergency? No, he's stable. OK, I think, that's great, but I'm going in anyway, because I want to be there for him.

I get to the hospital and go to my dad's room. He's in bed unconscious, and he's not looking well. I hold his hand and try to take in what I'm seeing. He's more yellow than I've ever seen, and I can hardly believe I'm thinking in these terms, but he looks almost gone. Like the end isn't far away. It's heart-breaking.

He's become more and more fragile recently, getting smaller and smaller as if he's shrivelling up. He's losing muscle in his face, and the skin across his cheeks and jaw is getting tighter and tighter, so you can almost see the bone through it.

The doctor comes in and tells me things are bad. I don't really listen to him enough to take in his words. Seeing my dad so close to death has rattled me. I don't ignore the doctor; I just can't focus on him. And anyway, I don't need to hear what the doctor has to say to know how serious this is. I can see how sick he is for myself.

But I do catch the end of what he says: 'All he can do now is rest. He should get as much rest as possible.'

Now I'm in two minds. Do I stay with him? Will that help? Will I make it worse? I talk to Phil, and he says I should definitely be there. He and I arrange things so that one of us is always at the hospital with my dad.

Over the next weeks, I'm between the hospital and home. For a while I even stop going out. When my dad is conscious we don't talk about much. It's, 'Hi, Dad,' and, 'All right, son?' and that's about it. We sit there barely talking, watching TV. He's not allowed to eat solids, but one of the few things he does say is to ask me to get him fruit pastilles and wine gums, which he's always loved, so every time I come in I bring him those sweets. I know I'm not supposed to be feeding him these things, but I can't help it. He looks so bad now – even more yellow and shrivelled – that I figure a few sweets won't be anything to worry about.

Towards the end of October I start getting regular calls from Phil saying Dad has taken a turn for the worse. Sometimes it's three o'clock in the morning, sometimes it's midday. I know it's a selfish thing to admit, but all this is pushing me close to breaking point. I don't have the words to describe how tired I am. Once or twice I get off the phone with Phil in the middle of the night and am so exhausted I instantly fall asleep again. When I wake up,

I'm frantic. Am I too late? I run out of the house, desperate.

This goes on and on. I haven't slept properly in months. I'm constantly stressed, emotional all the time, and it's getting worse and worse. I feel terrible, unhealthy and ruined physically and mentally. Life is brutal at the moment. My dad is dying, and I'm watching it happen. I'm living in a dark place, the worst I've ever known. And at the same time, I know that when he does go, it's going to be a hundred times worse than this. I feel like my soul is draining away.

And then a call comes that is different. It's the professor this time, and he tells me things are getting properly serious now. He is doing everything he can, but my dad isn't helping them. When he gets the chance, which is any time he's able to leave the hospital, he's drinking. The professor wants me to know they can only do so much for him.

This hurts, and drags me down even lower. But in a strange way, it helps me, because it makes me realize that it isn't just me that my dad doesn't want to get better for. It's Phil, his best mate, and the doctors too, especially the professor, who my dad is close to. Maybe there really isn't anything I can do, and alcohol is more important to him than all of us are. It's life or death now, and my dad must know that, but he's still not changing. I'm not the only one who's tried and failed. It's a terrible thing to say, but that comforts me slightly.

Maybe my dad's in denial, I think, and he still has faith

in the George Best myth and has told himself he's not going to go. But he must be in so much pain, and he must know what he looks like, so how can he not realize he's dying? It's impossible. And that means there must be awful trauma and anxiety going on in his head. I feel truly sorry for him because of what must be going on in his mind. There's no way he thinks he's pulling through this. He knows, I'm sure of it, and it must be torture.

Most days there's only the three of us around, Phil, the professor and me. We care about him, and he's hurting all of us, draining the life out of us. I'm in pieces, and the professor and Phil must be suffering too. My dad is an intelligent man, so he must know what he's doing to us. I can't imagine how that must be for him, because no matter what he says or does, I know he cares.

I'm very alone at the moment. I don't see much of Phil, because he and I are in the hospital at different times to make sure there's always someone there with my dad, and there isn't really anyone else around. I know there are other people who want to help out, and who truly love my dad, but the raw reality of these days, with him dying slowly in his hospital bed, is only really seen by me and Phil.

I don't know how Phil is coping, but I'm a mess. My mum isn't in the country, and I have no one else to talk to. We speak on the phone, but that's not the same as having her here in person. I don't know my dad's family well enough to talk to them, I'm not speaking to Alex because of the issues between her and my dad, I have no proper home, and no people around me to turn to. I'm on my own here, and it's horrible. It's been like this since I moved to the UK – I have no family here and no proper base, and I've always found it hard, no matter what my life might look like from the outside. Now that my dad is in the hospital and on his way out, it's worse than ever.

I cope by starting to go out again when I'm not needed at the hospital. It's the only thing I can do. If I go home from hospital to the place where I'm living at the moment and just stay in, I'll have too much time on my hands. I have no family to sit and worry with so that we can reassure each other. If I sit on my own, I'll get so depressed I'm worried I'll end up killing myself. So I do what I know. I go out and get wasted to take my mind off everything that's happening. I go out so I'm not alone.

I get grief from the press for going out while my dad is in hospital. But they don't know that I sit by his bedside all day every day, and I will go nuts if I spend time by myself, in silence, with just my thoughts for company. So I go out and drink to stop myself from going crazy, and to try to relax and distract myself from the pain of watching my dad die. When I'm out, I still worry about what's going on, but the blunt truth is the worry is easier to handle after a few drinks.

I get photographed whenever I go in and out of the hospital. I also get photographed when I'm out at night, and stories about me and different girls are always appearing. People lay into me in the papers and in person, asking what the hell I think I'm doing going out on the town while my dad is so ill? But these people don't know what my life is like. I am broke and completely alone. I know that if I go out to a club I will see people I know. I wouldn't call them friends – I don't have any really close friends – but they're there, and they know me, and that's something. I will talk to them, have a few drinks, relax and let off some steam.

If the people who criticize me really knew what my life is like, I don't believe they would have a problem with what I'm doing. But they don't even seem to want to try to see things from my point of view.

So my attitude hardens. If I want to go out and get wasted while my dad is in hospital, I will, and fuck you if you don't like it.

Another day, another call from Phil. But this time it's even more serious. I head straight in. My dad's now down in intensive care again, and we call his sister Barbara and his family in Northern Ireland and they come over. Barbara and her husband, Norman, have already been back and forwards a few times and they're always lovely to me, making sure I'm OK and that I know they're here to take some of the strain off Phil and me.

I hate to admit this, but even though I know they mean well, I feel resentful towards them. The issue is, I hardly know them, and that makes me think they're intruding. To me it feels like he's my dad, my special person, and now these people I hardly know are here and taking over from me. That's not fair on them, because they're not taking over, and they want to help, and I know my dad is glad they're here, but I can't help feeling like that. I'm jealous and possessive about my dad at the moment, and to my messed-up brain their arrival means my share of him has just got smaller. This is my dad, the person on whom all my hopes and dreams are focused, the one who all my life I've been trying to be close to, and just when I'm closer to him than I've ever been and am about to lose him for ever, I feel like someone else is pushing me to the side a little. I know it's selfish of me, and I know they're not doing that, but that's how I feel.

Days pass with my dad in intensive care, and all of us there with him. I sit there for hours and hours, by his bed, holding his hand. There are three other beds in the ward, all really sick people, and machines are beeping constantly. He's unconscious, and there's a tube down his throat and needles in his arms. These things are keeping him alive. He's tiny, just yellow skin and bone, and as dreadful as it is to say, he looks like something out of a horror film. He really does.

A few times, they're able to turn the life-support machine off, because my dad can manage without it. But every time this happens it's not long until they have to turn it back on again. This happens four or five times.

I'm spending hours in the ward, hours in the cafeteria getting tea, in the hospital lobby, coming in and out, hours in intensive care, over and over and over, for days and days and days. Everything is a blur.

On 20 November 2005, my dad has an interview

published in the *News of the World*. There is a photo of him lying in his hospital bed, with a warning: 'Don't die like me'. The picture doesn't have much of an effect on me, because I see him in real life every day. But to the many millions of people who aren't with him every day, the photo must be a terrible shock.

One day soon after, my dad is moved out of the room with the three other beds and into one on his own. I know how significant this is, and that makes me even happier to see my mum, who has come over from LA to be with me. She knows what's happening because I've kept her updated. She's the only person I've been able to talk to properly, and her being in the US hasn't made it easy. Seeing her makes me as happy as it's possible for me to feel at the moment.

Now she's here, I make an executive decision to invite her to the hospital to say goodbye to my dad. It's obviously the right thing to do, and I tell myself that she should come in to see him because she's the only woman he had a child with, and the only woman he ever truly loved. I don't know if this last part is true, but I like to think it is. I want to believe my mother stands above all the other women who've been in my dad's life. It's not that I don't like them, but I want her, and therefore us, our little family, to be special.

I don't tell my dad's family about her coming in. I know they haven't always got along too well, and I don't want to cause more problems, so I do it sneakily. They might well have said sure, of course she can come in, she was his wife and is the mother of his child. But I would rather not take the risk, so I invite her behind their backs. It's what I want, so I do it. The other thing is, I want someone to share the pain with. I don't know my dad's family, they're pretty much strangers to me, and my mum is my family, so I want her here.

My mum says of course, she'll definitely come in. I go to meet her outside the hospital. I know what a terrible state I must be in, and it must be hard for her to see me like this. I'm exhausted, terrified, emotionally drained, and just all round beaten. I must look horrendous. She hugs me, and in we go. There are press constantly outside the hospital now, paparazzi, reporters, news vans, all sorts, dozens of people. I try to ignore them.

We walk through the hospital, following the route I know so well, and I take my mum into my dad's room. I'm looking at her face when she sees my dad. She gasps, her hand goes to her mouth, and she says, 'Oh, George.' I don't know how long it's been since she last saw him, but it's obviously a huge shock to see him now. She remembers him when they were together, twenty-five years ago, when he was a very different man. She can see what alcohol has done to him, and it's devastating.

He looks at her, and I can tell he's happy to see her. His face doesn't show much, but his eyes light up as much as they can. He's at death's door now, and he knows it, so I hope he's happy to be looking at my mum, someone he had great times with and who has made the effort to come and see him. I don't know exactly what passes between them in that moment, but I think it's good. My dad turns to my mum as she walks in, she sits down, takes his hand, and that's the moment where I have to get out.

Looking at the two of them is too much for me. I can't take it. I have to leave the room. I say something like, 'I'll leave you two alone to do your thing,' trying to make it sound like I'm casually heading out to give them some privacy. But that's not it. The sight of them together is overwhelming. Amazing, in one way, that they're sitting there together, which is something I've always wanted, but indescribably sad at the same time, because of everything we've missed out on. In this little room, right now, is the family I could have had, and I can't handle it.

I leave my mum in there for an hour, and I expect she does exactly the same things I do, talking to him, stroking his hand and tidying his hair.

When I come back, my mum says her goodbyes. She asks if I want her to stick around, and I say it's OK, I have to do this by myself. I'm so glad she came. Just knowing she is close by makes a difference to me. I'm still miserable as hell, but at least I'm not alone now.

Chapter 16

'There's nothing else we can do. We're going to have to take him off life support.'

Professor Roger Williams

A couple of days later I come into the room when the machine is switched off. My dad is awake, but he looks awful, like nothing I've ever seen before. He's always been such a beautiful guy, but right now his face scares me. His cheekbones are sticking out, his eyes are yellow and wide open, and he's turning his head from left to right really quickly, like he's panicking about something. He looks terrifying, and terrified.

He sees me, and recognizes me. 'Bestie,' he says, desperation in his voice, 'you've got to help me. They're having fucking parties in here.'

'What do you mean?' I say. He's got me worried now. What are they doing in here?

'I heard them last night, Bestie, over there. They were having drinks, and there were girls, and they were having parties.'

'Dad, what are you talking about? I don't understand.'

There's a nurse with us, and she tells me he's hallucinating. He was probably lying there on his own while there were all these noises coming from the machines, and his messed-up mind turned those into visions of parties going on. I'm scared for him because of the state he must be in to have these hallucinations, but at the same time it makes me smile. Of all the things for him to have visions of, it has to be a party, with lots of girls and booze.

After a few minutes, he calms down and relaxes, and I go back to stroking his hand and pushing his hair behind his ear. A little later I go to the loo and when I come back he's asleep. His organs are working, and then not working, shutting down bit by bit as his body gradually loses the fight to stay alive.

I tell Phil about the hallucinations and we have a bit of a laugh about my dad imagining these parties going on, after the life he's had and the reasons why he's in here. We laugh because we're so desperate for something to laugh about, but at the same time we're terrified. I wouldn't have laughed if I'd known these are the last words he will ever say to me, because that's what they are.

From now on, my dad doesn't say anything. He's unconscious all the time. The nurses tell me I should talk to him, because he can hear me. I suspect they're saying that to comfort me, not because the words will actually get through. So probably for my sake as much as his, I talk to him quietly, whispering things in his ear. I say, I love you, I miss you, I'm sorry. I tell him things will be different when we leave here, even though I know it will never happen. You'll feel better then, I say, and we'll go to Manchester United together. I remind him of us riding that tandem at Hermosa Beach, I talk about restaurants, anything I can come up with that might spark something in his brain, a happy memory, or a bit more life. Anything to give him some kind of comfort, because physically he looks so bad.

Sometimes Phil's in there with me too, and then we'll both hold his hands. When I'm there on my own, I get up on my dad's bed with him, lie down and put his arm around my shoulders. I'm six foot three, twenty-four years old, and cuddling up to this tiny, frail man, but I feel like a little kid. I want to do something to make myself feel better and this is the best idea I have. I snuggle into the side of his chest, close my eyes and try to forget about everything else except the two of us together, here, now.

This is the first time I've ever had my dad's arm around me like this. I don't remember him ever holding me, not once, not even when I really was a little kid. There was the occasional awkward hug, but not much. Lying here, feeling my dad's arm around me, I get a tiny glimpse of what I've missed out on, how good and safe I would have felt if he'd been a different kind of father, and it tears me up.

At one point, when the machine is off, Barbara and Norman go back to Belfast to get the rest of the family. Phil calls Denis Law, my dad's old mate from Manchester United and a great guy, and Denis comes down. My granddad and uncles and aunts arrive too, his brother Ian and sister Julie among them. We don't want to admit it, the doctor hasn't said it, but we all know it's going to end soon. My brain hasn't accepted it, and I don't think anyone else's has either.

After my dad's family arrive, the hospital gives us two spare rooms upstairs from intensive care which we can use as a base, one with drinks and snacks, and the other with a couple of beds, a TV and a couch. Denis Law, the other family members, Phil and I are around all the time.

We all reach an agreement that Alex can come in. No matter what they're going through, she was his wife, and they were together for ten years, so she should come. I'm by the bed holding my dad's hand when she arrives, and she bursts into tears as soon as she walks through the door. She sits next to him and asks if I'm OK. I'm distraught, and so is she. I leave her alone with him.

The life-support machine keeps him going for a few more days. The doctors haven't turned it off for a while now, so he's completely dependent on it. Everyone's around, we're talking, but he's still alive. Even though all these people are here, whenever I'm alone with my dad I get straight back on the bed with him. My tears have run dry by now, and I feel like a shell.

Then one day I go upstairs to the room and lie down to sleep, fully clothed and with the lights on because I'm so exhausted. I wake up to Phil saying, 'Calum, you've got to come downstairs. We're having an emergency meeting.'

I go with Phil to the room off the intensive-care ward. I'm terrified about what's going to happen next. I'm exhausted, tired, confused, lost and dazed. I'm in a weird place, where everything is a blur. We go into the room and there are chairs all around. I'm in a corner one with Phil next to me and the family are in the rest. Professor Williams comes in. He sits down and says, 'There's nothing else we can do. We're going to have to take him off life support.'

I look around. I'm confused. What does that mean? No one is saying anything. And then I realize exactly what it means – this is the end. My head drops into my hands, I close my eyes, and I let out this huge noise, which is part scream and part roar of pure emotion. I start sobbing, no tears, just my body juddering. I feel a hand rubbing my back, which must be Phil.

It's finally going to happen. It's finally going to end, and I'm devastated. I can't move. I sit there, trying to get my head round what's going on. This is the end. This really is the end. I'm finally going to lose my dad. Everything is about to end. All that hope, all that anger, the sadness, the resentment, all that is over. I am so, so sad. And my mind starts playing tricks on me, throwing out cruel questions, like what could I have done differently? What could I have said to make him change? Is it my fault? Could I have saved him? Why didn't I try harder?

I don't know how long I sit there, going over and over these things, wondering what I did wrong, and contemplating the fact that my dad is about to die. Because it is a fact. No matter how much I don't want to believe this is real, it is. This is really happening, and it's happening now.

Eventually I stand up and walk through to the room where my dad is. I don't even notice if anyone else is in there. I sit next to him, lean forward and rest my forehead on the bed. I put his hand on the back of my head, and stay there, sobbing.

The next thing I know, everyone else is in there, Phil, my granddad, Barbara, his other siblings, Norman, and we're standing around the bed. They must be feeling awful too, especially my granddad, who's watching his son die, after watching his wife die in much the same way. No man – a husband and father – should have to see that. I feel so sorry for him. No one says anything. We don't need to.

One of the medical people turns the machine off, just flicks a switch, and it goes quiet. It's been helping my dad breathe, and as soon as it stops, he stops too. And that's it, over. Just like that, the room goes from him breathing with the help of this machine, to a still silence, and he dies. It's 25 November 2005, and he is fifty-nine years old.

I'm numb. I look at him and don't know what to do. I'm scared to touch his hand, in case it's cold. But I take it anyway. Oh my God, I think. My dad has just died. I've lost him. That's it.

The room empties, apart from me. On my own with him, I crawl up on the bed next to him, on his left-hand side, whereas I've been on his right the previous times. I put his arm round me, and hold him while he holds me.

As I'm lying there, all these thoughts start buzzing through my mind about what's just happened. I'm lying here with him, but he's not even here any more. I wonder where his spirit has gone? Where's his soul? Has he come out of his body? Has he gone somewhere? Can he see me? Or is that it, finished, and every part of his body and soul has been switched off, like a light going out? Has he gone completely?

I lie like that with my dad for twenty minutes, just holding him. I know he's dead, but in a way it doesn't feel real. I can't believe it's all over.

Barbara and Julie come in. They say they're going to take a lock of my dad's hair, and do I want one? Yes, sure, I say. I think it's a nice idea. We snip off little bits of his hair, and I put mine in a little plastic bag a nurse gives me. I put that in my pocket, and I know it's time to leave, but I don't want to go. I don't want to leave. This is the last time I'm ever going to have with my dad, and I don't want it to end.

Eventually I have to go. It's made clear to me, gently but firmly, that we need to leave the room. I say my last goodbye. I lean into his ear, say, 'I love you,' kiss his fore-head, and walk out of the room.

I go into the side room with everyone else, and I'm completely numb. I can't cry because I have no tears left. After a while one of the nurses says to me, 'I know this is a tough time, but you're his next of kin and you have to make the decision about whether or not you want to donate any of his organs.'

I don't know how to take this. Part of me loves the fact that I'm the one who's making this decision. I'm the next of kin, his only child, and this is an important decision. But I don't know what to do. I look at Phil. 'Calum, it's got to be your decision,' he says.

We should do this, I think. It's the right thing to do. I have to go into the next room, but I can't do it on my own. Barbara is kind and comes with me, and we have to fill out a form. They tell us that because of his illness, they don't think his vital organs will be of use. I ask what they will be able to use. His eyes, is the reply.

His eyes? They're his special thing. Everyone loves his eyes – he's Belfast's blue-eyed boy. Barbara knows this too, and at first we don't know what to do. We have a moment where we wonder if it's right or wrong. And then we decide very firmly that yes, it's right to make his eyes available, and I hope they will be used. He liked to give to people, and people gave so much to him too, so it's definitely the right thing to do. We agree that if someone can use them, they should have them.

Then we go back to the room upstairs. We're sitting

and standing around, all pretty quiet, but all shocked and devastated. I think some of us had come to terms with what was happening sooner than others and were more prepared. But not me. I'm a mess, shocked, furious, lost and bewildered. I'm angry he's gone. I'm angry that all my hopes and dreams of a life with my dad are over. I'm angry that it has all come to this. I left LA to come over here to see him. I was supposed to get to know him and grow with him. We were supposed to have a proper relationship, the one I'd dreamed of for so long, but it's over now. Ended for ever. I can't help being angry.

My hope is gone. The feeling I've had since I was a little boy, telling myself you'll get to know him one day, it'll happen, he'll want you around, which more recently has become he's George Best, he'll pull through, he always comes out on top, not long now till you start building a future together, and that's when you'll have the father you always wanted. All that is finished. It is never, ever going to happen. My hopes and dreams just died with my dad.

We're all standing around in the room when someone says we should make an announcement to the press out-side. I immediately say I want to do it and no one argues. I work out what I want to say, which isn't easy. I want to make sure I word this right for other people, as well as for myself. I know how much everyone loves him, and I want to say sorry to everyone for their loss, not just that my dad has died. He was an idol to so many people and I feel it's important to include them somehow. I call a friend of mine and he says I should make sure I say it's not just my loss. I've shared my dad with the world for my whole life and I want to share this too.

We all go outside as a family, and I announce that he has passed away and say, 'Not only have I lost my dad, but we've all lost a wonderful man. I'd just like to take the time to thank Professor Williams and Dr Akeel and everybody here at the Cromwell Hospital for doing everything they could do and to all the well-wishers and the fans . . . the letters and the flowers and the emails, it all means so much to us.' It's hard to get the words out, but I manage OK.

Denis Law adds something: 'It's an extremely sad day for the Best family. It was just a matter of time really. It was not if, it was when that things wouldn't go right. In the long run, after knowing him for a long time, it's the best thing that could have happened because he would have been slightly like a vegetable and he wouldn't have liked that. It's awful to say it sometimes but it was a blessing.'

When he says the word 'vegetable', I look over and think how politically incorrect was that? I don't mind, because Denis is a great guy who loves my dad, and he wouldn't have wanted to offend anyone. I know my dad wouldn't have been offended. In fact, I think he might have found it funny, and so it amuses me a little bit – I guess I need a laugh. But it definitely was the wrong thing to say. We go inside and Denis says, 'Oh God, I shouldn't have said "vegetable".' He's pretty mortified, but I don't think he gets any criticism for it, which is good. He'd just watched one of his oldest mates die, after all.

Then I have a moment with my granddad that really upsets me. I walk past him, and we start talking about where and how and when we're going to bury my dad. He says to me, without looking me in the eye, and in a hard voice, 'He might be your dad, but he's my son and we're burying him in Ireland.' It wasn't a caring, 'How do you feel about it, Calum? Where do you want to bury him? What are your thoughts?' It was, 'I don't care what you think or how you feel. This is what's happening,' and it really gets to me. I'm devastated right now, and I know my granddad is too, but that doesn't make this OK. I feel like he's telling me I don't matter, and that, where my dad is concerned, what I think isn't important.

It hurts me deeply. I've just made the decision about the organ donation, I've just spent all these months going in and out of hospital trying to look after my dad, I've spent the past twenty-four years trying and trying to be close to him, and now this within a few minutes of him dying. I go to the cafeteria, then out to the back of the hospital, sit on my own and burst into tears. I feel like my dad has been taken away from me again. I'm back to being not important. I might be being selfish now, wanting to be involved with everything, but if someone had said to me, 'We'd really like to bury George in Belfast, what do you think?' I'm sure I'd have said that's fine. It's the right place to bury him – the only place, really. I just don't like being told what's happening, and it makes me think my granddad doesn't care about me at all.

I pull myself together and go back into the hospital. By now my dad has been moved out of the room. I call a friend and ask him to come and pick me up. I say goodbye to everyone and tell them all I love them, because it seems like the right thing to do, and say please let me know about the next steps and what I need to do. Phil gives me a hug and says he'll be in touch later. I walk out of the hospital, and the press go crazy, cameras going off and questions being fired at me. My friend asks me if I'm OK and I say, 'I don't know. Just get me out of here.' And we drive away.

I go home and sit on my own, in a daze. Eventually I fall asleep, and the next day or two are a blur. I sleep, eat and try to relax. But I can't do anything properly. I'm a mess, living in a daze.

A couple of days after my dad's death, Phil calls to say I need to come to the hospital and pick up Dad's stuff; they won't release it to anyone else except me. I go to the hospital and they give me his black-and-red Umbro bag, which contains his black Reebok Classic trainers, a pair of black trousers with a belt, a white shirt, some toiletries, hand cream, and pills for his liver. Being back at the hospital is hard, but I'm proud to be picking up my dad's belongings. It puts an official stamp on him being my father. When legal things like this need to be done, no one apart from me can do them, because I'm his son, and I am proud of that.

Phil and I leave the hospital together. On the way out,

we thank the professor, the nurses and all the other staff we see. They've been so good to us, and tried so hard with my dad. I'm heartbroken for them too.

We stop and talk outside, on the roundabout by the main road. It's about 7pm, it's dark, and everything around us seems moody and grey. Phil's face is pale and I can see how distraught he is. We hug and he tells me how sorry he is, and I say I am too.

I'll look back on this moment and wish I'd said more than that to Phil. I am so lost in my own devastation that I don't show him the gratitude he deserves for what he did for my dad, for the friendship and loyalty he gave him for decades, and for what he did for me. Phil always looked out for me, and always tried to get me and my dad together. He included me in things whenever he could, and my words to him tonight don't do justice to what he did for us.

I think we're about to say goodbye, when Phil says, 'Your dad wanted you to have these,' and hands me the keys to my dad's flat.

I take the keys and don't know what to say. I look at them in my hand. I'm so tired and I'm too numb to react. I feel nothing. My dad wanted me to have his flat. I can't believe it, and its significance doesn't sink in. Phil says we need to meet back here tomorrow to go to the funeral parlour and finalize things, then we hug again and say goodbye.

Chapter 17

'There are little kids, people throwing roses, women
crying, men crying. It's so intense.'

Calum Best

I go to the flat on autopilot. It's in a basement by the river
in Chelsea and inside is dark and depressing, which
matches my mood perfectly. I sit on my dad's sofa and try
to get my head round everything.

The fact he's gone is beginning to sink in. All the
things I wanted for us are never going to happen. We will
never be the father and son I wanted us to be. There'll
be no more of me hoping things will be different, no
more hanging around waiting for him, no more wondering what's going to happen next between us. No more
asking myself does he love me, or does he hate me? That's
it, finished. I came to the UK to bond with him properly,
but it didn't happen and now he's dead so it never will.

By now I'm crying and crying, huge tears rolling down my face. But in the middle of all the crying and the pain, there's something else, an idea of how my life will be different without my dad. I'm gutted and my emotions are all over the place, but a little voice in me is saying maybe there's something good here for you, maybe now he's gone you don't have to worry so much, about his health or about the two of you. There'll be no more of your hopes being built up and then thrown back in your face. This is the final point. This is closure on all of that. Your life will be simpler now.

I hate myself for thinking like this. My dad has only been dead a few days – what's wrong with me? But I can't help it. I feel free in a way I never did before. And I realize that with this flat I have something else now: a base, some stability, a home. I feel a kind of relief, and then a new kind of hope.

Now Dad's dead I know I have to start again, and with the flat as my refuge I can do it in a better way. I'm crying, but at the same time there's a tiny bit of positivity inside me, like a tiny candle burning in a huge, dark room. Starting now, I could have a new life and this place, my dad's home, could be the beginning.

I realize something else: it took my dad dying for him finally to give me some security. How tragic is that?

I stand up and turn on the lights. My dad's stuff is still here, all around me. His sofa, his chairs, rugs, everything. It's weird looking at his things when he's no longer around. On the walls there's a mirror, some pictures and a big, brown-framed painting of him in his prime, playing for Manchester United. I remember it from his old flat in Oakley Street. It's a beautiful image and it reminds me how iconic he was in his playing days.

I have a strange thought: I'm never going to see him on TV again. It's not as if I used to see him on TV all the time, but just after I moved to the UK I saw him working as a pundit for a game on Sky and I was so proud that he was my dad, so seeing him on screen is a significant and happy memory for me. At the time I was pleased he was still involved with football because it would have made him happy, but that's never going to happen again. Just like we're not going to have any more moments where he asks me to come to a dinner with him, or go for lunch with him – those moments where I always thought to myself, is this it? Is this when our relationship starts properly? They'll never happen again.

I walk through to the bedroom. I look at his shower and remember the few times I used it. I wonder how he managed to live in such a small place. For a legend like him, this place, a one-bedroom flat, is tiny. It doesn't seem worthy of him. I try to think of any happy memories I have of this flat, of my dad here. There are none.

I go out the back, to his little terrace, and have a cigarette. Standing in the cold night air, the loneliness hits me. A fresh start is all well and good, but I'm alone. Totally isolated. Who can I turn to? Who can I talk to about this? There's no one. I am on my own.

I go inside and, on impulse, open the fridge. It's empty.

There's not even any out-of-date stuff. After everything he'd been through, this is how he lived, all the way to the end.

Suddenly I need to get out of here. I can't be on my own. Where can I go? The only person I have is my agent. He's not really a friend, just a person who I go out with to get pissed and laid. I know that if I stay here this evening I'm going to feel more and more like killing myself. At the same time, I know that going out isn't good for me. But I don't feel I have a choice.

I call my agent and we go out.

A couple of days later I talk to Phil again. He says there are some things my dad wanted me to have along with the flat. Hearing this makes me happy. Dad thought enough of me to want me to have these things – the flat and the other stuff.

But, Phil says, there might be a problem. Dad made two wills. The first one left everything to Alex unless they had separated, in which case Dad's sister Barbara would inherit it all and then divide it up between the family as she saw fit. That will was signed. The second one, which detailed what he wanted to leave to me, was never signed because they didn't want to tempt fate. They didn't want to make it official that my dad was going to die.

I'm not concerned about this, because I trust Phil completely and I know my dad did too. Also, I don't know anything about the legal side of things like this, so I assume that because that's what my dad wanted, that's what will happen. I don't know where any problems could come from.

The next day, I go to the funeral parlour, which is close to the hospital. Phil and I don't know which coffin to pick, so we ask the guy working there what people normally go for. He says they recommend this one, so we choose it. I am new to this, so I ask him what happens next. He says the next thing is they have to embalm my dad, which means draining his blood and filling him full of some kind of chemical to keep his body preserved. This is what they do for open-coffin funerals, which is what they seem to think we want. This freaks us both out, and Phil and I agree we don't want this, so we ask him not to do it and we choose another coffin. Then they say we have to decide what to do about the flowers that will go with the coffin. Phil asks me what I want them to spell out and I say just 'Dad'.

We leave the parlour and talk about what's happening next. Phil says we have to go to Belfast to bury my dad. He asks me who I want there with me, and I say three people – my mum, and my friends Dave and Adee, who are the guys I'm closest to at the moment. Everything is arranged for them to come over.

Before that, I head up to Manchester to make an appearance at the next Manchester United home game, because they want to do something in honour of my dad. It's on Wednesday, 30 November and by chance is against West Bromwich Albion, the team my dad made his debut against. I take two friends with me for support and we're all in the directors' box. Before kick-off, I'm taken down to join the players before walking out on to the pitch with them. I'm terrified because there are 75,000 people out there and they'll all be watching me. Then I start chatting with Ruud van Nistelrooy, one of the United players, and that calms me down. I'm thrilled talking to him and seeing people like Paul Scholes and Ryan Giggs so close by, but at the same time I'm an emotional wreck.

David Gill, the chairman, walks out next to me and I start crying immediately. My nose is running too and I realize I don't have any tissues. David notices and gives me his handkerchief, which I think is such a kind thing to do. I feel like he is taking care of me and right now that means so much. As we walk out the fans are cheering and singing and I applaud back to them. They're all holding up pictures of my dad – 75,000 of them – and it is amazingly powerful. I look up at the sky and think how mind-blowingly, overwhelmingly wonderful this is, and I'm smiling because I'm so touched by this display of love for him, but inside I'm so depressed and sad because they're holding up pictures of my dad who I'm never going to see again. I'm feeling every emotion you can think of all at the same time.

Later, I watch the scene on TV and one of the commentators says something which I'll never forget. He says how proud I must be, and that people should remember that they've lost a footballer but I've lost my dad. I want to shake the guy's hand for that because I feel like at least one person out there has some sympathy for me. Right now there aren't many of them around.

The day before the funeral, which happens on 3 December, Phil and I fly over with my dad's coffin, which we have to pick up from the funeral parlour. When we arrive there's a black hearse waiting for us outside, with my flowers in the window spelling out 'DAD', and a Northern Ireland flag on the coffin. We're flying from a private airfield just outside London and to get there we drive through the city. I stare out of the window, and every now and then someone catches my eye and recognizes me, which means they know it's my dad in the back. We get a few waves, and a few honked horns, and it makes me really proud. They're sad moments, but good ones too.

When we get to the airfield, the coffin is loaded on to the plane and Phil and I get in. I sit down in my seat, look back at my dad, and think how surreal all this is. The past few months have been such a blur I can hardly believe this is actually happening.

I put my seatbelt on and we take off. A few minutes into the flight, I go back and sit with my dad. I put my hand on his coffin, and have a quiet moment where I think about him and remember things. I try to focus on my good memories, and I talk to him in my head. I tell him I love him, and that he's going home, back to Belfast, just basic, simple words, and I think about what could and should have happened between us, and how there are no more chapters in this story. We're at the end now. The only thing that's reassuring me at the moment is knowing my mum will be in Belfast. Without her around, I'd be completely lost.

After a while, I go back to my seat and fall asleep. I wake up when we're landing in Belfast. I'm wearing black everything – black shirt, black tie, black jacket, black trousers – except for my shoes, which are white. I'm not sure why I chose that colour – I thought it was a good idea at the time, I suppose.

We land at an army base, where there are soldiers in smart uniforms and white gloves lined up waiting for us. I look across the runway and there's a fence with about twenty paparazzi on the other side, and I think what a big deal this must be for there to be so many of them here. What a weird situation this is. Bagpipes play as they take my dad's coffin out of the plane, and I start crying as Phil and I walk across the tarmac at the same pace as the soldiers carrying my dad. The coffin is put in the back of a hearse, and Phil and I get into another one, me still with tears in my eyes.

At this point the coffin goes to my granddad's house, while Phil and I go to check into our hotel, the Malmaison. I have no idea who has organized any of this – the hotel, the plane, the hearses, the soldiers, any of it. I don't know who's arranged things for my mum and my two friends either. I also don't know who's paying for it all. Everything is a blur to me, and has been for months now. I'm just going with it, trying my best to deal with how I feel, and I'm lucky that someone else is taking charge of the arrangements. Whoever it is, I'm very grateful to them.

We get to the hotel, where I meet up with my mum, Adee and Dave. It's so good to see them, especially my mum. She gives me a hug and asks if I'm OK. I'm not, but seeing her makes me think I will be.

After we check in, Phil gives me a pamphlet which has the itinerary for the day inside, including the plan for the funeral procession. I'm getting in the first family hearse with Barbara and my granddad, and then my dad's sisters Carol and Julie, his brother Ian and Barbara's husband, Norman, are in the second one. Hold on a second, I say, where's my mum? Phil says he's been told there's no space in the hearses for my mum, so she'll have to be in the bus, which is where he'll be. I understand it's family only, but my mum is family and I really need her with me.

She tells me not to worry about her, she'll be fine, and to just go in the hearse. I say no, I'm really not having this, I need her with me. I don't want to make a huge scene, so I go to the front desk of the hotel reception and say I need a phone number for a high-end taxi company. They call a guy for me and tell him Calum and Angie Best need him to pick them up for the funeral.

I look at the itinerary again and see that someone has chosen a poem for me to read during the service. I haven't seen it before, and I don't like the feeling that someone else is in control of this. After finding out my mum is in the bus, and now this, I'm really not happy with how things are going. I have no say at all in what's happening. No one has asked me. I don't seem to matter at all. This is what I was afraid would happen, how I was afraid I would feel.

I ask my mum what to do about the poem. It's a perfectly nice poem, but it's not my choice. It's not personal to me. My mum says that since my dad died she's been getting messages from all kinds of people sending condolences, saying how sorry they are that my dad has passed away, and among them was a poem sent by a woman from Belfast, which she'd written herself. My mum says she thinks the poem is special, so why don't I have a look at it? I go to my room and read the poem, and it's brilliant. It's sincere, genuine, kind-hearted and lovely, and completely original. I know this is what I want to read at the funeral. I get the hotel to make me a photocopy of it and put the piece of paper in my pamphlet. I don't tell anyone else.

The time comes for us to leave. We're going to my granddad's house first, for a family moment, before going in procession with the coffin to the funeral, which will be at Stormont, the Northern Ireland parliamentary building. At this point I don't know much at all about Stormont. I don't know how big it is, or what it looks like. I don't know that it's been the home of the Northern Ireland parliament on and off since 1921, and that my dad's funeral, on 3 December 2005, is the first time it has been used for anything other than political or governmental business since the Second World War. They chose Stormont because of the number of people expected to show up.

Phil, Adee and Dave go there separately, and my mum and I say we'll see them later. Outside the hotel a silver Mercedes with a taxi sign on top is waiting for us. I say hello to the driver, who's a local Belfast guy, and tell him I need him to take us to my granddad's house, to wait outside, and then to follow the hearses to Stormont. He'll be in the parade, and I ask if he's OK with that. His jaw drops. 'Jesus,' he says, 'it would be my absolute pleasure. When I came into work today I did not think this would be my job.' I thank him, and seeing the look on his face is a really special moment.

I'm worrying myself sick about so many things. If they're not letting my mum into the hearse, how will the rest of today go? How am I going to cope at the funeral? Will I break down? Will I keep myself together in front of all the guests? So many things could go wrong.

I know today is a big deal, because I've seen all the media coverage, I've seen the soldiers and the paparazzi at the airport, I know about the guests, and I know Stormont is an incredibly important place, but it's not until we turn the corner on to the road where my granddad's house is that I realize just how massive my dad's funeral is. There are thousands of people crammed into this little street of terraced houses. Oh my God, I think. Can I handle this? My mum holds my hand and tells me everything will be OK.

We're driving super-slowly because of all the people, and I'm looking out of the window trying to make eye contact with them, and I'm nodding at everyone I possibly can, wanting them to know how grateful I am that they're here. There are little kids, people throwing roses, women crying, men crying. It's so intense, and incredibly emotional.

We pull up to the house and my mum says, 'You go in. I'll wait here.' I say hold on, I'm not sure about that, and get out of the car. I look around and say thank you to as many people as I possibly can.

I go up to the front door, and the first person I see is Norman, who's there with Barbara and Julie. Inside and to the left is my dad's coffin. I can't bring myself to look at it. I say out loud, 'I'm going to get my mum,' to no one in particular. Norman, who's standing close by, stops me and says, 'No,' in a really stern, authoritative voice, 'this is for family only,' and now I really lose it.

'What do you mean family only? This is my mother, this is who I'm here because of. She and my dad are the reason I'm on this earth. I'm my dad's only son, of course she's family.' I'm so confused about all this, especially about why it's Norman telling me my mum isn't allowed in, when he's a guy who I don't know, and who is family in this situation in the same way my mum is, except without a child involved. Who is he to tell me my mum can't come in here? But they won't budge. My mum isn't allowed in.

I go through the house and out the back to be on my own. I can't stand this. It's not right. Julie comes out to see me, and I look at her and see her eyes which are so similar to my dad's, and I see my dad in her, and I'm comforted. Julie's always a very caring person, and is very reassuring and nurturing to me, and maybe that's why I break down. I start crying hysterically, bawling my eyes out. She says she's so sorry for what was just said and done inside the house, and through my tears I say over and over, 'This is not right, this is not right.'

I go back through the house, not making eye contact with anyone. I walk out of the front with tears running down my face, and I see thousands of people, and suddenly I feel like I'm under a huge microscope, being looked at by every single one of them. I go to the car and say to my mum, 'I'm so sorry, they told me you're not allowed to come inside.' My mum smiles and says, 'It's OK, son, don't worry, son.' She makes a point of calling me 'son', and I'm so glad she's there, because she's the only person who stops me from feeling alone.

I say it's not OK, and she should be in there with me, and she keeps on saying it, being sweet and loving, 'It's OK, son, it's OK.' I calm down and tell her I'll be back soon. And so my poor mum has to wait in the car for an hour, outside the house.

Back in the house, I go straight out the back and smoke. I eat some food, but I don't mingle with anyone. I'm furious, but I'm also thinking about the bigger picture and what's still to come today, the journey up to Stormont and then the funeral itself.

The hour passes quickly. My dad's coffin is taken out of the front door to the hearse, then we get in the cars and start on our way. This journey is when the number of people my dad's life touched hits me the hardest. From the moment we leave to when we arrive at Stormont, the streets are lined with thousands and thousands of people, hundreds of thousands of them. I open my window and try my best to look at as many as possible, and to say thank you for being there. My mum is waving, taking it all in her stride and doing exactly the right thing, and I'm looking at her and saying, 'Can you believe this?'

My mood has turned from me being angry and upset to being overwhelmed by how brilliant this is. The love and admiration being shown for my dad is incredible. I don't think he would have expected this. He knew people loved him, and how famous he was, but I don't think he would have thought the whole of Belfast would come out for him, because that's what it feels like – the entire city is here. I'm sure he didn't know how loved he was, and that is so sad. He might have made more of an effort to live.

The hearses and our car are in a police convoy, which blocks traffic lights to make sure the road is constantly flowing. People are throwing roses and other things, and someone throws a little green football which comes through my window and hits me in the face, which makes me laugh. A picture of me holding the green ball and looking out of the window appears in the paper the next day.

The drive goes on for a good while, and as we get to the end I'm thinking that's it, the main fuss is over. But it's not. The biggest moment comes when we turn into the drive leading up to Stormont. It's a breathtaking sight – a big black fence around an estate, and then the long drive with perfect grass and trees on each side, leading up to Stormont itself, which looks like a huge stately home, with massive pillars in the middle and dozens of windows spreading out on each side. It's spectacular. People are climbing up the fence so they can get a glimpse inside to see what's going on, as if it's a rock concert.

The streets have been lined all the way here, but the lines were mostly only a couple of people deep. At Stormont, on both sides of the drive there is row after row after row after row of people. It is beautiful. My dad is getting the send-off of all send-offs. Later I read that there were more than 25,000 people there inside the grounds alone, which is astonishing. I am so proud of him, and I'm so glad I'm sharing this moment with my mum.

Chapter 18

'A woman comes up to me and says, "I think it's absolutely disgusting that you're out partying only a few hours after you buried your dad." I'm too drunk to reply, but what I think, and what I want to say, is that I'm not partying, I'm drinking to avoid reality.'

Calum Best

Outside Stormont, there are two big TV screens up for the crowds to watch the funeral. I realize I'm going to be on those screens, and it's not just the people inside I need to be nervous about speaking in front of; it's the crowds outside too. I don't like speaking in public at any time – it terrifies me – and this is on a different scale to anything I've ever imagined. I am petrified. I tell myself I can do this, I'll be fine.

We pull up at the top of the drive. There are soldiers

lined up and bagpipes playing, and I'm trying my best not to lose it. At the top of the stairs, when we enter the building, it becomes my turn to carry the coffin. It's me, Phil and Ian on one side, and Norman and my granddad on the other. We carry it inside and the place is full already. There are people crying, and I see Sir Alex Ferguson, the Manchester United team, and loads of different faces. Stormont is done up beautifully. It's like a king has died, not a footballer.

The coffin is taken from us and put on its stand at the front. I sit down in my seat, next to my granddad and Barbara. The funeral starts with some songs – 'You Raise Me Up' is one – and it blurs by until it's my turn. I go up and read the poem chosen for me, and I'm nervous, but the words don't mean much to me so it's OK. It's a nice poem, just not personal to me.

When I finish it and everyone's waiting for me to come down, I say I have something else I want to read. I tell them that this poem was written by a lovely lady from Belfast and it has a lot of significance for me. I start the poem and quickly get choked up. I try to carry on, but I don't think I'm going to be able to finish. I feel a single tear going down my face as I continue, and I concentrate on each word, taking them one at a time, and eventually I get to the end. The poem is called 'Farewell Our Friend' and Julie McClelland is the kind lady who wrote it:

> Farewell our friend, but not goodbye.
> Your time has come, your soul must fly.

253

To dance with angels, find the sun,
but how we'll miss our special one.

He walks among us just a while,
weaved your magic, made us smile.
Your life was so full of light and tears,
we lived it through you, through the years.

The golden days, they went so fast.
The precious times, why can't they last?
So many loved you, did you know?
We were not ready to let you go.

The stars from Heaven are only lent.
A gift from God, that's why they're sent.
We won't forget our Belfast boy,
he filled our lives with so much joy.

Your star will shine now in the sky.
Farewell our friend, but not goodbye.

I look at my mum when it ends. She's crying, and I'm only just holding myself together. I'm so relieved it's over. I could so easily have collapsed halfway through. So much of it felt so personal for me, and so real. It's amazing that a woman who never met my dad or me could make such a connection. My mum was right about it being a special poem. A few days after the funeral, Julie McClelland gets in touch with my mum to say how happy she was that I read her poem out, which is lovely.

Eamonn Holmes and Barbara speak, and then it's Professor Williams's turn. He says, 'Doctors are said never to get too close to their patients. It's not that easy when the patient is somebody like George Best. Hi, Prof, hi, George, that's how it was. I think he got too well with the transplant and the temptations of life overtook him again and then it was the beginning of the end.'

Denis Law and Bobby McAlinden, who was with my dad when he met my mum in the US all those years ago, say a few words too. They all talk about how special my dad was, how he had a unique charm, and as I listen to them all I think of is how much I wish I'd had more time with him.

There are songs sung, more people speak, and then we leave Stormont to go and bury my dad at the Roselawn Cemetery. This is a private affair, just for the family, and so it's the two hearses, and then me and my mum.

My dad is lowered into the ground, and by now I am totally numb. I have no more feelings, even as I watch him being placed in the grave and covered up, and I know that this really is the absolute end, that he will never, ever be seen again. It's raw, but I'm so drained of all emotions now that I barely know what I'm feeling. The past few weeks and months have been such a blur, and the past couple of days have been so intense.

Now is when things go downhill. The next part of the day is a celebration of his life at a golf resort. We all go back to the hotel first, and my mum is going to stay there. This is where we say goodbye to our driver and his silver Mercedes. He was a nice guy all day, and tried to keep our spirits up, which I was really grateful for. I say, 'Thank you so much for today,' and ask him how much it will be. He says absolutely no way am I paying him. It was his honour to be part of George Best's funeral, and he never thought anything like this would happen to him. My dad was his idol. On a difficult day, this is a lovely moment. I make him take a tip off me and we say goodbye. He is a good man, and I am glad that driving us made him happy. It was another reminder of how loved my dad was.

I say goodbye to my mum, and Dave has to go back to London, so Adee comes with me to the party. When we arrive there, it's packed. I see all these familiar faces, the famous ones who were at the funeral. But I don't talk to anyone, I just start drinking. One Guinness becomes two, becomes three, four, eight, ten – I don't know how many I go through. I'm drinking as hard as I can to drown my sorrows. I team up with Alex Higgins, the snooker player and another Northern Ireland sports legend with a drink problem. There's something about him which reminds me of my dad, and we sit together in a corner, not really talking, just clinking our glasses together every now and then and saying, 'Here's to Bestie,' to each other.

I stay with Alex for the whole evening and get completely wasted. I speak to a few people, but I can't remember who they were or what I said. Literally, not a single word. All I remember is drinking Guinness with Alex Higgins.

At the end, Alex says it would be great if I would go with him across Belfast to see a different side of the city. I'm not in the mood to go home, so Adee and I go with Alex to what feels like the seediest of seedy pubs somewhere in Belfast, and I drink and drink and drink. We go on to a nightclub – I don't know what it's called or where it is – and I go nuts. I've taken off my jacket, my shirt and my vest, and I'm holding a bottle of booze. I'm staggering around, saying I don't know what to I don't know who, when a woman comes up to me and says, 'I think it's absolutely disgusting that you're out partying only a few hours after you buried your dad.' I'm too drunk to reply, but what I think, and what I want to say, is that I'm not partying, I'm drinking to avoid reality. If I wasn't out, I'd be on my own in my room, and that is not a good place for me. I'm drinking so I can try to forget. Anyone who looks at me right now and thinks I'm partying doesn't know me at all.

Someone drives me back to the hotel, and I crash out. At about 11am, someone knocks on my door because we have to get to the airport. I quickly pull on some clothes and get out of there. We fly back to London, and that's it, the funeral is over.

A couple of weeks after that, when I'm back in London and my mum has gone home to the US, I get a letter from a lawyer asking that I return everything I have of my dad's that is part of his estate. This includes the keys to the flat. The letter also mentions the bag he had with him at the hospital. It's a cheap bag and only has toiletries and a few clothes in it, but the lawyers want it anyway. Any belongings I have from inside the hospital room, anything at all, it all has to go. Someone tells me they're doing this so they can get my dad's estate in one big pool before it's divided up, so there's nothing to worry about.

But now I have lawyers on my back, Phil's warning runs through my mind again. The second will – the one that mentioned me – wasn't signed. Right there my gut tells me this is going to be a struggle. In fact, I might not get anything from my dad after all. I am gutted. My fresh start is falling apart already.

People have been asking me how the will works and every time I've said I don't know, but what I do know is that my dad wanted me to have his flat, so it's mine. In my head, that was settled. But now it's being taken away.

It's just before Christmas. My dad has been dead nearly a month and I'm a mess, going out drinking and taking drugs every night. I'm living in a two-bedroom flat off Brompton Road in Chelsea, a very nice area. But the flat's empty, except for a single bed and a TV. That's it, nothing else. The kitchen has nothing in it. One bedroom has nothing in it. The other has the bed, with no sheets or anything other than the mattress. And the living room has the TV in it and absolutely nothing else. I'm living there with a friend and we argue about food and rent money all the time because we spend everything we have on going out. We even take turns in the bed.

I have a shaved head and I'm not getting any modelling work at the moment. I'm still earning money from doing personal appearances in nightclubs every weekend, which means Friday and Saturday nights are spent out in places like Manchester or Liverpool, getting paid in cash and then blowing most of it in a casino or a strip joint and then coming back down to London again with just enough left to last me until the next weekend.

I've fallen hard off the rails in the few weeks since my dad died, even by my standards, and I'm painfully aware of what's happening to me. But I don't know what to do about it. I don't know how I'd cope with all the thoughts and emotions in my head if I wasn't drowning them out like this.

Just before Christmas, my flatmate goes away for a short while and I'm left on my own. These next few days are probably the lowest and worst of my whole life.

The only friends I have are people I know from being out in the nightclubs, so that's where I go, because I don't want to be alone. Every day I wake up at three in the afternoon, get a bite to eat and then wait until it's time to go out again. I walk from our flat on Brompton Road to a club in Knightsbridge, because I don't have enough cash to pay for a taxi just for myself. Later on, I might use my last few pounds to take a girl home with me. If I'm not with anyone, I'll walk home alone.

On 23 December, John Benson, a guy who works in the music industry, invites me over to eat with him and his family on Christmas Day. He's a true friend and a good guy. I would love to spend Christmas Day with him, but I don't have the money to get to his house.

That night I go out and get wasted, as usual. The next morning, Christmas Eve, I wake up and look in the kitchen. I find baked beans and bread, and nothing else. This is so depressing. I go to the bathroom and look in the mirror. I am about to cry but I don't want to. I want to be stronger than that. I fight off the tears.

I consider my life. It's Christmas Eve and I'm alone. My mum is on the other side of the world, and no one here wants to see me. I'm hungover to hell. No clubs are open so I'm not going to see my friends tonight. And are they really my friends anyway? I don't know any more. I have one invitation to Christmas dinner and I can't afford to get there.

Two voices start talking in my head, one after the other, the two halves of my split personality.

One says: *So you lost your dad, big deal. Shit happens. Get on with it. This is life. You can handle this. Pick yourself up and be a man.*

Then the other one kicks in: *You're pathetic. You're a loser. This is all your fault. You're worthless. You deserve to be alone.*

Now I can't fight the tears any more. Still looking in

the mirror, I start sobbing. I stand there with tears pouring down my face for what feels like hours.

Later, when I've pulled myself together, I go out and buy the cheapest packet of cigarettes I can find. I come home and make my beans on toast. I move my bed into the front room so I can sit on it and watch TV and I settle in for Christmas on my own. But I'm lucky to have someone like John around. On Christmas Day he sends a taxi for me, and I spend the day at his house with his lovely family.

Early in 2006, I get the news I've been dreading. I'm not getting my dad's flat. In fact, I'm getting nothing, except for the watch he was given for the 1994 World Cup in the US, the one he wore that day he came to coach my team. I talk to Phil about it and he tells me the will that was signed is the one that stands, and that means my dad's sister Barbara is the beneficiary. It quickly becomes apparent that I get nothing.

I ask what happens to the business we were setting up. The lawyers have taken all that, all his image rights. And I have nothing? Phil nods. Phil too is left with nothing, which is wrong. He was my dad's best friend and right hand for twenty years. He deserves more than this. In a way I'm angrier for him than I am about anything else.

The word angry doesn't tell the whole story of how I feel. I am devastated. I am furious. I have nothing of my dad's, nothing to remember him by. I remember seeing the pictures in Phil's office that day we signed the papers for the company. My dad's and Pelé's footprints together, how cool is that? How cool is that picture of him with the guys from Oasis? If only I could have some of those memories. I'm his son, after all.

I'm angry with Barbara. I think to myself, who is she to come and take all my dad's stuff away from me? I don't even know her. My granddad's words about burying my dad in Ireland pop back into my head, reinforcing the feeling that they don't care what I think about anything. These people seem to think I'm not part of their family. But I was my dad's next of kin. How can I have ended up with nothing?

I just want some memories. I want to feel like I mattered to my dad and am part of him. That's all. Something I can put on my mantelpiece and look at to remind myself of him and which I can give to my children when I tell them about their granddad the legendary footballer. This shouldn't be happening. But there's nothing I can do about it. The will is binding. I have the watch, and nothing else.

Chapter 19

'I didn't move over to the UK to be known as George Best's son. I came here to get to know him, and I only planned to be here for a couple of years. Now, five years later, he's dead and my life is turning to shit.'

Calum Best

The new year, 2006, starts with me falling deeper and deeper into a dark hole. I have to earn a living, so I carry on doing nightclub appearances on Thursdays, Fridays and Saturdays. These are in different cities around the country, so usually there's travelling involved between each one, and every night is heavy. They follow the same pattern. We go to the nightclub and I get on stage for the first part of the PA, which is the question and answer session. I hate this part. I get so anxious beforehand that I have to have a few drinks to get myself in the right mood. I'm not a singer, or an actor, so performing in front of an audience isn't my thing, and sometimes there are thousands of people in these clubs.

Once I've got past this bit, and am off the stage, it's really fun to be part of these nights. Everyone's out for a good time, and when people come up and talk to me I like being the centre of attention.

After the questions on stage, you sit down for a meet and greet. People queue up behind a screen, then come in to say a quick hello and take a picture. It's a great way to meet girls and I spend time with different girls all over the place, trying to cover up the fact I'm lonely. Months pass in a fog.

In March, there's a memorial for my dad at Manchester Cathedral. A dinner is held the night before, where things are auctioned off to raise money for charity. It's full of football legends like Sir Bobby Robson and current Manchester United stars and the manager Sir Alex Ferguson. I am in a pretty bad way, so don't do much mingling. Paul Gascoigne comes and says hello early on and stays with me for the whole evening. He sits next to me and looks after me, putting his hand on my shoulder and just making sure I'm OK and not alone. He's obviously a good guy and the fact that he's also a football legend makes what he's doing even more special. The evening could have been much more difficult without him. He is a comfort to me and obviously understands what my dad went through, which makes the terrible problems he has with alcohol over the next few years even sadder.

The dinner ends at about 11pm and I go back to my hotel. But I'm alone and I can't stand it, so I text some friends, ask where the good places are and head out. I buy a bottle of Jack Daniel's from the first shop I see and then walk into the city centre, drinking it as I go. The rest of the night is a blur.

The next morning I can't find the suit I brought for the memorial. I gave it to the hotel's dry cleaners, but they put it somewhere they shouldn't have and it takes a long and painful series of calls to reception to work out where it is. The result is that I'm late for the actual memorial service, which I'm gutted about. I walk in while it's going on, past the whole Manchester United squad and famous face after famous face, and take my seat at the front next to my granddad, who nods to me. That's all, just a nod. I hardly know him and I'm mortified about what he'll think of me, and pretty soon the intensity of the day and all my emotions get the better of me and I burst into tears. I sit there thinking about my dad and what's going on in my life and I feel terrible, I mean in-the-gutter shitty, about all of it. The memorial ends and I talk to a few people, but I'm not really all there. I head back to London and the blur continues.

Not long after that, I'm offered *Celebrity Love Island* again, for another £50,000, and I have to say yes. I got so much work off the back of the first one that I'd be stupid to turn it down. And I have no other big plans, so I need the money.

The evening before I leave for Fiji, I go out with some

friends and the night doesn't end until 7pm the following evening, when I have to leave for the airport. We have been drinking and doing lines of cocaine for almost twenty-four hours, which is a perfect example of how out of control I am.

The weeks in Fiji are good for me. I like being away from London. Being away is healthier, and distance between me and my life and reputation in the UK gives me some perspective on how being the son of George Best has worked out for me. By which I mean badly. I'm a mess, and seriously, deeply unhappy.

I have a great time in Fiji again. I feel liberated being out of London and away from all the stress. I relax and start to feel well, physically and mentally. My good mood must come across on screen, because somehow I win the show. Before I came out, I was not expecting this and it gives my confidence a boost. It makes me feel like I could do something good with my life, if only I can think of what that might be and then get myself in better shape.

But when I come back, it's on with the nights out again. I can see no other option for me. If I sit down and think for too long about what I want to do with my life, if I try to be sensible, I'm immediately confronted with what's happened over the past few years, how I fucked things up, and I can't stand it. How do I cope with this feeling? I go to parties and clubs and get wasted all the time. This is what it means to be the son of George Best.

I get stick from the press constantly for it, mainly to do

with me being a chip off the old block for living such a debauched life, but I know why I'm getting wasted. It's not to have a good time; it's because I'm hiding. They don't know what my life is like. They see me as the son of George Best, the legend, and assume I have a place to go to grieve, that I sit at home in front of the fire surrounded by people who love me. But my life is not like that. People who don't know me assume I'm a hellraiser in the way they think my dad was. But I'm not what they think I am, and I expect deep down my dad wasn't what they thought he was either.

After *Love Island*, I do an interview with *OK!* magazine, and when I look at the pictures I realize what a dark place I'm in. I look depressed, I have bags under my eyes, my skin is bad, and I'm all puffed up. I'm in terrible shape, but I don't know what to do about it. For a good year, I'm out every single night.

Off the back of *Love Island*, I bring out a fragrance with my name on and it starts to do well. I spend quite a lot of time travelling around promoting it and I'm really happy that it's a success. The money is very welcome, but I also enjoy the feeling of being involved in starting something successful.

In October, I go to do a PA at a nightclub in Wales and I'm staying in the Hilton in Cardiff. After the question and answer part, I'm sitting down meeting people when an absolutely beautiful girl comes through. She's incredible. Immediately I know I'm not going to look at another girl tonight. 'You're gorgeous,' I say. 'Why don't you and your friends stay in the VIP section with us?'

The girls stay, the meet and greet goes on, and when it finishes I go and hang out with them. At about two or three in the morning a guy who owns a bar down the road says we can go for a lock-in at his place. Off we go, me with this super-hot girl, my friends, her friends and the guy who owns the bar. It's about ten people in total.

We go into this empty nightclub, the guy turns on the music and the lights, someone gets behind the bar and starts dishing out drinks, I'm kissing this gorgeous girl and the night is going well. There's a bit of coke around and everyone is having a great time. A while later, three of the guys disappear into the office with one of the girls.

I decide to leave with the girl. I can't wait to be alone with her. We go back to the hotel, have a great, great time together and then fall asleep. What a beautiful night, I think before I doze off.

At six in the morning, probably only an hour after I went to sleep, BANG! My door is kicked down and four police officers, two men and two women, storm in. I'm terrified, and start jabbering, 'What the fuck is going on? What the fuck?'

One of the policemen says, 'Mr Best, we're taking you down to the station for questioning.'

I'm scared and confused. 'What? How? Who?'

'Mr Best, we'll talk at the station.'

'But I didn't do anything. I was with her all night.'

I point at the girl in bed next to me. She is still

beautiful, but the look on her face isn't great. This clearly isn't what she was expecting from the morning after a night with me. She's terrified.

I come out of the room and the police say they're going to take me out of the hotel's back exit so I don't get any more drama, which I really appreciate. There's an unmarked police car with two more female police officers inside and I get in. We drive to the police station, go into their underground car park and then I am taken up to give them a statement. They ask for a full account of what happened last night. I have no idea what I'm supposed to have done, or even why I'm here. I'm so scared I don't hold anything back. I tell them everything – the PA, the question and answer, the girl, the after-party, the coke, back to the hotel. All of it.

They tell me that the girl who disappeared into the office with three guys is now claiming she was raped, by all of them. It's a very serious matter.

My stomach drops. 'I know nothing about that,' I say. 'Absolutely nothing.'

I really don't. I didn't see anything that went on in that office. But I'm scared anyway. They tell me to stay there for twenty minutes while they go and ask some more questions. I sit there on my own, stewing badly. What happened in that office? I have no idea about any of it. I'm not even sure which girl it was who went in there.

Eventually, the policewomen come back and both are much more relaxed. They tell me one of the men filmed what went on in the office with his phone, and it turns out the girl who claimed she was raped was in fact very happy to get involved with two of the guys. Everyone was drunk and wild, but it was obvious from the recording that nothing happened that was against her will. She was very happy about everything.

It's a huge relief. But the really crap part for me is that when the police asked the girl who raped her, she said she didn't know any of their names, except that she was there with Calum Best and his friends. That was why I had the door of my hotel room beaten in and why I was dragged out of bed so early.

Once they know no crime was committed at all, and that I wasn't even in the room when no crime was committed, the police's attitude to me changes dramatically. Now we're friends. Now they want pictures. I sit there and do photos with both female officers and a male officer. I'm asked to sign something, and then they give me stuff – a Welsh police hat, and a neon Welsh police jacket. They hand them over as souvenirs. It becomes a laugh.

I go back to the hotel at about midday and my mate is there and we're talking to each other about what a bizarre situation that was. The girl I spent the night with is long gone, and I don't see her again, which is a shame.

The newspapers haven't had a good word to say about me for a long time, and I hate it. They paint a picture of me that isn't accurate, and it upsets me. What happens in the wake of this is a perfect example, because not long after there's a story in the paper with the headline, 'Calum is quizzed on "rape" claim'. That's awful – it makes it seem that I've been accused of rape, which is obviously not true. The story itself doesn't exactly backtrack on that implication. It says: 'PLAYBOY Calum Best was woken up by eight cops in his hotel bedroom and quizzed over a nightclub rape claim. The officers spoke to Best – son of football legend George – and his agent. However the girl who cried rape later dropped her allegation – and it is thought Best was only quizzed as a possible witness.'

This isn't fair. If you compare what actually happened with that headline, it's seriously misleading. The fact is there was no rape at all, and I wasn't accused of one, but the headline doesn't say that. Newspapers and magazines are now using anything like this to make me look bad, because it fits the version of me they like to write about, just like they used to turn the spotlight on anything my dad did wrong. But that version is warped. I'm not that guy.

The press carry on kicking me, and I go on holiday to Spain to get away from everything. While I'm there, a journalist from the *News of the World* calls me and says he has proof I've been doing cocaine. I hang up on him, in shock. I'm terrified about that coming out – I haven't been caught with drugs yet, only girls. The repercussions of that kind of story could be awful for me. I don't know what to do. The journalist continues to call, time after time. Each call makes me more and more anxious. Finally, on about the fiftieth call, I answer and am given an ultimatum: either I do an interview, confess and say I do coke, or they will run the story anyway and it will be ten times worse. I am completely cornered, so I agree to talk to him and he gets on a plane to Spain.

But at the last minute, nerves get the better of me and I pull out of the interview, just before I'm meant to do it. I call Alex, my dad's ex, for some advice, because it's playing on my mind. She tells me not to worry, and to go and see a girlfriend of hers who lives close to where I'm staying. She says her friend is lovely and I can chill out at her house, away from all the stress. I go to this girl's house, we have a few drinks, and I relax. I explain to her why that journalist is on my case, and I tell her about some of my issues to do with my dad and how I've been taking drugs. I trust her because she's a friend of Alex's, and I talk quite openly with her about my life and what I'm doing. We end up sleeping together. Next morning we say goodbye and that's that, I think.

But the next weekend a story appears in the *News of the World* based on what I said to her. This includes me saying about a good friend of mine, who'd let me stay in his house and had been really kind to me, that he smokes weed all day and takes cocaine at night, and that he's been a bad influence on me. I'm devastated, and he's furious, which I don't blame him for.

I'm so angry with the girl for setting me up – she recorded the whole thing and sold the tape. I can't believe someone who seemed like a decent person would behave like that. I know I'm not an angel, but I would never do that to someone. I know nothing about lawyers or privacy, so can't do anything to defend myself. I just have to take it and move on. I'm really upset and embarrassed that it's come out, and I feel like I've let down my friend, which he didn't deserve. It's just one more stress to add to everything else.

Life carries on and I'm still out of control. And then something happens which leads up to the lowest moments I ever have with the press, and some of the worst of my life.

It starts at the club I go to every Monday night. I know everyone here, it's like my local, so I'm always at a table. This group of people come in and sit down at the table next to us. There's a girl and some gay guys. I catch the girl's eye and she smiles. I know who this is – it's Lindsay Lohan. Everyone knows who she is.

A few minutes later, one of her security guys comes over and tells me Lindsay would like me to join her. I politely say no thanks, I'm good here. I'm playing it cool in front of my mates. I don't want to look like I've come running just because I've been asked over by Lindsay Lohan.

A bit later she comes over and sits next to me. We get on well immediately. We have a good chat, some banter, and she asks me to come back to her hotel for a party. We go back there and are photographed going in. We spend the next few nights hanging out together, and then she goes back to the US. A few days later she asks me to come over to New York to go to a film premiere with her. I fly over, and we're pictured together. Then we fly to Barbados for the opening of the Atlantis Hotel.

After our trip to Barbados, photographs appear of us frolicking in the sea with a headline, 'How did Calum get this girl?' as if to say what the hell is she doing with him? I think, wow, you guys must hate me so much. And I don't really know what I've done to deserve that. Why not be happy for us?

I'm called a 'seedy lothario' all the time and it kills me. I hate that label so, so much, and it's being called that over and over and over again that makes me think I need to change the way I behave. Those two words make my skin crawl. The thing is, I really don't think I'm a seedy lothario. I'm just a good guy who likes girls and a good time.

I don't have a PR adviser, or a lawyer, so there's no one to put my case forward, and the journalists carry on writing what they want to write. None of them really know me. They think they do – and I know I give them plenty of ammunition for the stories they write – but the real me isn't the one they describe.

For a while I didn't mind being known as a playboy. I liked the naughtiness that came with it. And the association people made between me and my dad. I had a bit of cash, could get girls when I wanted, and was welcomed into any club. But when 'playboy' turned into 'seedy lothario', that was when I stopped being happy. That's not fun.

All this makes me think about two things. First, my

mum raised me well. She raised me to be a good guy and respectful to women. She did not raise me to be a seedy lothario, and that's not what I am. The second thing is, what has my life become? I didn't move over to the UK to be known as George Best's son. I came here to get to know him, and I only planned to be here for a couple of years. Now, five years later, he's dead and my life is turning to shit.

I'm not even helping myself now. It looks like I might be starting something with Lindsay, but I don't treat her well. When we go out I flirt with other girls, sometimes in front of her, and one day she catches me hanging out with another girl in my hotel room. Nothing happens between me and the other girl but I'm still a terrible boyfriend and after a few intense weeks and lots of arguments we part on bad terms.

I go back to the UK expecting that to be the end of it. But we carry on messaging each other, and I realize what an idiot I've been for treating her badly. We had a good thing going, and I don't want to lose her.

I decide to try to make it up to her, so I go to Theo Fennell and buy a diamond lock and key, spending thousands of pounds that I don't really have. The lock is for her to wear, and the key is for me. It's her birthday and I know she's in Malibu, so I fly over there. We kiss, and we make up. But things aren't simple, because the two of us together are combustible. At this moment in our lives, we're both a bit nuts. We both like to party a lot and it makes things tempestuous.

I go back to London and head out to my usual Wednesday-night spot. I spend every Wednesday night here now. I go with the same group of guys, we drink, get high and get debaucherous. One of my friends and I meet two girls. We know they are escorts, but we're not paying them, we're all just having a good time. The four of us go back to a hotel and things go from there.

The next day, I regret what happened, because of Lindsay. It's the first time I've been with another girl since we met and I wish I hadn't done it. But it's done now and I can't change anything, so I decide to try to forget it.

Two days later, I fly to Los Angeles to do an interview and photo shoot with Lindsay for *OK!* magazine. This is a big deal for me, because it's the first time the American press has been interested in me, and we're getting £100,000 each. I'm not sure where it will lead, if anywhere, but I do know it's worth seeing what happens.

I get to my hotel, the Roosevelt, in the middle of the day on Saturday. I check in and then I get a call. My agent tells me one of the girls filmed everything that night and she's taken it to the *News of the World*. She had a camera set up in a corner of the room and got the whole lot. I feel like I've been hit round the face. All that, on video? I'm fucked. Completely and utterly fucked. And I'm here, in LA for a photo shoot with Lindsay, who I'm supposed to be with. I have never been this fucked before.

My agent goes on to say the paper has given me a choice. Either I do a piece for them saying I'm addicted to booze, drugs and women, or they'll put the video out.

The video is bad, and I really don't want people seeing it. I don't want to be known for what's in it. So either the world sees that, or I tell the paper I'm addicted to cocaine, booze and women. Not a difficult choice, and my agent agrees. I don't think anyone will be surprised to hear I have problems in those areas and, he says, the story will run and then be forgotten pretty quickly. So I agree to it.

Later that day, I turn on the TV in my hotel room. It's the cable channel E! and they're running through their ten biggest showbiz stories of the day. At number ten is me, under the headline 'Calum At His Worst'. They have stills of the video. Stills of that damn video, on televisions all across the US, which means they're being shown all around the world.

There's one of me in a towel, one of me doing a line of coke. I want to scream. I realize my mum is going to see this, and my grandma is going to see this. My grandma. She'll be so upset. I can't stand the thought of what will be going through their minds. And then there's my career. What am I going to be able to do after this? I've been caught on tape with drugs and hookers. No one cares that we weren't paying them. They were still hookers. Where can I go from here? I am now really, truly fucked. Then I get a call from *OK!* cancelling the interview. No great surprise.

I'm sitting there, on my own, in that hotel room, wondering what to do next. I have a return ticket to London. Do I want to go straight back there? What's there for me? I'd end up going straight out and getting in more trouble. The thought depresses me so much I feel like I'm hungover already.

I've humiliated myself in front of everyone – family, friends, the entire world. Everyone I care about will know about this. What will they think of me? This must have been how my dad felt when he was being splashed all over the papers for whatever new scrape he got himself into.

My career is in tatters, and it's all my fault. I did this to myself. No one forced me to go back to that hotel with those girls. No one forced me to take cocaine. They were my decisions. My choices. I did this damage. I realize I'm behaving just like my dad. I'm destroying myself. No one is doing it to me. I'm doing all this to myself and I have no one else to blame. I am in a dark place.

OK! say they think we might be able to do the shoot in rehab, if I'll go. But Lindsay says she doesn't want to do it any more. After everything she's read about me, I don't blame her. So here I am, in LA on my own. I have a bungalow suite at the Roosevelt Hotel, and a credit card.

I get the news about the shoot, put the phone down and walk out on to my balcony because I need some air. The room feels like a prison right now. My balcony over-looks the pool and there's a daytime pool party going on down there; the sun is shining and girls in bikinis are dancing around. I look a bit closer and I recognize a guy, a good friend of mine I haven't seen for ages. And then another one, and another. I can't believe they're all here. I shout down to them, and they're shocked to see me. They had no idea I was in LA, let alone in the same hotel. I tell them to come up to my suite, and the party starts again.

Chapter 20

'A few years ago, the press loved me. I was charming,
good-looking Calum, but now I'm the seediest guy
in the world, a seedy lothario, a scumbag, a guy
whose dad was great but who's a loser and a waste
of space.'

Calum Best

I spend the next month staying at the hotel and partying. I
eat out every night, I go to Malibu Beach and I see old
friends from all over the place. I'm by the pool every day,
ordering food and drinks for everyone. I don't care about
anything – I just go for it. I drop a few hundred here and
there without any thought. I have breakfast on room
service every day. It's thirty days of carnage. I'm beginning
to understand the vicious circle that my dad got caught
in.

I'm not off my face for the entire time, though, and

over those weeks I do some thinking. I realize I have to sort myself out. I can't go on like this. I need to change things, but I don't know how. I can't face involving my mum in any of the things going on in my life. I'm too ashamed to get in touch with her. I have no one to give me any advice. No lawyer to advise me on how to handle the papers – I don't know how things like that work. The only advice I've had has come from agents, who say it's best not to fight them, because if you do you'll become their enemy and that will make things a hundred times worse. So I just let things go again and again and again. Of course they have printed stuff about me that is true, and I know I can't complain about most of it, especially when girls sell stories about me. But there have been lots of lies too. And they hurt. Maybe ignoring them has been the wrong thing to do, because it certainly hasn't stopped me from getting nailed by the papers this time.

Maybe I should have fought back, so they knew I wouldn't just take it. But then again, even if I had fought back, I would probably still have ended up in that hotel room with those girls. The papers didn't do that. I did. I should have known better.

I also think about me and girls. If this mess has taught me one thing, it's that I don't want a girlfriend. Something in me means that no matter who the girl is, I don't want to be serious with her. It doesn't even matter that it's Lindsay Lohan, a sweet, gorgeous girl who has all this great stuff going on around her. That doesn't change my mind. I don't want anyone.

It's possible that my commitment issues stem from deep, dark stuff to do with my dad, such as his lack of commitment to me, but I don't think it's that simple. I've always been around women, and comfortable with them. I was raised by my mum, I was around Cher, who always had women around her. I loved her female backing dancers. Ever since I've been old enough, I've enjoyed sleeping with girls. But I'm not a bad guy: I've never lied to anyone to get them into bed; I've never said I love you when I didn't mean it.

As I've said, since I moved to London I've never really had close friends, and being with different girls gives me company. Maybe on some level there is a bit of this which traces back to my dad. But I don't think I can blame him for all of it – the things I've done and the trouble I've got myself into are my responsibility.

I don't know if Lindsay would have got serious even if I'd wanted to. I think she liked me more than any other guy who was around at the time, but I don't know how deep her feelings went, probably because we never actually got that close. We didn't spend any full-on one-on-one time together, so never had any really bonding moments. No walks or hanging out watching movies – any of the things couples do together. Our relationship was about the lifestyle, being at certain places, attending events, partying and meeting people. She has a mad life, running around the world all the time. Everyone has their nose in her business, so there was no chance for something real to build between us. But I did spend enough time with her to know she's a lovely girl.

While I'm still in LA, I apologize to her and say we should stay in touch. I mean it – I really am sorry. Lindsay tells me I must be seriously messed up to be such an asshole. Maybe she's right, but I don't know what to do about it. At least things between us are OK now. We might never be best friends, but I hope we'll stay in contact.

A few weeks later, when I'm back in the UK, just being friends becomes impossible, because stories appear about a sex video of me and Lindsay. According to the press, I recorded it and have put a clip online. I'm the bad guy and get all the blame. I fit the bill – I'm the sleazy lothario who just got caught with drugs and hookers, so of course I did the video.

Lindsay now hates me. Our new friendship is over. She gives interviews saying I did terrible things when I was with her, that she thought I was a good guy when we first met but I turned out to be the worst. I try to contact her but she won't get in touch with me, so the only communication we have is through stories in the press which are full of lies.

At one stage I text her and say, 'Do you really think that's you and me?' because it's not. The guy in the clip is not me. Even if the girl is her – and I can't tell if it is or isn't – then it's still absolutely nothing to do with me. I'm not in it, I didn't film it, and I didn't release it. I am entirely innocent, and I am desperate for her to know this. But she doesn't reply to my messages. It occurs to me that maybe she's been told not to by her people. After all these stories, I might now be too toxic for her to be associated with. Whether or not the story is true doesn't matter any more. The mud has stuck. My reputation is so bad she can't even be in contact with me.

I know I deserve some of the reputation I have. Maybe even a lot of it. But this situation isn't right. It's damaging and humiliating, and because of the internet the story has gone all round the world. Who's going to give me any kind of work after this? No one. But what can I do? I have no one to call on who has experience of these things and can help me set the record straight. So the stories are left out there, and I have that label for ever – the sleazy guy who put out a sex video of Lindsay Lohan. The way people see it is that if anybody was going to do something like that, I'm the guy. But it wasn't me. None of it.

Not long after this, I get stung by the press again. I'm leaving a nightclub with Elizabeth Jagger, who's been a friend for a few years, and on the way out we get a bit naughty. It's twenty seconds' worth of pretty innocent fooling around, that's all. But without us realizing, it's caught on camera. I find this out because the *News of the World* gets hold of the tape. One of the journalists calls me and says, 'We've got the tape and here's what I suggest we do to make you both look good. We'll write the story so it sounds like the information has come from a source, which means it will be someone saying, "Calum feels this way about Liz," or "Calum can't believe this has happened, he's so embarrassed," but the information will have come from you. You'll know it's all true and accurate, your name won't be mentioned, you can be nice about Liz and we'll get our story.' And he says they'll give me two grand.

I'm absolutely broke at the moment, so two grand in cash for making a story that is going to appear anyway sound better for me and Liz sounds like a good deal. I go and meet the journalist at a hotel and tell him how much I like Liz, what a great girl she is, how we're young and silly and everyone makes mistakes, thinking this is going to be one of those 'Calum told friends' deals as promised. He gives me two grand, and we're all good. One of his colleagues is there to witness the deal and that's that.

A couple of days later, I'm in Stringfellows late on Saturday night and someone comes in with the next day's *News of the World*. I open it and there's a picture of me with my mouth open under the headline 'CALUM CONFESSES'. The quotes are all attributed to me; there are no friends or sources, none of what we agreed. They've made it look like I've done a kiss-and-tell, like I've ratted out a famous girl for cash, which I didn't and would never do.

The tape never gets out, which I think is thanks to Elizabeth's parents and their lawyers. She doesn't speak to me again, and I'm pretty sure she and her friends will always think that I am a scumbag who sold the story.

It now feels like I'm getting slated in the papers every

single day. People are putting the boot in all the time, and my self-worth is as low as it can be. I feel like I'm not good enough, I feel like my work – nightclub appearances, interviews and the odd TV job – is shit and I look like shit. The fact I'm drunk most of the time is messing with my emotions, and I'm a mess. When I'm out and pissed, I'm as confident as hell, but in my day-to-day life, I'm depressed, anxious and paranoid about what people are saying. I used to worry about what people around us thought of my dad. Now I'm worrying about me. People put me down all the time, and I've become really quick at picking up on it. There's nothing going on that could build my confidence.

I know that in some ways I'm asking for it, because I come out of nightclubs and say, 'Fuck you,' to the cameras. But that's my way of coping with everything. People cope in different ways, and this is how I do it. But it's not who I really am.

A few years ago, the press loved me. I was charming, good-looking Calum, but now I'm the seediest guy in the world, a seedy lothario, a scumbag, a guy whose dad was great but who's a loser and a waste of space. I don't get abuse walking down the street, but I know people are seeing me and thinking bad things. I learn this from experience, and sometimes I choose to ignore it. For example, one day I'm in the airport and out of the corner of my eye I see two people clock me. I've learned to be able to tell if people's reactions to me are positive or negative without looking straight at them, and this time it's definitely negative. They look at me with contempt. Nine times out of ten this happens, and it always affects me. It hurts. I now think the majority of people out there hate me, and so I turn down work because of it. I don't want to face these people who think so little of me.

I turn down some TV stuff, different appearances, things which might have taken me to better things. I know what I'm doing with my life is nothing compared to what my dad did, what he achieved and how loved he was, and that makes me feel even worse. I used to think he'd failed me, but maybe it's me that's failed him. I'm too nervous and afraid to try anything. I have no pride in myself, no belief in myself.

So many lies are written about me in the papers, but there's nothing I can do about it, because I don't know how. I'm accused of doing nasty things, like throwing a drink in a girl's face because she wasn't giving me enough attention, which I absolutely did not do, but it makes for a good story. I am spiralling further and further down.

A friend of mine recommends that I go and get some acupuncture done. He thinks it might be good for me, so I give it a try. I sit with this woman, who's really warm and lovely, and I open up to her. I explain that I'm so anxious and depressed that I walk around with my head down because I'm worried people will see me and think, 'There's that **** Calum Best.' She looks shocked, and says that is one of the saddest things she's ever heard, and that to counter it I should stand in front of the mirror every day and say to myself, 'I'm a beautiful man, and I deserve to do well.'

My immediate reaction is absolutely no way am I doing something like that. But a few days later, when I'm feeling down, I try it, just in case. I do it a couple of times, and no, it's definitely not for me. I just feel stupid.

Chapter 21

'I realize that the position I'm in, where people know who my dad is and who I am, means I can help people who are going through things similar to what happened to me. And if I can, I should at least try.'

Calum Best

My mum had moved back from the States in June 2006, when I was already in a bad way. She knew I was a mess, and eventually she got so worried she decided to pack up and move back to the UK to be with me. For the first four months after she arrived she stayed in a hotel, and spent some time in hospital. She made sure I knew where she was and that she was around if I wanted her, but I didn't see her at all during this period, didn't visit her. Nothing. I couldn't face her. I was too ashamed.

I hardly see her for the next year and a half, literally

once or twice. We go through periods where we don't talk for months and months, maybe close to a year, even though we're now in the same country. She gets a call from me every once in a while, but that's all. That's how lost I am. I'm pushing away the most important person in the world, the one who knows me the best and who cares about me more than anyone else does, because I don't want her to see what I have become. I don't realize it at the time, but in a way I'm doing exactly what my dad did to me.

When we were young my mum and I were super-close. And when we don't talk for long periods, it's never because we fall out. It's my fault. Not ours, not hers; my fault. When things get really shitty, I don't know how to talk to her. I don't know what to say about what's going on in my life. I don't want to admit the truth, because if I tell her I'll have to face up to it myself, and I'm not ready to do that. I tell myself I'm busy doing my thing, trying to figure my life out, but in reality I'm not figuring out anything at all.

Shortly after she arrives, I hit another low when a friend of mine is arrested on suspicion of rape. Under the headline 'Girl "raped as Calum Best slept feet away"', the story begins with the line 'Cops are to interview Calum Best after a woman claimed she was raped'. The story is picked up by different papers, and every time it appears there's a picture of my face next to it. I am deeply upset by this, because it's so unfair, on both of us.

My friend spends six weeks in jail on remand, and it's

an unbelievably stressful time for him. He says all along that he is innocent and, sure enough, just before the trial is due to start, the girl drops the charges. She admits there was no rape. So the truth of it was my friend did nothing wrong, and neither did I. All I did was be asleep in a room in a flat when a girl in a different room didn't get raped. Yet my face is plastered all over the papers next to this horrible story, the implication being that somehow I was part of it.

I don't know what I can do to stop things like this happening. It's awful feeling so helpless. When girls I've been with sell stories about me, it's not as bad as this. I'd rather they didn't, sure, but I know I can't complain about it. But this is different, and it makes me feel like everyone is going to hate me even more than they already do. It's miserable.

By late 2007, my mum has moved to a place in Kew, on the edge of south-west London, by the river. Just before Christmas we talk for the first time in ages, and it's obvious what a state I'm in. She says, 'For God's sake, Calum, come and see me, come and stay with me.'

Until now she's been gently telling me she's there if I need her. But it's different now. This time I have to go. I can't see a way through the mess I'm in, and I need her, so I pack a bag and go to Kew. As soon as I get there it's awkward. I don't know how to act around my mum any more. I'm not comfortable with her. I am upset with myself for what I've done, for how I've let her down over the past few years. She's a wonderful woman who's never done anything but love me and look after me and I've treated her terribly. I feel awful about it, and part of me wants to run away and hide from her. But that's what I've been doing for too long. I wonder if this is the kind of feeling my dad had about me, and which made him drink even more to get away from the pain.

One night she says, 'Let's go for a walk down the river.' We take the dogs and walk in silence. It's a clear night, the river is to our left and the lights of London are in the distance – a view that has always brought butterflies to my stomach. Then my mum says, 'I'm so happy to have you back,' and something in me clicks. Suddenly this feels like a huge moment. This is the first time we've bonded for I don't know how long. It's the first time I've had someone who really loved me around for years. My mum is my family and I haven't been with her. I realize what I've been missing.

But it is still awkward. She puts her arm around me while we walk, and I'm uncomfortable with her doing that. I realize I've become so detached from any kind of real, caring emotion that I don't know how to deal with it. My mum asks me if I'm OK with her having her arm round me, and the honest answer is I don't know, I can feel all kinds of emotions bubbling up. But I do feel safe.

She starts talking again. 'You deserve to be better than this,' she says. 'You deserve to be happier. Things are going to change for you. We can do this together. I can take care of you, I can help you. I love you, and I'm here for you.'

I feel a spark appear in me, like a little light being switched on. I realize there's someone here who really cares about me, and that my life can be better. I can be better. My dad has gone, but I need to close that off now, I need to move on.

My mum can see how desperately I need help, but she knows she has to tread carefully. I'm stubborn, and can't be told what to do, so she doesn't nag me or boss me around. As we walk, she gives me options. I could do this or that, or maybe think about this, or maybe it's time to look into that, and whatever it is I decide to do, she'll be there for me.

She's desperate for me to deal with all the stuff I have inside me before I turn into the same kind of alcoholic my father was. I saw what happened to him, and I know how that story ends, but I don't really understand how terrifying this must be for her, to feel like I might be straying down that same path.

We walk and talk for two hours, and I feel like a different person when we get back to her house. I'm still a bit uncomfortable, not really knowing how to take it all in or how to make the change, but I know I want to change. I look around her flat and it's the kind of homely environment I haven't been in for years. I live in a flat with a bed, a TV and nothing else. But this is a home. There are little bits around that I recognize from LA – a couple of candelabras and a needlepoint on the wall. It's warm, the TV is on, the sofa is comfortable, her little dog Chester is around, my mum asks what I want to eat so she can cook it for me, and the whole thing is lovely. Being here with her is so good.

I want to smoke – I smoke a lot – but I'm not sure if I can smoke in front of my mum. But I figure I'm twenty-six years old now and I've been doing far worse things for the past few years, so what does one cigarette matter? I go out the back and have a cigarette and she doesn't say anything. Her silence tells me it's OK, I'm welcome no matter what.

I love being in this environment and, as I stand in her little courtyard, something happens to me. It's a kind of epiphany. I'm telling myself, Calum, it's time to change. Your mum's here, she loves you, she's got your back. There's a lovely little home here for you whenever you need it. That's what you've been missing for so long – a base, something to lean on, someone to turn to. So let's change. You can be better now. It's a pretty intense moment, in a good way. I feel like a completely different person when I head back to my flat a couple of days later.

It's funny how the universe works, because a few weeks after this I go to see my agency to talk about what I can do next. I'm hungry for the opportunity to turn things around. They say it's funny timing, because they just had a call from these two women who make true-life documentaries, about serious subjects like cancer, AIDS in Africa and so on, and there's an opportunity for me to make a film where I talk about kids who grow up with alcoholic parents.

At first, I think how can I do that? I can't talk about that. I imagine the anxiety it would cause me to dig up all those demons and I think no way, never. I can't do something like that. I won't be able to handle it. I don't say any of this, though. I just think it. What I say is, 'OK, sounds interesting. Let me call my mum.'

I call her and tell her about the opportunity and she says, 'Of course you should do it. You've got to do it.'

I go and meet the two women, Joanna Grace and Katy Sheppard, and they're great – lovely, caring, softly spoken people who make me feel really good about the whole thing. I feel like they'll make it so much easier for me to deal with. They know I'm concerned about how doing the programme will make me look, and how it will make my dad look, and they reassure me that it will be fine. They will come up with the content, the questions, and all they need me to do is wear my heart on my sleeve, be honest and open. They say the film will be shown on BBC One and we'll have to travel round the UK for the next four or five months to make it. We'll be talking to charities and kids who were worse off than I was and it will be really hard for me, but it'll be a learning process. They say they hope the process will help me find answers to questions I have about my dad and me and alcohol, and maybe even some closure. It's the right time for me to do something like this, so I say yes, I'm in.

Before we start, in spring 2008, I sign up to do an MTV show called *Totally Calum Best*. The idea is I will stay away from girls (and myself, if you know what I mean) for fifty days and fifty nights. It plays on my reputation for being a sex addict, which I'm not, but it makes a good pitch for a show. I'm not ecstatically happy about the project, but I decide to do it because I need the work, and having my own show on MTV is a great opportunity. I also hope I'll be able to present a side of myself that people don't know. The real me, I suppose. I want people to know I'm not a 'seedy lothario' or a sex addict.

The show is filmed in LA, and I'm put up in a ridiculously nice two-bedroom house, just over the Hollywood Hills on the Valley side. The place has a pool, huge open spaces, French windows, a great view, and must be worth a few million.

MTV's publicity people tell me they have set up an opportunity for me to do an interview with a woman from the *Observer*, Polly Vernon. They've never had one of their shows publicized like this in that paper, so they're keen for me to do it, even though the people who read it aren't likely to watch the show. The *Observer* isn't my usual terrain, and they warn me Polly might not like me very much. She has a reputation for being a feminist, and it's likely I'm in for a slating.

I decide to do it anyway because Polly is actually going to spend some time with me rather than just read newspaper stories about me, so I figure it's worth the effort. If she gets to know me a bit and still wants to slate me, fair enough. At least I'll have had a chance to be myself and not the person the press seem to think I am.

Polly flies in at noon on a day we're not filming, and I ask the PR lady to tell her to meet me and my friend Adee Phelan, who's staying with me, by the pool at the Mondrian Hotel, where she's staying.

At midday, we're waiting and Polly shows up. We're there, in shades and covered in tattoos, and I expect she looks at us and thinks we're a pair of reprobates – not impressive at all. We introduce ourselves, get some drinks and start talking. About twenty minutes in, she suggests we postpone the interview and just enjoy some time by the pool. She's really cool, and has great banter, so we spend the afternoon in the sun, having a few drinks, swimming a bit, and having a good laugh.

Later in the afternoon, she goes back into the hotel and we tell her to come to our house at 7pm for dinner. I make her linguine with chicken and chorizo – I try really hard to cook something good – and we carry on the interview as we eat. After the meal, I say, 'Why don't you come out with us?' and she says she'd like that. I get us a table at a club, and we all head out together. We have more drinks, and pretty soon we're dancing on tables and having a great time. I look at Polly dancing, and I really hope I've won her over. She looks like she's enjoying herself, which is a good sign.

I read the interview a few weeks later, and I'm really happy with it. It starts with a lot of talk about me shagging, which is funny, because she's a good writer. Then she takes the piss out of my accent, the show, and me in general, which is also funny. After that, she writes this:

> There are many reasons not to like Calum Best. There's the transatlantic twang and the petulant, spoiled, too-tanned, too-good good looks. He has inherited celebrity from a man who earned it properly, with a singular talent, and the legitimacy of George Best's fame serves to reinforce the pointlessness of his son by comparison. And, in a double whammy, George's reputation also serves to taint Calum's, because George Best died of liver failure in pitiful, ugly circumstances. All that, and then there's the prolific, feckless shagging.
>
> But then you meet Calum Best, and bam, you do like him, despite yourself. I'm a big fan, five whole minutes in. He is sweet, he is friendly, he is immediately, patently, desperate to like you, and desperate to be liked back. He's attentive, he's interested, there's a bass line of gentleness to him. He listens to you, he teases you: 'Is "sanctimonious" your favourite word, Polly?' he says, after I use it twice in a sentence. He's preposterously flirtatious, but there's no real sexual intent there; I suspect that flirting is one of the many, many things that Calum Best does to try and make more people like him.

I'm really pleased with it. I liked Polly a lot, and I'm so glad she took the time to get to know me. She makes some sharp observations about me, how I'm struggling to find something to do with my life that will make me happy; how I'm lonely and not very happy at the moment; and that I'm insecure about what people think of me, and that I like to be liked. She also points out that I manage to succeed at the task the show set for me and do nothing sexual for the whole fifty days.

After the show, I stay on in LA for a couple of weeks, hanging out with my friends. I check into the Mondrian Hotel for the whole period, and by the time I leave I've spent virtually all my fee from MTV. That's not clever, but at least things are looking up.

When I get back to the UK, we start filming the documentary. I spend the next five months travelling around with the two producers finding out more about other people and more about myself. As I try to turn my life around, this proves to be the best thing I could possibly have done. It stops me from carrying on with the serious downward spiral I've been on since my dad died. The experience shows me another path, one where there are great opportunities and happier, better things. I realize that the position I'm in, where people know who my dad is and who I am, means I can help people who are going through things similar to what happened to me. And if I can, I should at least try.

I have been wondering how to better myself, how to give myself a sense of purpose, and this has provided me with an answer: I can help others. It's a slightly spiritual thing, I suppose, which I get from my mum, which means that by putting positive things out into the universe, positive things will happen to me and for me. This makes sense to me now. Instead of drinking through the fear, the worry and depression, I want to use this opportunity to try to do something better. I might not have the power to achieve anything, but I have to try. I want to use my father's name and people's interest in me to do something good.

Chapter 22

'Most importantly, I am given the chance to do
what I really want, which is to use my name, the
one I have because of my dad, to do some good.'

Calum Best

I'm very proud of the film, and of my part in it. But
something happens off camera that shows how I can still
lose control badly.

It starts when we go to Manchester about two months
into filming, in autumn 2008. We've already been all over
the country and the pressure is getting to me. Before
every interview I'm nervous and anxious about how I'm
going to talk to the person. I'm desperate not to say anything that will upset them or make them feel bad. After
two months of this, I'm finding it tough. But I won't give
up. I'm too stubborn to say I need some time out. Instead,
I carry on until I break.

Manchester is a difficult place for me. There are so many associations with my dad there, such as the traumatic trip when he left me at the hotel when I was eleven, to his memorial service. It's full of demons for me.

We check into the Malmaison Hotel and I'm staying in the Best suite. That's Best, not best – it's named after my dad and there are pictures of him all over the place. It's a strange experience, but it's a great hotel, a lovely place, and was my dad's favourite. None of this helps my state of mind.

Earlier that day, I called a girl I knew in Manchester to tell her I was coming to town. I need to let off steam and she's good fun. She said to me what a coincidence: she's staying at the Malmaison too, with three friends of hers, two girls and a guy. I think to myself I could go and see her for a while; it wouldn't have to be a crazy night. I've been filming so much over the past couple of months, I could just drop in for an hour to relax.

That evening, when it's time to go to bed, the producers ask me if I'll be OK. I say yes, sure, I'll be fine, I'll go straight to bed. At about 10pm, we all say goodnight and go to our rooms.

Except I don't go to my room. I go straight to the girls' room. As I walk down the corridor, I know I shouldn't be doing this. I should be sleeping, getting ready for tomorrow. I owe the people I'm working with that much. But I can't help myself. I don't want just to go to my room and be alone with my thoughts and memories.

I get into the room, and there's a pile of coke on the table. They offer me some, but I haven't even had a drink today, so I say no. I've been off drink and drugs while I'm making the film because I want to do it properly. It's been hard, but I'm happy with how I'm doing. But the girls get upset and have a go at me for spoiling the party. I don't have the strength to stand up to them, so I have a whisky from the mini-bar. Straight down it goes, and oh, that tastes good. I have another, a double. That tastes even better.

Fuck it, I think, and I get stuck in.

At 6am I'm still in the room, wired out of my head. I have a moment where I realize I have to be up in two hours, so finally I go to bed. I try to go to sleep but I'm still buzzing so much from the cocaine that I can't. I lie in bed and all I can think about is how I have to be up in two hours so I can go to a school – a school, for fuck's sake – and do some filming about being the son of an alcoholic parent and I'm going to show up off my nut. I'm ashamed, and terrified. I'm a mess and I'm desperate to get some rest. The anxiety is awful.

Finally, my eyes close and I go to sleep.

And then bang, the phone rings and I'm awake. I must have slept for thirty seconds, maybe even less. It's one of the producers asking if I'm ready. Sure, I say, I'll be right down. I am completely embarrassed. They have been so good to me over the past couple of months, and this is how I repay them.

An hour later I appear in the lobby, petrified of their

reaction. I can see from the expressions on their faces how rough I look. I wait for the shouting to start, but it doesn't. One of them is so caring; she doesn't make a fuss, she doesn't get angry. 'How can we fix this?' she says, and gets me coffee and Gatorade, anything that might make me feel better.

We get in the car and luckily it's a thirty-minute drive so I get a bit more sleep. When we arrive I get out and look at myself. I'm in a bad way. My eyes are red and I look awful. But I go in and film with the kids, play games with them and do all the things I'm supposed to do. All the time, I feel horrendous, physically and about myself. We film for about six hours and at the end I say to the girls, 'I'm so sorry.'

'You're such a nightmare,' they say, but with smiles. They can't tell me how they really feel because we still have filming to do. It's only when we finish the documentary that they tell me how horrendous that day was.

We get the film done in the end and I'm very proud of it, but it's been tough. I've been fighting my demons all the way through, doing OK and nearly getting there and then breaking spectacularly. Realistically, I was never going to be able to jump from my old lifestyle to being completely clean and sober for six months. That was never going to happen. I knew I was going to try my hardest and I did. I wore my heart on my sleeve, and when I spoke to the three young girls mentioned earlier who told me stories about their lives I felt incredibly lucky to have had it as easy as I did with my dad. Their stories broke my heart. I tried my best to make them feel good, just like I tried with everyone I talked to. But it just took that one night in Manchester for me to break. Did it ruin the whole thing for me? No, of course not. But I regret that night hugely. I'm ashamed of myself for it.

Maybe if we'd been in another city it wouldn't have happened. Manchester was a difficult place for me, and those girls being in the same hotel as me could be seen as bad luck. But I could easily have not knocked on their door. That was my choice, and I did the wrong thing. I knew I could go and spend the night being naughty, so I did.

Years later, when I watch the show back, I can see I was fresh out of a dark place. I have bags under my eyes, they look a bit fuzzy, I have a double chin, bad skin and so on. The clip of me reading at my dad's funeral is me in the darkest of all the dark places I have ever been, and that was at the end of 2005. I don't even recognize the guy standing there, I was so lost. When we finish the film, it's 2009, nearly four years later, and I am still not out of that dark place.

I go on BBC News and *This Morning* and a few other programmes to promote the film and I'm so nervous every time. I don't want to say the wrong thing, I don't want to embarrass myself, but most of all I don't want people to think I'm trashing my dad's memory by talking about my relationship with him. But I get through it. I'm prepared, I know statistics and I've got more comfortable talking about this stuff, so it's OK.

I'm prouder of that film than of anything else I've ever done. It first went out on BBC One prime time as part of *Children in Need* and was later repeated on BBC Three. One of the senior guys at the BBC writes me a letter saying how proud they are of it.

Most importantly, I am given the chance to do what I really want, which is to use my name, the one I have because of my dad, to do some good. After the programme I become a patron for NACOA, the National Association for Children of Alcoholics. When they ask me, I cannot say yes quickly enough. I hope I can be useful to them. Being George Best's son makes me an ideal person for them. In a strange way, as much as I hate my dad's drinking and I wish more than anything that he had never touched a drop, I'm grateful for this opportunity. This is how I should be using his name. This is what I want to be known for, for doing some good, for making a difference.

One of the first things NACOA ask me to do is an after-dinner speech a couple of months later. Elle Macpherson is also a patron, and she and I are speaking one after the other. The dinner is at Battersea Power Station, and it's not until I arrive that I realize how big the event is. There are thousands of people there. Thousands.

How am I going to get through this? How can I get all those people to pay attention to me? What if they already hate me? And how am I going to talk to them about why you shouldn't let your kids see you drink when they're out there getting pissed?

Elle speaks first, and I can see she is super-nervous, trembling before she goes on. That makes me feel slightly better, that this hugely famous woman who's known around the world is nervous. That makes it OK for me to be nervous too.

Then it's my turn. I mumble a bit at the start, and try to make a joke about how I'm talking about alcohol while all the people out there are drinking. After a couple of minutes I relax and it seems to go OK. At one point I see some guy at a table close to the front telling his mate what a wanker I am, but I ignore them and try to talk to the people who are interested in what I'm saying, and I think I do quite well. Making the speech is really hard for me. I am so self-conscious up there, worrying about how I'm being judged, whether people will listen to me or take anything I say seriously, but I get through it. To say I don't enjoy the experience is a massive understatement, but as soon as it's over I know one thing for certain: I want to do more.

As 2010 starts, things are improving. I'm struggling financially, finding it hard to get much work, but I'm happier than I've been for as long as I can remember. I'm healthier, going out much less and not hitting it as hard as I used to; I've started eating better and working out; and I'm excited about each day. I've started to make some real friends and to top it off one of them asks if I want to play some football. I say hell yes, I'd love to. And so I go to play six-a-side on a Tuesday night in

Kensington, and it's brilliant. I get such a thrill from playing.

I've started going to the gym, thanks to my mum and Mark. Because they are both trainers, they run a gym and are always encouraging me to exercise more. I'm feeling great, so I ask around my other friends to see if there are any more football games going on. Someone says yes, we have a game every Monday, and there's an occasional one on Wednesdays, so pretty soon I'm playing two or three nights a week.

This habit stays with me. It becomes part of my routine every week, and I love every second. It reminds me of being back in Malibu on the Bluffs, the carefree days when I'd throw my boots in the back of my truck and drive up to play with my friends. In those days I used to buzz about playing football, and I feel that now too. I fell off it for years, but now I'm back playing I'm thrilled with it.

But it's not all good. There are things from my past that still hang over me. I have all these ideas for things I can do, businesses such as my fragrances I want to try to make something of, and my confidence is coming back, but I'm struggling to make money, while at the same time I'm trying to figure out what to do with my life. It's hard. I want to do something amazing, which lives up to what my dad did, but I know I'm not my dad. I don't have his talent.

How could anyone live up to a father like George Best? This has bothered me all my life, because I've felt so small in comparison to him. Modelling and reality TV don't look like much next to his football career. But now I realize that's OK. What I do with my life doesn't have to be measured against what my dad did with his. I'm a different person, and I have to figure out who I am, who I want to be and what I can do. In a strange way, I feel like I'm breaking free.

One thing holding me back is my reputation. It is still a problem. The years of making mistakes that were splashed all over the papers mean no one wants to touch me. I have gone from being welcomed into every club in London to being turned away. It happens twice in the same night in 2010 – I turn up to clubs where I am on the guest list only to be told I'm not the kind of person they want inside.

Ten years ago, every door I saw was open for me. I can't believe how much things have changed. I think back to when I first got to London at nineteen years of age. I had a call from Fendi, inviting me to this luxurious party at a mansion in the countryside. They paid for my driver and my hotel. People like Lionel Richie, Jude Law, Sienna Miller and all kinds of other big names were there. I was doing shoots with Mario Testino, campaigns for Burberry. Ten years later, I'm being turned away from clubs. How did this happen?

I know I shouldn't have done a lot of what I did, but relative to what a lot of people do, I haven't done anything that bad. I was a young guy who had oppor-tunities, and I took them, probably too often. If I'd been a rock star, I don't think anyone would care about any of it. But because I'm the son of a legend, and I was given a lot of attention as a result, people seem to hate it, and I've ended up with a seedy reputation that really isn't me. People who think that of me are judging me on a small part of my character. I understand why they make that judgement, because thanks to the media that's all they see of me. But I do still feel resentful about this sometimes, and I try to use that feeling as fuel to make me work harder.

My father isn't an excuse to ruin myself any more. Instead, I'm trying to do positive things with my time, taking responsibility for myself. I start working on a film about my dad because it's something I would love to do, and end up hooking up with a top producer. I go to the gym and play football regularly, so I feel good. I have a couple of hair transplants, because my hair has been falling out, which I hate, so I'm happy about how I look. I do the London Marathon twice for the Children's Trust, I trek through Vietnam for the same charity in 2010, and I carry on doing after-dinner speeches for NACOA. In my own small way, bit by bit, I'm getting better all the time.

A friend of mine mentions he's doing an acting class and I decide to have a go too. My confidence is coming back as a result of the changes I'm going through. I've gone from being in a nightclub every single night, drunk and on drugs all the time, to not even wanting to be in one. I don't even want to meet girls any more. I'm beginning to understand why I did what I did when I was younger, how unhappy, angry and afraid I was. Now I don't want to be around the kind of draining people I used to see in clubs. I like being in at night. I'm in good shape, and I like spending evenings cooking dinner after football, or after the gym. I like waking up early with a clear head. I read *The Secret*, and a few other self-help books, and they're all part of the change I'm going through.

I go to the acting class, and I enjoy it. I'm not so good at being told what to do, but at least I'm taking that first step, because things can grow naturally from there. I'm becoming more comfortable with myself, and that's feeding through to every part of my life. It's about me getting out and being confident and active after years of being low.

One day in 2011 I'm in London and bump into a guy I used to know from parties a few years ago, and he's a casting director. This meeting, which might be important, comes about because I am being active in good areas – I've been to one meeting with good people and am on my way to another one when I bump into him. He says he remembers seeing me completely wasted six years ago, and it's nice to see me looking so well. That feels really good.

A few days later, I go to a meeting at the Soho Hotel about me going to a speedboat event in Bahrain, and while I'm there I bump into an old friend of mine, a film-maker called Arran Anyrin Bowyn. 'Good to see you,' he says. It's late morning, and I'm in a suit and looking fresh and well, and I can tell he's surprised – he knew a very different me a few years ago. Arran asks what I'm doing, and I tell him bits and pieces, and then I mention the acting class. He says great, and he has an audition for me, but if I try out I have to smash it. I have to be better than good. 'Tell me when and where, and I'll try my hardest,' I say.

The audition comes round a few weeks later. It's in a hotel room, and at the start they hand me my script and I'm given a few minutes to prepare. It's only ten lines and I'm nervous as hell, but I'm determined to give it everything. I focus, and I really try to do my best. At the end, the people watching thank me and I leave. I have no idea how well it went – it was my first time, so how can I know?

Three days later, I get a call from Arran and he tells me I got the part. He liked me, and his investors did too. They have faith in me and want me on board. I'm thrilled, absolutely thrilled, because Arran is a serious guy, a very talented filmmaker who is going places. I feel like this little bit of success shows I'm on the right path. This is something that happened because I've been trying hard in general, looking after myself and doing good things with good people, and it makes me want to do even more good things.

In summer 2014, we make the film. It's set in a gypsy camp and is about my character waking up there after being attacked. He falls in love with the daughter of one of the main gypsy guys, but she's already engaged. It's then about the confrontation between my character and the fiancé. The girl's part is taken by Alexandra Weaver, and her dad is played by Paddy Doherty.

It's starting off as a short film, where they film us doing a few scenes, and hopefully that will get some investment in the project so we can make the full film. I don't know whether it will work, but they're good guys, and the director is excellent. We shoot over a weekend in Wales. We work sixteen-hour days on it, and at the end of each one I'm exhausted, but I feel great because I've put in a hard day's work. I'm grafting for things, and I like it. I might not end up being an actor, much as I would love to be one, but the point is I'm trying hard at it, and at other things. I used to be like that when I was younger, a grafter, and all the London craziness made me lose track of that. Now I like who I am and what I'm doing. When I walk down the road, I don't hide my face any more. People might still look at me and think I'm George Best's loser son, but I know I'm living the right way now.

All my life, my dad has affected everything I do. Until he died, I always had hope for us, for what we could be, and when I lost him I lost all that. I thought fuck the world and everyone in it, fuck you all. I messed everything up, including myself. I didn't care about anything for ages, and then one day I thought to myself, hold on, this isn't right. I had times on my own where I asked myself, what are you doing? Where are you going from here? No one likes you, the press talk crap about you every day, and you deserve better.

Next my mum came back, and that gave me a bit of confidence. Then I did *Brought Up By Booze*, and that gave me a little more. I met young children who'd suffered all kinds of physical and sexual abuse because of alcohol, and it made me think to myself that I didn't have it that tough, that in a lot of ways I'm all right. Compared to them, and a lot of other people, I'm lucky. And that helped me feel better about what happened with my dad.

Bit by bit, I got better. I started to take care of myself and all these little additional positive things started happening.

When I was twenty-seven and stopped going to night-clubs, I was so drained by it all that I couldn't stand the idea of going to one again. But I do like to party now. I don't do it often, but when the time is right I go for it. I don't think I'll ever change that, and I'm not sure I want to either, because I know how much fun it is with the right people. I just do it differently now, not so often and not so hard.

But at the same time, I know that when I'm sober, when I haven't drunk for a month, which happens every now and then, my head is clear and I'm buzzing with energy and ideas. I feel like I'm capable of so much, but if I have one messy night my brain goes back to how it used to be. It's about finding the right balance, which is hard, but I'm getting there.

* * *

My life is heading in the right direction now, and the satisfying thing is knowing that if any of the things I'm working on take off, it will be because I've made it happen. I've pushed these things and worked at them, whether it's my acting, or the film about my dad, or the clothing line I'm starting, or my new range of health supplements, or my fragrance. These are all things I've grafted for over the years. I've battled through so much to get to this point.

But there is one huge issue that I still have to deal with: tax. Or rather, the fact I haven't paid any. For years I've been conscious that at some point someone from the government is going to tap me on the shoulder and ask for money. When I first started earning in this country, my agent told me I needed to do something about tax, to make sure I took care of what needed to be done. But I didn't listen.

In the early days, I would often end up with cash in my hand after a job, whether it was from a nightclub or because I'd been given a cheque after a bit of modelling work and had cashed it. At that point, I would think, 'Great, I've got this cash, let's go out,' and I'd blow it all straight away. Even when I opened a bank account, I carried on burning through my money and only very rarely thought about things like tax. It was always there at the back of my mind, and I knew that one day I would have to deal with it. I just kept putting it off and putting it off, telling myself that one day I would earn enough to pay it all back, and more. I was also aware that I wasn't saving anything, not only for tax, but for the future. I spent and spent, as fast as the money came in, and sometimes faster than that. This is exactly the same pattern of behaviour that saw my dad go bankrupt twice. Back then, I didn't realize how stupid I was being.

In 2007 I got a letter saying I had to complete a tax return. I contacted an accountant and he went through my stuff, told me what I had to do, but then I didn't contact him for a year. In 2008 I got another letter, and did the same thing with the accountant. In 2009 the accountant got my tax returns ready again, and when it came to my turn to sign things and send them off, I didn't do it. Same in 2010. I could see that I owed money in tax and would have to pay the accountant for what he'd done, but I didn't have the money, so I didn't finish the paperwork and just let things drift. I would tell myself that one of my next jobs would bring in enough to pay all these things off, but it never happened. I put it off time after time.

In 2011, things start getting serious. The letters change and now say I could be in trouble. I've been in the system for a few years – they know how much tax I owe. It's a serious amount of money now, mainly because of *Celebrity Love Island* and the nightclub appearances. Yet again, I don't do anything.

In 2012, the letter is even more serious. They need to be paid, and the amount I owe is now over £100,000. I am terrified. This thing is now out of control. I speak to my accountant and he tells me yes, I'm in deep trouble, but I'm also lucky to have been left alone for so long, so someone seems to be looking out for me. We joke about how my case must be being handled by the Belfast office and one of my dad's fans is helping me out. Jokes don't change the fact that I owe this money, and there's not a chance of me being able to pay it. I am broke. I'm not doing any TV work or nightclub appearances any more.

From 2010 to 2012 I have no money at all, apart from money from the fragrance I launched with my name on. That comes in once a year, every December, about £60,000, and by the time I get it I owe so much that most of it goes immediately. But I also do stupid things, like going on expensive holidays, so I'm not helping myself. I struggle for the rest of the year. I'm late with rent virtually every month – sometimes I'm three or four months in arrears – I can't pay my bills, I can't go anywhere, and things are really difficult. I still get free trips to places, so in some ways it looks like I'm still living the dream, but the reality is I'm skint.

Finally, in 2012, bankruptcy is mentioned. I'm given a date when I have to be in court. They want £160,000.

This is really tough, and scary, but at the same time I'm much stronger mentally now than I used to be. I'm more comfortable in my own skin, and about who I am as a person. I'm going out less, I'm healthier, my mum is around, and my life is better than it's ever been before, so I can handle it. This bankruptcy is something from when I was younger that is now coming back to bite me.

It's not how I live now. My mum says bankruptcy is the last bit of my past that I have to deal with and she's right – I have to sort this out. I'll do what I have to do, and then I can move on.

My accountant tries hard to get it settled without me being declared bankrupt, but it doesn't work because the money I offer is based on future earnings from a contract that is about to be signed, rather than on money I already have or earnings from a signed contract. I'm disappointed, but I can totally see their point. I owe all this money and can't pay it, so in November 2013 I'm declared bankrupt. It will last a year, it will be painful financially, but I'll get through it eventually. I can't wait for it to be over. To me it feels like the last thing left of the old me, and I'm looking to the future now. I'm not going to go down the same path my dad did, because I know how that story ends.

Chapter 23

'When I meet someone, I'm digging myself out of a big, deep hole before we've even started, and that screws things up immediately. People think they know what I'm like, but they don't.'

Calum Best

As I get older I start to care less about what people think, and I decide to do what will make me happy. The papers are still on my case from time to time, and whenever I give an interview it gets twisted to mean something I didn't intend. But things have changed. It doesn't bother me like it used to, and now I have Twitter, which has been great for me. It gives me the chance to say what I want to the world, to put my side out there. When I first signed up, I often got abusive messages, but by 2014 it's virtually all good. I get tweets from guys about the beard I grew, my clothes, my work or my dad, and it's almost all positive. Every now and then someone says something bad, but these days I don't let it affect me. Once, a guy came on and said I'd wasted my dad's fortune. Usually I wouldn't bother replying, but I did because his comment was so wrong it was funny. I said something like, mate, do your research. My dad had no fortune, and left me nothing. The fact I'm laughing about something like this is a good sign – it means I'm becoming more comfortable with my dad's legacy.

My dad's will wasn't sorted out properly until 2010, when all the debts had been paid and some memorabilia sold off to raise cash. This broke my heart. No one asked me if I wanted to keep anything, or if I minded about different things being sold. I wasn't consulted about anything. It's hard for me to know there are all these things around – trophies, signatures, boots, rights, and so on – but none of them are mine. I don't want cash, I just want something that was his, something to hold on to. A connection. Most fathers want to leave something for their son after they've worked for their whole lives. But my dad didn't, and it hurts. It always will.

In 2014, in the middle of my term of bankruptcy, something happens that adds to the hurt I feel about all this. My fragrances have been going since 2005 now. I help create the smells, I'm involved with the design, I do appearances to promote them and to meet people who are interested in them, and there's a company behind it that manufactures and distributes the products. My name is on the bottles and boxes, and I like doing it. They sell well in Ireland, and have been important income for me.

In 2013, during my bankruptcy proceedings, our contract ended. I was then contacted by someone else in Ireland who wanted me to start doing my Best fragrance with another company, which I was very happy to do, not least because the money is useful. Now, in 2014, I find out that the previous company has started doing a George Best fragrance. I am furious about this – these people are using my dad's name without permission. I can't let this go on.

I'm keen to build bridges with Barbara, so I decide to tell her about it and hope we can get back on good terms as a result. I send her a message, saying I hope you're well, and I wanted you to know that a company has started doing this George Best fragrance and you might want to get your lawyers to take a look at it. I know she now has a deal with IMG, the huge sports marketing company, to license my dad's image, so I expect they'd also want to know this is going on. I add that I'm doing well, I'm clear-headed and healthy, and I say I would love to be involved with my dad's stuff somehow. I don't want money, I just desperately want to be part of it, and maybe to use his name for something positive.

She replies quite quickly, and I'm really encouraged. She's friendly, says thank you, and asks what I had in mind. I reply saying I have good ideas, I'm enthusiastic, and being my dad's only son might make me useful. I add information about the George Best fragrance, saying it's being launched on a certain date. She replies saying, yes, we know about it, it's our deal.

I am stunned. For a while I look at the message in shock. They did this with her blessing? I can't believe it. I don't know all the details about the George Best fragrance, but it's not hard to imagine it competing against mine for sales. My fragrance is pretty much my livelihood at the moment.

Barbara also says IMG will be in touch with me as they're dealing with my dad's estate. But nothing comes. Maybe Barbara and Norman think I'm still the same lost soul I was for those years after my dad died and believe I can't be trusted to do anything with my dad's estate. But I'm not like that now. I've changed, for the better. I don't care what they think of me. What I care about is being involved somehow with my dad's estate.

It's a horrible situation. I wish I could just pack it all away, say it's the past, and move on, but I can't. I don't know what will happen in the future with this, but one thing seems certain: whatever is done with my dad's estate won't have anything to do with me, and I'll have to live with it.

As if this wasn't painful enough, my bankruptcy trustee finds out about the watch my dad left me and says I'm going to have to sell it, and that whatever we get for it will go towards paying off my debt. He takes the watch and starts arranging the sale. He says it should fetch £5,000, which seems a shockingly small amount to me. If it's worth so little, can't I just keep it and pay the money a different way, over a longer period? No, apparently not. I'm devastated. This watch is all I have, and it's going.

For a few months I'm in turmoil because of all this. The £80,000 I'm owed by the fragrance company hasn't come through yet, and I'm desperate for it to arrive because I don't want to lose that watch. I keep asking the trustee for updates, and eventually he tells me to mind my own business, because the watch isn't my possession any more. He doesn't seem to understand or care how I feel about the watch, even though I've told him it's the only thing my dad left me. It's one of the very few assets I have, so it has to be sold. In the end, in the autumn of 2014, it is put up for sale for £6,000. I'm gutted.

Maybe it's the universe telling me to let go of the watch, and with it all the baggage I have related to my dad. I hope so, because I can't see any other positive side to this.

My mum is a huge help to me, and I'm so glad she's around. I don't know where I would be without her. I really don't – I was in such a dark place before we had that walk by the river. What would have happened to me if she'd stayed in the US? The thought scares me.

Moving over here for me was a bigger deal for her than I've let on. It was a huge life change for her, and for Mark, who she is still with. He came on to the scene when I was young and has been pretty much constant ever since. But when I moved out at eighteen, I lost contact with Mark and, to an extent, my mum. I ventured off into the world to do my thing. When I landed in Milan, the first person I called was my mum, but we were not in touch constantly, not at all. It was on and off, but I never worried about her because Mark was there to take care of her. He's a solid guy, and I was reassured knowing he was around.

After I left home, they moved together from Malibu to the Valley. My mum wanted eventually to live out on a ranch in the Colorado Hills, so they saved up with that dream as their goal. Finally they bought one, and Mark went out there first to start things up. But that was the point where my mum changed her plans so she could come to London to take care of me. Her long-held plans went out of the window. For a while, she and Mark lived on opposite sides of the ocean, which must have been tough, and finally she decided to stay over here permanently, for me.

Mark's dream life with my mum on the ranch vanished into thin air as well, and he decided to move over here too so he could be with her. He turned his life upside down for my mum, who turned her life upside down for me, and I'll always be grateful to both of them.

After a while my mum and Mark move to Henley-on-Thames, and being here is the only time I can find any kind of total peace. I switch off completely. There's nowhere else in the world I can do this, even now, at the age of thirty-three. It's quiet, in the country, my mum is there, there are dogs around, my brain goes silent, and I can sleep for days.

My mum and Mark have been together for fifteen years now, and I love that he's there to take care of her. He always thinks of the best for her; he suggests planning surprises for her birthday and that kind of thing. He also tries to come up with ideas for my business. I'm glad he's around. I see him a lot, we work out together and message all the time. He's an important person in my life.

So I'm healthy now, and looking after myself, and making good friends. But I'm still single, and lonely. In a way, I'm trying to reteach myself things, which sounds odd for a man my age, but it's true. I've spent most of the past eighteen years drinking, taking drugs and sleeping with girls all over the place. Now I want a normal relationship, a girlfriend to spend evenings with, someone who knows me and accepts me, who I can hang out with and cook for. But I don't know how to have one. Where do you begin?

The trouble is, every time I meet somebody, I'm starting from way below square one. All the girls I meet know who I am and assume I only want sex. I can understand why they would think that – I deserve that reputation – but I'm not that guy any more. I've changed. The problem is I don't know how to convince a girl I've changed. When I meet someone, I'm digging myself out of a big, deep hole before we've even started, and that screws things up immediately. People think they know what I'm like, but they don't. I'll just carry on trying to find the right one, which is a girl who accepts me and makes me not want anyone else. I'm still young, so I'm sure it will happen. I hope it does.

I am definitely changing for the better. I talk to my mum every day, and I say to her that now I'm in all the time, and living well, I'd like a dog. I have always wanted one and feel ready for the responsibility, which is a good sign. I was raised with dogs. My earliest memories involve my mum's German shepherd, Dallas, in our house in northern California. We had four or five as I was growing up: Jessie, Paris, Nero, and my dog, Havoc. He was an Akita, and I named him that because I was a little troublemaker. He would get in the back of my truck when I went out, and he slept in my room. When I left home, he stayed with my mum, and I've always missed him.

Now my mum is in Henley, she has a gorgeous white German shepherd called Cosmo, and I love seeing him. Spending time with dogs always puts me in a good mood, so I decide to get one. A few months after I mention the idea to my mum, this guy gets in touch to say he has a white German shepherd called Jessie, who needs a home. My mum and I go to meet her, and she is beautiful. She's skittish and nervous and jumpy, but I adore her immediately. We take her, then on the way home I start to wonder if it was such a good idea. She's energetic and nervous, and barks at other dogs. But we stick at it and build a bond over the next few months. She needs some security, and I start to really love her.

But there's a problem. I live in a first-floor flat, with no garden, and Jessie is a one-year-old dog full of energy, who needs space and exercise. I am out quite a lot during the day for work, and I travel a bit, and she's always by the door waiting for me when I get back. Sometimes it's hours, and I start to feel bad. It's not right.

I go to stay with my mum for Christmas 2013 and Jessie has the most amazing time. She loves my mum's dog – she only has one now – and loves running around the hills near the house, where they walk Cosmo. I realize she'd be better off here, with another dog, with all this space, and with people who are around more than I am. My mum and Mark are more than happy to take her, so she stays there now and is so happy. I see Jessie all the time and it's great, even though I miss her.

The circumstances aren't right yet for me to have a dog. I've moved house again since then, but it's still a flat so I'm not ready. Maybe at my next place I'll have space for her. It'll happen one day, when the time is right.

I never asked my dad about the daughter he supposedly had but never met, and he never brought it up, so we never, ever talked about it, which was typical for us. But over the years I heard the story a few more times. Apparently a baby was born after he had a brief fling with a woman in the sixties and she got pregnant. She decided to keep the child, a little girl, but didn't want my dad to have anything to do with her. The mother didn't want her daughter to have to grow up being George Best's child. She was happy getting on with her life without him. She didn't want the fame, and didn't want anything from my dad, so she raised her on her own.

My mum has never believed it's true, and I'm pretty sure she's right. I can easily see how my dad would have used something like this to manipulate people into letting him drink, telling them about the daughter he never met and how that was the greatest regret of his life, so they would feel sorry for him and excuse the alcoholism. I also can't see how this daughter would never have been found, even if she didn't want to be. The press were all over my dad's life for years, and if she really existed, then surely they'd have tracked her down. To me, that makes it unlikely that the story is true.

For a long time I didn't even think about the possibility of having a sister. My family is small: there's been me and my mum, and a few relatives in California. I don't speak to my dad's relatives, so when he died it was like I lost half my family.

If my mum and I are wrong, and I really do have a sister out there somewhere, I'd love to meet her. If someone told me her name and where she is, I'd contact her tomorrow. In a heartbeat. It would be awesome to have a sister. If I could have another connection to my dad, even though it's someone who never met him, if I could have another person in my life who's my blood relative, I would definitely try. Maybe she wouldn't want to know me, but I would try.

She might be married with kids, and our lives might be so, so different, but wow, a sister? I would love that. Maybe she'll read this and get in touch. Maybe she knows she's George Best's daughter, and knows who I am, and hasn't reached out because she doesn't want to, or she's nervous, or worried. I don't know. All I do know is, if she does exist, I'd love to hear from her. You never know what might happen.

Chapter 24

'Calum, you were the love of George's life. He adored you. He just wasn't able to show it, and that meant you never got to see it.'

Phil Hughes

It's early 2015 now, and I'm a few months away from great things happening. I'm out of bankruptcy, and all the projects I've been working so hard on are coming together. My new line of Best Life health and fitness supplements are out, I have a new fragrance deal, I've started acting and been in a short film, I'm making a film about my dad with the producers of *The King's Speech*, I've been on *Celebrity Big Brother*, and there's this book. I'm happy, and proud of what I'm doing. These are all great projects, all things that could change my life.

I've come such a long way since my dad died. That was the only time I was ever truly sad. Until then, I always had hope. I hoped he would change and would want to be with me. To talk to me properly, to have dinner together in a way that wasn't awkward, to go on holiday without having to worry about whether or not he was drinking, to do the normal boring stuff fathers and sons do together. I didn't want anything flashy, just him. When he died, I lost that hope, and it was the worst, but things are now, finally, getting much better. My mum says I'm like an onion being peeled. Making *Brought Up By Booze* was the first layer coming off. More have come off since, and I'll keep going even though I don't know how many there are.

I still don't understand my dad properly. On the football pitch, he was in control. He knew what he was doing. But away from it, he was a lost soul. He tried to be a good husband and father to my mum and me, but he couldn't do it. He didn't know how to deal with what life gave him. I don't think he was close to his family – when he and my mum were together, she only remembers him visiting Belfast once, and that was after his mum died. Barbara even admitted at his funeral that she had denied being his sister for most of her life. I don't know how close they can have been if that really was what happened. I think my dad was very lonely for a lot of his life, even though there were always people around who wanted to be close to him and who really cared about him.

The longer he went on drinking, the worse he got. He got further and further away from the man he wanted to be – the legendary footballer, the good father, the great guy who everyone loves – and knowing that was happening messed with his head. In the end, he didn't like reality, and that's why he drank so much. He hated what he'd become and drank to protect himself from that, and the more he drank, the worse his life got. The worse his life got, the more he hated what he'd become, and so he drank even more to protect himself. It was a vicious circle. Maybe if he'd been less intelligent, he might have been OK, because he wouldn't have thought about things so deeply. But he was a clever man, and he understood what was going on around him very well. The shame he felt made him drink even more.

I know that in the years after he moved to Manchester from Belfast when he was fifteen, and when his career took off, he gradually visited his own family less and less. He pulled away from them, moved to the US, and eventually settled in London. Maybe he pulled away from me in the same way – he just couldn't handle having people around him that he really cared about.

His mother dying when he was thirty-two, in 1978, the year he married my mum, must have been horrific for him, especially as her death was caused by alcoholism and he already had serious problems with drink. I know he loved his parents, and his brother and sisters, and I know he loved me. He just didn't know how to show it, and maybe he didn't think he was worthy of our love, because with us he was just George the man, the father, son and brother, with the same kinds of flaws all men have. Maybe he thought that man wasn't worth much, because he didn't match up to the standards set by George Best the legendary footballer. But those standards were a myth. No one is that perfect, and that wasn't what I wanted anyway. All I ever wanted was my dad.

I hate to say this, but in the end my dad wasn't a good human being, and he caused terrible pain to the very last people he should have been hurting. But he also caused terrible pain – possibly even the most – to himself, by making the choices he did. I know he didn't want his life to turn out the way it did. George Best the footballer was a god. But George Best the father and husband wasn't.

My dad lived a strange life. He wasn't wealthy. He didn't own the kind of properties his equivalent would have today. That flat in Chelsea was it, and it wasn't very impressive. The place was mostly owned by the mortgage company, and it was shabby. But he didn't care. He didn't even have a washing machine. He was terrible with money. He didn't budget, and always forgot to pay his bills. He was paid for work in cash and loved to carry a big wad of it around with him. For an alcoholic, this wasn't clever, and I dread to think how many times he was robbed, or lost it, or gambled the lot. He went bankrupt twice. Hopefully that's something we won't have in common.

I am so proud of my dad, of what he achieved, of how loved he was, and I know some people will hate me for what I've said about him. I'm dreading that. But I didn't write this book to trash his name. I wanted to write it to tell the truth about what my life was like as his son, so I can move on. Now, finally, I am doing that.

I have always had to tread so carefully when I talk to people about my dad, because everyone thinks he was a legend in every way, so aren't I lucky to have been the great man's son? No one cares what kind of dad he was. To them, he's just George Best, legendary footballer, and I am proud to be that man's son. But he was a shit dad to me. I had a hard time with him. There was no silver spoon, and I want people to know that, not so that I ruin his legacy, but so they understand me better, and know that their perceptions and judgements about who I am aren't necessarily right.

I will always be sad about losing my dad, but I've accepted I can't change the past and I've learned to live with it. For so many years, being George Best's son took me to extremes, of happiness and sadness, of anger, pride, shame, disappointment and a whole load of other emotions. Being his son was amazing, because he was a legend, and I know deep down he was a good man, but being his son was also awful, because he was an alcoholic.

These days I don't feel those extreme emotions about him any more, and that's the biggest change in me. I'm proud of my dad, I love my dad, and I always will. Just like I will always wish things could have worked out differently. But I've accepted they didn't and my emotions aren't volatile any more. I don't go to those extremes when I think about him because I've made peace with what happened. I know that he wanted to be a good dad, but he couldn't, because of alcohol. Understanding and accepting that means I will never think of being George Best's son as a burden or a curse. It's an honour, because of what people thought of him, but mainly it's just part of who I am.

Phil Hughes, who knew my dad as well as anyone in the world, is convinced he loved me, and was kind enough to say this about my dad and me: 'Calum, you were the love of George's life. He adored you. He just wasn't able to show it, and that meant you never got to see it.'

That says it all.

Acknowledgements

I would like to thank the following people for their help and support with this book and many other things as well: Angie Best, Mark Miller, Adam O'Rourke, Phil Hughes, Professor Roger Williams, Fraser Carruthers, Jermaine Davis, John Benson, Mimi McDonald Janes, Lyndy Dangerfield, Doug Young and Henry Vines at Transworld, Erin McKee, Celia Walden and Humfrey Hunter.

Picture Acknowledgements

All images copyright of Eddie Sanderson/Scopefeatures.com unless otherwise stated.

Page 1: bottom left © Tom Wargacki/WireImage/Getty Images

Page 4: top left © Brendan Beirne/REX; top right © Pacemaker Press, Belfast; bottom © Bob Aylott/Express Newspapers/N&S Syndication

Page 5: top right © News (UK) Ltd/REX

Page 6: top © Xposurephotos.com; bottom © Frank Doran/ REX

Page 7: top left © News of the World; top right © Andrew Parsons/PA-Pool/Getty Images; left © Adrian Dennis/AFP/ Getty Images; bottom © PA Archive

Page 8: top © True Vision Productions; bottom © BBC Northern Ireland/Press Eye

Index